WOMEN, WORK, AND GLOBALIZATION

Women increasingly make up a significant percentage of the labor force throughout the world. This transformation is impacting everyone's lives. This book examines the resulting gender role, work, and family issues from a comparative worldwide perspective. Working allows women to earn an income, acquire new skills, and forge social connections. It also brings challenges such as simultaneously managing domestic responsibilities and family relationships. The social, political, and economic implications of this global transformation are explored from an interdisciplinary perspective in this book. The commonalities and the differences of women's experiences depending on their social class, education, and location in industrialized *and* developing countries are highlighted throughout. Practical implications are examined including the consequences of these changes for men. Vignettes and case studies from around the world bring the topics to life. The book argues that despite policy reforms and a rhetoric of equality, women still have unique experiences from men both at work and at home.

Women, Work, and Globalization explores:

- key issues surrounding work and families from a *global cross-cultural* perspective;
- the positive and negative repercussions of more women in the global workforce;
- the spread of women's empowerment on changes in ideologies and behaviors throughout the world;
- key literature from family studies, organizational psychology, sociology, anthropology, and economics;
- the changing role of men in the global work–family arena;
- the impact of sexual trafficking and exploitation, care labor, and transnational migration on women;
- best practices and policies that have benefited women, men, and their families.

Part I reviews the research on gender in the industrialized and developing world, global changes that pertain to women's gender roles, women's labor market participation, globalization, and the spread of the women's movement. Issues that pertain to women in a globalized world including gender socialization, sexual trafficking and exploitation, labor migration and transnational motherhood, and the complexities entailed in care labor are explored in Part II. Programs and policies that have effectively assisted women are explored in Part III including initiatives instituted by NGOs and governments in developing countries, and (programs) policies that help women balance work and family in industrialized countries. The book concludes with suggestions for global initiatives that assist women in balancing work and family responsibilities while decreasing their vulnerabilities.

This book is intended as a supplemental text for advanced undergraduate and/or graduate courses in Women/Gender Issues, Work and Family, Gender and Families, Global Families, Family Diversity, Multicultural Families, and Urban Sociology taught in Psychology, Human Development and Family Studies, Gender and/or Women's Studies, Business, Sociology, Social Work, Political Science, and Anthropology. Researchers, policy makers, and practitioners in these fields will also appreciate this thought-provoking book.

Bahira Sherif Trask is Professor of Human Development and Family Studies at the University of Delaware.

WOMEN, WORK, AND GLOBALIZATION

Challenges and Opportunities

Bahira Sherif Trask

Routledge
Taylor & Francis Group

NEW YORK AND LONDON

First published 2014
by Routledge
711 Third Avenue, New York, NY 10017

and by Routledge
27 Church Road, Hove, East Sussex BN3 2FA

Routledge is an imprint of the Taylor & Francis Group, an informa business

© 2014 Taylor & Francis

Library of Congress Cataloging in Publication Data

A catalog record for this book has been requsted

ISBN: 978-0-415-88337-5 (hbk)
ISBN: 978-0-415-88338-2 (pbk)
ISBN: 978-1-315-88234-5 (ebk)

Typeset in Sabon
by Cenveo Publisher Services

CONTENTS

v

ABOUT THE AUTHOR

Bahira Sherif Trask is an author, professor, and speaker on issues of globalization, gender, and work and family. She holds a BA in Political Science from Yale University and a PhD in Cultural Anthropology from the University of Pennsylvania. Dr. Trask is currently a full professor of Human Development and Family Studies at the University of Delaware. She is also the author and editor of four other books including *Globalization and Families* (2010), and she has published over 50 peer-reviewed articles, chapters, and review articles on globalization, cultural and family diversity, gender roles, and work and family life in significant edited volumes and handbooks. Dr. Trask regularly speaks about the complex issues facing working families, and women in particular, to audiences at international organizations such as the United Nations, at major corporations such as DuPont and Microsoft, and at international conferences all over the world. In August 2012, she gave a TEDx lecture on Global Family Changes that has been widely viewed.

Much of Dr. Trask's scholarship has been informed through participation with a number of international, national, and community-based research projects that focus on diversity, gender and work, and strengthening low-income families. Dr. Trask's involvement on these projects reflects her belief that academics need to apply their knowledge toward bettering social conditions.

PREFACE

There are few social phenomena that are as clearly obvious, as highly debated, and as controversial as the rapid increase of women in the paid workforce around the world. Moreover, today working outside of the home is not just a strategy of survival for many women. Instead, it is becoming central to their identities: working allows women to earn an income, acquire new skills, forge social connections, and empowers them in many cases. However, working outside of the home is accompanied by other challenges: foremost for most women is the problem of simultaneously managing domestic responsibilities and negotiating their relationships with spouses, children, and extended family members.

While most people are aware of this fact of contemporary social life, the wide-ranging implications of this global transformation are poorly understood. This book examines this phenomenon from a unique interdisciplinary vantage point: it highlights some of the commonalities of women's experiences in the industrialized and developing world and emphasizes the multiplicity of women's experiences depending on their social class, education, geographical position, and a myriad of other factors. Most importantly, this work analyzes the close relationship between globalization and the ideologies and practical implications of women's participation in the paid labor force. This work argues that despite policy changes and a rhetoric of equality, women still have unique experiences from men both at work and at home. There is no question that there are increased educational and work opportunities for many women around the world today. Yet, globalization has also made certain groups of women more vulnerable to economic and social exploitation. While there is some awareness of these issues, there is much debate about how to resolve such complex matters. This book advances the dialogue on women and globalization by first examining these issues from a comparative worldwide perspective and then by suggesting that despite many of the negative connotations associated with globalization, globalization also provides the mechanisms to effect positive changes for women and their families.

Intended Audience

The primary audience for *Women, Work, and Globalization* are scholars and advanced undergraduate and graduate students who are interested in gaining a comprehensive understanding of the changes in gender roles, work and family issues, and the role of globalization in both the industrialized and the developing world. Researchers, policy makers, and practitioners will also find the ideas introduced in this book accessible and thought provoking. *Women, Work, and Globalization* is intended to expand the subject matter covered in courses such as Women/Gender Issues, Work and Family, Gender and Families, Global/International Families, Family Diversity, Multicultural Families, Global Social Policies, and Urban Sociology taught in departments of sociology, psychology, human development and family studies, gender and/or women's studies, business, social work, political science, policy, and anthropology. This work is also conceived as foundational to individuals who are interested in global affairs and the development literature. The opening vignettes, case studies, and final synopsis in each chapter will assist readers in following what are at times complex concepts and arguments.

Women, Work, and Globalization draws on research from anthropology, sociology, and feminist economics, as well as case studies found in the development literature. It highlights the processes of globalization and why it is critical to specifically examine women's experiences. However, it is not meant as a treatise on women's rights nor does it argue that most women are in any manner victims of globalization. Instead, the book emphasizes that macro processes are intimately related to changes in individual's lives and that gender, class, regional location, and ideology are closely intertwined. Another emphasis of this work is on agency: women are not just the passive recipients of the effects of global processes. Instead, they are an integral part of a dynamic system, in part influencing the progression of global changes.

While globalization is a divisive term that suggests to some the growing inequalities between individuals and societies, others see globalization as a positive force that is associated with growing prosperity and interconnectedness. In this book I argue that globalization processes with respect to women are contradictory. Some women, depending on their geographic location, their backgrounds, and their socio-economic class have benefited from the changes brought on through global forces. Other women have become increasingly disadvantaged and their fates have worsened. It is thus impossible to speak of a universal experience, or of the improvement or worsening of the situation of women in a globalizing context. Forgotten in many discussions about the relationship between globalization and the situation of women are also the implications for men. In a rapidly changing work and social environment, men have become more vulnerable to economic dislocation and their traditional primary roles as providers and breadwinners are being challenged. This creates serious questions about normative family and social ideologies and roles, and the long-term viability of current work and family models and policies.

Why the Focus on Women?

This book focuses specifically on the situation of women in an increasingly globalized world. This focus is an outgrowth of my previous book on the relationship between globalization and families. As I conducted my research, I realized that globalization is bringing about intrinsic changes that are altering social life in unforeseen ways. Many of these changes are very specific to women. While feminist economists have recently highlighted the gendered nature of globalization, much of this discussion has not yet been incorporated into the mainstream debates about globalization. Nor has the relationship between women's labor force participation from a global perspective been widely analyzed to include the social implications and repercussions of these changes. This is extremely surprising given the current situation. For instance, in the United States, women are now more prominently represented in the labor force than men. The same is true in higher education, where the national average with respect to college students is approximately 60 percent female to 40 percent male. Other Western countries are moving in the same direction. However, maybe most strikingly, it is in the developing world that we are witnessing a very slow but distinctive move in the same direction. For example, some studies are now suggesting that in places like Bangladesh girls are outperforming boys in schools and are even more likely to continue their education than boys. These transformations are occurring within contexts where being female may still mean that a girl receives less food than the males in her family, or where her brother will be taken to the doctor for health care and she will not.

The complexity of the situation becomes very evident when we turn back to looking right here at home. Despite the success of women in the educational domain, women continue to face specific gender-related challenges both at work and at home. For instance, in the United States only 17 percent of American Fortune 500 board seats are currently occupied by women and only 3 percent of board chairs are held by women. The recent lack of women in President Obama's cabinet has also evoked discussion both at home and abroad. What we find is that women have both made progress and continue to face specific types of prejudice and discrimination. While mainstream rhetoric points to gender norms with respect to behavior and women's supposed "lack of desire for leadership positions," empirical evidence paints a different picture. Women's experiences, opportunities, and challenges are very much influenced by social class and social location. However, even these important factors do not tell the whole story. Women across the geographic and economic spectrum are trying to negotiate a work–life balance, and they face specific obstacles along the way. Even the most successful women who can outsource most of their domestic responsibilities have to find a way to make peace with what are perceived as normative gender roles, that is, that women are supposed to be the main caregivers in families. They do so against a backdrop of contradictory ideological persuasions that posit that women are empowered through working and that women bear the primary responsibility for making sure that their family lives are in order. Moreover, this model of work–family negotiation is spreading across the world. Increasingly, a shared experience for women is to continually debate when, where, and how to best use their energy: at home and at work.

While women have very contradictory experiences with respect to balancing work and family life, this time of globalization also provides new opportunities. The same processes that are creating a global labor market are also intertwined with mechanisms that allow new concepts about human rights, women's rights and empowerment, and economic resourcefulness to spread. Moreover, increasingly individuals are able to come together in global spaces and react to those aspects of their lives that they are dissatisfied with. Throughout this book I argue that there is a democratization of voices occurring that is in constant dialectic with the material and social aspects of globalization. The rapidity of the changes makes this a very complex process. But embedded in this transformation are the seeds for positive change and the potential to create a more socially just world that is characterized by equality between women and men, and where there is a lessening of the social and economic gaps between regions, countries, and individuals.

Content

Women, Work, and Globalization is divided into three parts. The first section, Chapters 1 to 3, gives an overview of the scholarship on the study of gender in the industrialized and developing world, global changes that pertain to women's gender roles, women's labor market participation, globalization, neoliberalism, and the spread of the women's movement. The second section of the book, Chapters 4 to 7, focuses on specific issues that pertain to women in a globalized world, including gender socialization, sexual trafficking and exploitation, labor migration and transnational motherhood, and the complexities entailed in care labor. The third section of the book, Chapters 8 to 10, details programs and policies that have effectively assisted girls and women in attaining skills and education in the developing and industrialized world. Chapter 8 focuses specifically on initiatives that have been instituted by NGOs and governments in developing countries. Chapter 9 is concerned with policies and programs that help women balance work and family in the industrialized countries, and Chapter 10 suggests future directions with respect to crafting successful global policies that assist women balance work and family responsibilities while decreasing their vulnerabilities.

This is a timely moment to build on the many opportune initiatives that are already underway. We need to highlight these programs and policies and build on their successes. It is also imperative, however, to raise awareness of the challenges that so many women face. By engaging in transnational dialogue and collaborations, we can all work together to move women and their families to a better quality of life.

ACKNOWLEDGMENTS

I would like to take this opportunity to especially thank Debra Riegert, my editor at Routledge, for encouraging me to write this book. She was the one who approached me with the idea and has consistently encouraged and cheered me on. Thank you! I am also grateful to Lee Transue and Miren Alberro, Debra's new assistants, as they were very prompt and helpful right from the start.

I am extremely thankful to my colleagues and friends Monika Shafi, Michael Ferrari, and Ralph Ferretti. Each of them regularly checked in on me and encouraged me to keep writing even when I was feeling that balancing a book, a job, and a family was too much for me! I also appreciated the support provided by Lynn Okagaki, Rob Palkovitz, Bob Hampel, Donald Unger, Martha Buell, Barbara Settles, Ruben Viramontez Anguillano, and Olena Nesteruk. Each of them took an interest in my book and tried in various ways to be very supportive. Jennifer Gallo-Fox came in at the end but ended up reading several chapters and providing valuable feedback. I also want to thank the following reviewers: Sandra J. Bailey (Montana State University), Tara Newman (Stephen F. Austin State University), Cynthia Schmiege (University of Idaho), Lynn Walter (University of Wisconsin–Green Bay), Anisa M. Zvonkovic (Texas Tech University), and one anonymous reviewer. Thanks also to Sarah Yarrusso and Tammy Salzbrenner at the University of Delaware for helping keep me organized at work and taking an active interest in the progress of this book.

I am also extremely grateful to my graduate students, especially Nikki DiGregorio for her support throughout this process. Nikki read a draft of this manuscript and gave me helpful feedback. I would also like to thank Laura Finan who worked as my teaching assistant over the last year, and whose cheerful encouragement kept me going. Much appreciation goes to Melina McConatha Rosle, Bethany Willis-Hepp, and Megan Barolet-Fogarty. Each of them cheered me on in different ways.

I would also like to express my gratitude to my old roommates and friends from Yale, Brendan Damon Ethington and Deborah Michals, for their friendship throughout this process. They literally and figuratively held my hand when I was most down. I am also appreciative of the encouragement provided by Nancy McKeon, Julie Donofrio, Joan Sharp, and Marilyn Bensman. They were consistently supportive and took an active interest in my work. In the same spirit I would like to acknowledge my colleagues at NCFR, especially Diane Cushman, Nancy Gonzalez, Jeanne Strand, and Cindy Winter for continually encouraging me and providing whatever supports possible. Diane, in particular, is extremely interested in work–family issues and several of her observations assisted me in reframing some of the topics covered in this book.

I also need to thank my parents, Ingeborg and Ahmed, Tarek and Sophie, and Richard, for encouraging me to continue writing despite various personal obstacles. Finally, I would like to thank my children, Ian and Julia. They are now old enough to understand that I was working on a book and they checked in on my progress every night. Having girl–boy twins, I very much hope that *both* grow up in a world where they will have equivalent opportunities to pursue their talents and desires while maintaining happy personal lives.

I am *more* appreciative to everyone around me for their support and friendship than they will all ever know.

Part I

AN OVERVIEW OF GENDER, WORK–FAMILY ISSUES, AND GLOBAL RESTRUCTURING

1

PERSPECTIVES ON WOMEN, WORK–FAMILY LIFE, AND GLOBAL TRANSFORMATIONS

At a recent speaking event in the United States, I began my talk with a vignette about women from a village in northern Mexico who transitioned from a traditional rural lifestyle to working in an export processing plant. I described how these women are now balancing long one and a half hour commutes with strenuous hours in a factory, while still maintaining all their domestic responsibilities. In my talk I did not pass judgment about their lifestyles or if their quality of life had improved or declined. However, as soon as I finished my speech, I was surrounded by a sizeable group of American women, most probably in their mid-thirties and visibly upset. They asked me why I had used Mexican women for my work–family example, when I was obviously describing their lives as well. They followed me to dinner still recounting the complexities of their daily routines and they asked me "Did the feminist movement really help us?"

I left the evening event disturbed and puzzled. As a scholar of family life, and of the work–family–gender–globalization intersection specifically, I was not able to conclusively answer their question. On the one hand, women's lives have obviously improved—my generation in particular has benefited from increased opportunities in every sphere of our lives. I was able to attend an Ivy League institution and later on obtain a PhD and a professorship due in large part to the efforts of women who are only slightly older than I am. On the other hand, every woman I know, no matter how rich or poor she is, is struggling in some manner to balance work and family responsibilities. Of course, it is not just women who are overburdened. Several recent surveys of American life have indicated that young professional fathers are now the most stressed group of individuals in the United States.[1]

As I reflected on the questions posed to me by the thirty-something women after my talk, I also in my mind compared the lives of these women to what I knew from my field research of low-income women in several countries in the developing world.[2] Many of the women I had encountered had few if any opportunities. They had married young, had had many children, and were burdened by heavy domestic responsibilities. Other women that I met were working but at unsatisfying jobs and always concurrently taking care of their households. Moreover, I realized, my observations are not unique or unusual. A significant feminist and development literature indicates that millions of women in the developing world have exploitative, low-paying jobs without any form of benefits and still are obligated to meet all their traditional family duties. The story, however, is more complex than meets the eye: a substantial number of these women who are negotiating low-paying jobs and family life report that earning an income and interacting with others in the public sphere is an improvement over the more traditional lives of their mothers (Ganguly-Scrase, 2003).

In 1999, the Noble Prize winner Amartya Sen suggested that:

> working outside the home and earning an independent income tend to have a clear impact on enhancing the social standing of a woman in the household and the society. Her contribution to the prosperity of the family is then more visible, and she also has more voice, because of being less dependent on others. Further, outside employment often has useful "educational" effects, in terms of exposure to the world outside the household, thus making her agency more effective.
>
> (p. 192)

In other words, Sen highlighted the fact that working outside of the home, even in what middle-class Westerners may see as an exploitative job, makes some women feel empowered. By earning an income and interacting with others in a more public arena, they feel that they are assisting themselves and their families to obtain a better place in this world. In fact, many of these women, despite the complex conditions under which they work, are extremely grateful to have as they see it "a chance" in life to "get out of their houses."

I begin with these examples to illustrate the complexity of the current situation: women's increased participation in the paid labor force is a multifaceted phenomenon. While working for pay and maintaining one's domestic responsibilities is becoming an increasingly normative experience from a global perspective, we cannot speak of employment as universally empowering to women, nor can we say that women are victims of a new globalized market economy. The opportunities and challenges that accompany this phenomenon vary depending on region, social class, education, race and ethnicity, and individual circumstances. That said, the increase in women's labor force participation is an unprecedented global phenomenon.

Between 1960 and 2010 the labor force participation of women jumped from 31 to 49 percent on the North American continent, from 32 to 53 percent in European countries, from 26 to 38 percent in much of the Caribbean, from 16 to 35 percent in Central America, from 17 to 26 percent in the Middle East and North Africa, from 27 to 64 percent in Oceania, from 21 to 59 percent in South America, and increased slightly in sub-Saharan Africa to about 62 percent (United Nations, 2010; ILO, 2013).[3] These rough aggregate statistics indicate that, in virtually every part of the world, women's labor force participation has increased. However, they do not illustrate intra-region variation or the real enormity of the phenomenon. For instance, in the United States, more than 61 percent of mothers with children under the age of 18 now work outside of the home, a figure that just 30 years ago was almost unimaginable (Statisticbrain, 2013).[4] Simultaneously, men are losing their once taken-for-granted role as the primary or only breadwinner in the family. As women move into the public sphere, every aspect of the social fabric of their societies is being irrevocably altered.[5] While there is awareness of these transformations, much of the dialogue on these issues is limited in scope, and primarily restricted to changes in the Western world. Moreover, the long-range implications of this trend are not well understood.

The immense transformation of the global labor force is accompanied by a re-negotiation of roles in families and new conceptualizations of what is public and private. Responsibilities that were traditionally perceived as private and part of the family domain, such as caregiving, are increasingly the focus of public attention. The lines between work and family life are being blurred and the blueprints for how to manage both are being renegotiated. These immense changes have not just affected women and their families. Instead, communities, employers, and governments around the globe are being forced to react to these social transformations. Some of the responses have been dramatic—for instance, in some countries new policies have been put into place that specifically focus on helping individuals balance their work–family responsibilities. But in other places, these changes despite their impacts on family life have been virtually ignored, or even brought on violent social repercussions.

Even within the family realm, there has been a wide range of responses. In Western middle-class families we are witnessing a slow shift away from patriarchal norms to more egalitarian decision-making and role distribution between women and men. However, in many parts of the world, as was illustrated in the introductory Mexican example, women are now working outside of the home while still being responsible for their domestic responsibilities with little if any assistance from men. Complicating this discussion further is that due to regional, societal, and class differences, it is difficult to pinpoint which policy responses and best practices with respect to work and family negotiation are most promising and would assist individuals achieve a higher quality of life.

Different contexts have elicited varied policy and programmatic responses from states and employers. Some policies and initiatives have been transformative in a positive sense, and have eased the burden on working individuals, and others have been virtually ineffective. What we can say conclusively is that there is no one-size-fits-all solution. However, given the enormity of the social changes around us, it is imperative to highlight, from a *global* cross-cultural perspective, some of the most significant issues around the work–family intersection and to point to possible policy and programmatic solutions. Critical components of this discussion are the role of globalization in spreading new ideologies with respect to work and gender and the transformation of market economies. Moreover, as I pointed out in the preface, globalization has had specific repercussions for women. This work examines that premise and the underlying causes of this phenomenon. It also highlights some of the opportunities and complex challenges for women that have accompanied globalization.

The Global Nature of the Social Transformation

The unparalleled global social transformation we are in the midst of is the consequence of the convergence of a variety of economic and ideological factors. As women in high- and low-income countries become increasingly active in the formal and informal paid labor force, the labor force participation of men has decreased in most regions (Standing, 1999).[6] This social transformation is intimately related to widespread economic and market changes, the global spread of neoliberal and feminist ideologies, and increasingly advanced communication and information technologies. These global changes are transforming ideas about the role of work in individual's lives, appropriate gender roles in families and communities, and the types of supports and practices that increase worker productivity while simultaneously improving the quality of life. The discussions and analyses in this book highlight the enormity of the changes, some of the challenges particularly for women, and the multifaceted nature of the responses.

It is important to begin with the understanding that the social transformation we are in the midst of is not homogeneous in nature. For instance, with respect to gender relations, some regions and even within some arenas of social life, values and practices are rapidly moving toward an increased emphasis on gender equity and parity in the workplace and the home. In other places, however, nationalistic responses have reinforced traditional norms and ideals, particularly with respect to the appropriate roles of women and men in families, communities, and society. These responses are usually understood as a reaction to the spread of Western ideas such as democratization, individualism, and consumerism.

6

However, the situation is more complex than these simplistic explanations imply. Within the same society, for instance, there may be a range of responses varying by social class, region, or ethnic group. A problematic aspect of this transformation is that it is often understood as a Western phenomenon and is treated as such in a burgeoning work–family literature. The increasing entrance of women into the labor force in low-income countries is primarily captured in what is referred to as the "development" literature. Dichotomizing this dialogue does not allow us to explore commonalities in the experiences of women or the intricate ways in which they may actually be interacting with one another.

The unprecedented gendered shift to an increasingly feminized labor force is tied to a variety of new phenomena, including neoliberal conceptions of the marketplace and the spread of Western feminist ideologies that emphasize female empowerment through education and employment. As more women enter the paid labor force and participate in the more public sphere, their self-perceptions are being altered, as are their relationships with men in and outside of families. These social transformations are also playing themselves out in other arenas such as economic, political, and community life. This is not to imply that the large number of women in the global workforce is necessarily just a positive phenomenon. Quite the contrary, many women, particularly poor women in low-income countries and economically marginalized women in high-income countries, are often exploited through the circumstances caused by recent global flows and restructuring. In addition, women's high degree of participation in the global labor force signifies a need for new types of social arrangements with respect to caring labor and nurturance, a predicament that affects families at every level of society. Nonetheless, the extent and global reach of the rearrangement of the social roles of women and men as well as the long-term implications of this change are unique in the history of recent civilization.

In order to understand the complex nature of this aspect of the social transformation within which we find ourselves, it is instructive to draw from interdisciplinary sources such as feminist economics, the work–family literature, and anthropological and sociological perspectives on globalization and gender trends. By focusing on the relationship between economic restructuring, labor market informalization, the feminization of the labor force, changing gender constructions, and the transformation of work and family life, we can better understand the trajectory of changes with respect to gender issues, with the ultimate goal being creating mechanisms and policies that support individuals as they maneuver this new and rapidly changing landscape. While there is much discussion about work–family issues in academic and policy circles, most has focused on the Western world, and primarily the United States. This limited focus has obscured developments in other parts of the world. Much of the world's population lives in low-income countries in the developing world and the experiences of those individuals stand in stark contrast to those who reside in industrialized societies. In particular, many women in other parts of the world do not experience the same degree of equality, choice, and progress in either their work or family lives that have come to be taken for granted over the last several decades by Western women. And even in the West, social positioning plays an important role in the experiences of women and men.

Western Historical Roots of the Gendered Division of Labor

In order to better understand the enormity of the changes we are in the midst of, and to comprehend why so much Western research and policy has had difficulty breaking away from a nostalgic rendition of the traditional breadwinner–homemaker family of the past, it is instructive to revisit some of the past antecedents to contemporary social life. Historically, over the last two hundred years in the West, women were primarily defined by their reproductive activities. However, anthropological evidence indicates that this pattern has not held true for non-industrial societies (Wood & Eagly, 2002). Cross-cultural reports reveal that in many places women have always contributed substantially to the family economy, and may even be the primary providers in most gathering societies. I begin with this fact to negate the popular psychological Western conception that women have traditionally relied on men for subsistence due to their biological dispositions to nurture their young. While in Western industrialized economies men's main role has been to provide resources for their families as their wives were engaged in domestic life, this pattern is only specific to a certain point in time and place.

Much of what is believed in the West about the "appropriate" roles of women and men has its intellectual and material roots in the era of industrialization. From the end of the eighteenth century onward, the growth of capitalist industrialism was accompanied by technical innovations, the development of the factory system, and an independent wage labor system. Technical and social advances led to a swift increase in productivity and the accumulation of wealth by a relatively small elite. During this period, families lost their productive functions and became units of consumption. A growing number of households became more nuclear and focused increasingly on the obligations of parents and children. Nuclear small families were believed to be the family form that was more compatible with the increased demands of production in capitalist societies. Social scientists such as Talcott Parsons suggested that nuclear families with their increased potential for mobility and fewer traditional obligations were more suited for this new economy (1949). This social transformation was accompanied by a growing focus on market relations: "Instead of economy being embedded in social relations, social relations are embedded in the economic system" (Polanyi, 1944, p. 57).

An emergent belief in the market was ideologically accompanied with political liberalism. This perspective emphasized the contractual rights of free and autonomous individuals who had the right to own property. However, women originally were not included in this definition and according to the law were subordinate to men. Crompton (2006) highlights a quote by Mary Astell who asked in the eighteenth century: "if *all Men are born free,* how is it that all Women are born Slaves?" While in the Western tradition women had been naturally considered inferior to men, the shift to a market economy also gave rise to a new manner of thinking about the roles of women and men. Women's roles in the family as nurturers and carers took on increased importance, accompanied by new beliefs about their moral superiority. This shift became known as the concept of "separate spheres" (Hattery, 2001) with men thought to be more dominant and better suited for the public sphere of work, and women, because of their innate nature, best located in the private sphere of the home. This move was accompanied by the development of the male breadwinner division of labor with men's focus being on paid employment while women were to be responsible for the unpaid work of caring for family and domestic obligations. Women were no longer regarded as inferior to men, however, this model still presumed innate and natural physical, spiritual, and psychological differences between the sexes (Crompton, 2006).

This specialization model was accompanied by the physical separation of women from economic and political activities. While it is important to note that many poorer families were unable in practice to adhere to such an arrangement, throughout the course of the twentieth century this model became the ideological basis of much Western social and economic policy. Educational systems, pension plans, and health-care programs were organized around the concept of a male wage earner, who now earned a "family" wage, and his dependent wife and children received benefits as such.[7] States in the Western world supported this arrangement that included social protections for vulnerable individuals. Often referred to as Fordism, this was a system that emerged after World War II in the West and was characterized by mass production, the full employment of males, an emphasis on the state as the provider of a social safety net, and increased personal consumption. An integral and often forgotten aspect of this system was the role of the state in reinforcing social relations and social connectedness (Thompson, 2003). In other words, the state was understood as a critical component of supporting family and community life.

In the last several decades of the twentieth century, the male-breadwinner/female-homemaker model of family life started to disintegrate concurrently with a retreat by nation-states from Fordist ideology and policies. Women in massive numbers joined the paid labor force while states began to withdraw support services. As gender relations and their associated norms and values in the West morphed into new configurations that highlighted equity, autonomy, and self-empowerment, new and old challenges coincided. Primarily, unpaid reproductive labor and caring work for the young, disabled, and elderly, obligations that had been traditionally allocated as the responsibility of women, continued to be assigned to the female sphere. This has raised complex questions about labor force participation, gender roles, family life, and state supports.[8] A concurrent set of transformations also affected the roles of men. The administrative and managerial positions in workplaces that offered stable, lifetime careers with benefits, as well as many unskilled and semi-skilled jobs especially in manufacturing, began to disappear and in their stead only jobs in the much lower-paying service sector emerged. Jobs in the service sector were characterized by their flexibility, a lack of benefits, and the dominant presence of women and young people. These flexible jobs gave complete control to the employer who could determine the number of hours worked and which tasks needed to be completed. It is important to note that transformations in the workplace were only one aspect of larger more intrinsic ideological and economic changes that were reflected in social rearrangements at every level of Western societies. We will examine how these changes have come about and why they have also spread to non-Western societies. However, in order to understand these transformations it is also necessary to examine the philosophical underpinnings that have set the stage for the transformative aspects of globalization.

The Rise of the Importance of Diversity and Individual Agency

The 1980s and 1990s witnessed a revolution in social thought with a shift toward understanding the production of meaning and perspectives. In other words, instead of only studying institutions, meanings, symbols, and representations came to be understood as central to conceptualizing and understanding social life. Writers such as Foucault called into question long-standing beliefs about the objectivity of scientific thought, and instead argued that knowledge is diverse and relative; in other words, that there is no such thing as an "objective truth." This intellectual shift was associated with the dawn of postmodernism and led to a questioning of social scientific meta-theories. Cultural relativity became the foundational aspect of this new approach and the boundaries between cultural understandings and economic life shifted. According to these new social scientific interpretations, economic behavior was driven by cultural imperatives and needed to be understood from that perspective (Crompton, 2006). For instance, this led to a new understanding of markets: that markets are not a neutral force but instead are characterized by winners and losers and are controlled by subjective players. Drawing on proponents of globalization theory such as Giddens (1991), theoretical analysis also now turned to a consideration of which "new" types of behaviors would allow individuals to be more successful in contemporary economically driven environments.

A renewed focus on cultural explanations of behavior was accompanied by an increased interest in identity politics. Instead of an earlier focus on Marxist, class-oriented principles, issues such as the environment and the rights of self-identified minorities such as various ethnic and gay groups grew in importance. The shift from a "politics of redistribution" to a "politics of identity or recognition" led to a convergence of various political streams that now concurrently supported neoliberal conceptions of the market with an emphasis on individual rather than collective action. This move also meshed well with arguments that had criticized collective social welfare nets as disempowering vulnerable individuals (Crompton, 2006). As will be discussed extensively further on, a mainstay of contemporary economic and ideological thought has become the concept of the individual who takes care of his or herself without having to rely on the assistance of a larger entity such as the nation-state. This belief is closely related to what has become known as reflexive modernity, and is associated with the concept of "choice" and the individual's rational ability to make something of themselves (Beck, Giddens, & Lash, 1994). From this perspective neither family responsibilities nor the constraints of a place of employment determine an individual's life course. Instead, "the positioning of individuals via class and status mechanisms is replaced by a focus on the construction of individual identities" (Crompton, 2006, p. 9). In other words, individual agency and motivation become the critical aspects that either further or constrain lifetime opportunities and advancement.

This emphasis in social thought on culture, individual agency, and choice needs to be contextually understood as a retreat from earlier ideological stances in the 1960s and 1970s, most often based on Marxist thought, whence the material basis of life was assumed to govern individual experience, that is, the system determines life outcomes, and thus, needed to be rethought and restructured. Instead, the foundational concept of redistribution has been replaced by a new focus on the role of cultural relativism and how due to cultural devaluing certain groups have lost access to resources, power, and prestige. This approach moves away from suggesting that by redistributing resources we can redress inequalities in social relations, and instead advocates that recognition of a group is the key to righting injustices. This contemporary approach to social justice is controversial however. As Fraser (2000) explains:

> the current reality, in which marketization has pervaded all societies to some degree, at least partially decoupling economic mechanisms of distribution from cultural patterns of value and prestige. Partially independent of such patterns, markets follow a logic of their own, neither wholly constrained by culture nor

subordinated to it; as a result they generate economic inequalities that are not mere expressions of identity hierarchies. Under these conditions, the idea that one could remedy all mal-distribution by means of a politics of recognition is deeply deluded: its net result can only be to displace struggles for economic justice.

(pp. 111–112)

Fraser continues by suggesting that this single-minded focus on identity recognition effectively also erases intra-group variation: "The overall effect is to impose a single, drastically simplified group-identity which denies the complexity of people's lives, the multiplicity of their identifications and the cross-pulls of their various affiliations" (p. 112).

She points out instead, that a true social justice approach needs two components: a dimension of recognition and a dimension of distribution. This perspective allows us to understand societies as complex arenas that contain intertwined cultural and economic aspects. However, she also suggests that in market societies, economic distribution becomes in part decoupled from non-market arenas in which interactions based on customary values and beliefs may dominate. In other words, under capitalism, cultural values and patterns do not necessarily always determine economic allotments, and class disparities do not just mirror status hierarchies. We need to understand the relationship between both—between economic arrangements and culturally based status recognition—in order to redress injustices to individuals and groups.

Analyzing social interactions from economic *and* cultural perspectives allows us to better understand the effects of institutionalized norms on capacities for interaction while moving away from essentializing existing configurations. Thus, throughout this work, we will focus on the material, the ideological, and the cultural underpinnings of gender relations in the spheres of the marketplace, communities, and families. This approach allows us to develop a more nuanced understanding of current social transformations, and will let us speculate on those strategies that may best mitigate the more harmful aspects of the changes we find ourselves amidst.

Family Life and Rational Choice

Since a primary focus of this book is on the work–family intersection from a cross-cultural perspective, it is instructive to examine current conceptualizations and arguments around family life. While there is much dispute around the definition and usage of the term "family," ethnographic work indicates that most individuals live in some form of close contact with principal others with whom they are related through a combination of emotional attachments, economics and/or blood ties. In both Western and non-Western societies, the early socialization of children is centered in

12

families, and family contact remains a primary source of social identification throughout most individual's lives. Despite this fact, contemporary social scientists such as Beck (1992) and Giddens (1991, 2003) argue that a defining feature of Western societies is an increased emphasis on individuation, deciding on one's own unique life course, decoupled from family responsibilities and normative prescriptions and roles. From this perspective, family affiliations are decreasing in importance, and personal choices and inclinations are becoming the foundational aspects of people's lives. Adherents to this perspective point to rising divorce rates, increases in out-of-wedlock births, cohabitation, and a whole myriad of interpersonal behaviors as evidence that families are decreasing in importance on both an individual and a societal level. They also suggest that the increasing number of women in the paid labor force in the West is an indication that women are exercising their "choices" and constructing new identities and lifestyles for themselves that are weakening families.[9]

This ideological perspective on the role of women in families disregards the context within which individuals make choices related to employment decisions. For instance, many women take on part-time rather than full-time employment in order to balance their work and family lives. Moreover, as will be discussed in greater detail, choosing to work outside of the home is often primarily a financial decision, driven by economic contexts that require any kind of income in order for individuals and their families to survive. Exercising choice with respect to employment decisions is fundamentally a very ethnocentric Western perspective: in many parts of the world, individuals have far less control over their lives than Westerners (or at least a certain segment of rather well-to-do Westerners) do. The choices they make are primarily determined within the context of family membership and the normative rules of their cultures, and are not based on individual wishes or Western notions of self-realization. Especially in non-Western contexts, women, and in particular poor women, often have very little choice with respect to their life trajectories or the extent to which they can absolve themselves of their family obligations (Edgar, 2004). These women often have few if any material resources and they are in constant survival mode. Their life course is often governed by the fact that they are female in cultures where initially their fathers and later their husbands still have primary control over their lives. This observation is not meant to obscure the role of personal agency in these women's lives, but just to highlight that there are still many cultural contexts where the mere fact of being female has serious social implications that differ from the contemporary Western experience.

Despite the many changes in the West, Crompton (2006) points out that with respect to employment decisions, many Western women also must negotiate personal choice and external constraints. In particular, when it comes to caring responsibilities, women will balance these duties with work obligations by drawing on a moral framework that is not just based on personal choice and the maximization of personal benefit. Seconding the arguments of Duncan (2003) and Finch and Mason (1993), Crompton suggests that family responsibilities are not just rights and obligations but instead are developed over time, and contain material and moral elements. Moreover, when considering their choices, individuals also develop their own identities as a mother or father, career woman, caretaker, and so on. In other words, individuals are not operating in a vacuum, obsessed only by rational calculations. Instead, choices are made relationally to oneself, significant others, and some form of a normative cultural framework. This complex relationship is found at all class levels and across societies. For example, what constitutes a "good" mother may differ over time and place, but all working women with children will make choices as to the extent that they wish to adhere to their contemporary cultural frame of reference in relation to their employment decisions and the amount of effort and energy they wish to invest in each arena.

As this brief discussion indicates, contemporary changes in Western and non-Western family arrangements and women's employment patterns are intimately related to a constellation of other issues. Castells (2000), for example, highlights the decline of patriarchy and the influx of women in the labor force as principal components of restructured societies and the new world that we operate in. Some social theorists such as Giddens (2003) point to the relationship between women in the paid labor force and the increased individualization of Western societies, while others suggest that in non-Western countries gender roles are strongly influenced by former experiences with colonialism and other repressive regimes, as well as contemporary notions of neoliberalism (Beneria, 2003). We will examine all of these arguments in greater detail in later chapters. However, in order to understand how gender roles are being re-conceptualized and why this is such a controversial issue in both industrialized and developing countries, it is necessary to revisit some of the foundational writings on gender.

Gender as an Organizing Principle

Throughout this work the concept of gender is used as the central organizing category to discuss changes in work and family life and their interrelationship with economic, political, and social life. At this point gender is defined as "socially learned behavior and expectations that distinguish between masculinity and femininity" (Peterson & Runyan, 1993, p. 5) and is understood to be significant on three distinct levels: gender as critical to ideology and in particular to social processes, practices, and beliefs; gender as a vital part of social relations; and gender as the social construction of male and female bodies (Marchand & Runyan, 2000). The focus on gender is necessary in order to better understand the circumstances that govern the lives of so many women around the world. In spite of some utopian feminist writings, we do not live in a gender-neutral world, and in fact the role of women in public and private spheres remains a hotly debated topic. Specifically, the massive move of women into the paid labor force has been accompanied by concerns around the negotiation of caring responsibilities and associated changes to the roles of men and children.

Observations on the transformation of gender roles are coupled with intensive debates around the restructuring of societies and the need for social policies that can support new types of families. These deliberations are occurring in environments where programs and policies that support individuals and families have often actually decreased. While most work–family and gender-focused discussions and analyses emphasize the changing roles of women, it is important to note that men's roles have also been profoundly affected by these transformations. Any analysis that does not take into account this dualistic relational perspective cannot adequately reflect the revolutionary changes that are taking place in so many places around the globe. As an aside, it is important to note that throughout much contemporary scholarship, gender has become a proxy term for women. However, we cannot understand social life by only examining the condition and circumstances of one group without explicit reference to their other relationships. As ideologies with respect to women and their roles and status change, men are implicated as well. We are, thus, really looking at a complete shift in gender relations that has significant repercussions beyond the individual and societal levels.

That the issue of gender is central to understanding global restructuring can be seen in the many political discussions that repeatedly highlight the role of women and the democratization of societies. Time after time, the status of women and their rights becomes a focal point with respect to understanding how to advance societies and create supportive social policies. For instance, Hirdman (1998) introduced the concept of a "gender contract," arguing that during the Fordist period, Western societies subscribed to a breadwinner–homemaker contract whose primary purpose was to support state conceptions of creating "good citizens" and "good workers." Families were the mechanism for this process and were organized on gendered lines. Now this contract is rapidly fading away and being replaced by an "equality" or "citizen-worker" contract that focuses on people's relationships to employment rather than family roles (Crompton, 2006). Importantly, Crompton highlights the fact that in our contemporary environment it is not enough just to focus on gender. Instead, "these developments must be examined in parallel with other aspects of change, particularly in relation to class and the structuring of inequality" (Crompton, 2006, p. 14).

Gender is never just a stand-alone concept. It is intimately connected with the ideology, economics, politics, and policies of a time, and, thus, needs to be understood and examined from this perspective.

Doing Gender

The starting point for any analyses that focus primarily on gender is the "doing gender" perspective that was first pioneered in the late 1980s. This is a significant concept because it introduced the idea that gender is actively created; in other words, gender is not a fixed entity. West and Zimmerman (1987) explain:

> We contend that the "doing" of gender is undertaken by women and men whose competence as members of society is hostage to its production. Doing gender involves a complex of socially guided perceptual, interactional, and micro-political activities that cast particular pursuits as expressions of masculine and feminine "natures."
>
> When we view gender as an accomplishment, an achieved property of situated conduct, our attention shifts from matters internal to the individual and focuses on interactional and, ultimately, institutional arenas ... Rather than as a property of individuals, we conceive of gender as an emergent feature of social situations: both as an outcome of and a rationale for various social arrangements and as a means of legitimating one of the most fundamental divisions of society.
>
> (p. 126)

This approach to conceptualizing gender still has contemporary validity. It is also a useful historical and cross-cultural concept for understanding variations in gender roles and gendered behavior. The "doing gender" perspective highlights the social construction of gender. In other words, it allows us to understand that gender is created through interactions between individuals. We ascribe meaning to those interactions depending on context: primarily time and place. From this perspective, gender is not a static concept but instead is continually changing in response to a variety of stimuli. Moreover, gender is *accomplished* by individuals. They conduct themselves in such a manner that befits certain customary expectations. Culture provides normative guidelines and they influence and regulate appropriate gender behaviors.[10]

An extensive feminist literature has now incorporated the "doing gender" approach into social analyses of domestic relationships. Sullivan (2006), however, critiques these investigations. She proposes that most scholarly treatises on gender emphasize almost exclusively "how contextual behaviors lead to the reproduction of existing structures of gender inequality, rather than on their possible contribution to processes of differentiation and change in those structures" (Sullivan, 2006, p. 11). There is, thus, a serious omission in scholarship: we focus on how existing gender constructions are maintained and reproduced in social contexts such as families instead of exploring how gender ideologies are changing in contemporary contexts, or on how to effect change with respect to gender norms and behaviors.

Gender and Interconnectedness

An integral aspect of understanding gender is its multifaceted nature. Gender is not a stand-alone concept. Instead, it is intimately tied to images, ideas, institutions, and practices. Conceptualizations about gender identity and appropriate gender roles vary over time and place and are tied to other social processes. This dynamic relationship allows us to understand why globalization has played such an integral part in the spread of new images and practices with respect to gender, and why in so many places this is leading to a re-conceptualization of gender, with very specific repercussions for women and men. While global processes may seem uniform and homogeneous (for instance, the freer flow of capital or the spread of certain beliefs or images through communication technologies), these same developments have very different impacts depending on local contexts. As certain ideas or practices are disseminated around the globe, they are not necessarily universally embraced and may be altered through the process. For instance, as will be seen in Chapter 3, feminist gender ideologies have had a mixed reception in different societies around the globe. The consequences of this transfer of ideas are also often quite different than their originators may have intended them to be. Thus, global flows and transformations are complex and dynamic, and cannot simplistically be characterized as beneficial or oppressive to any one group. By deconstructing dominant discourses on the empowerment of women through paid work, or the detrimental effects of globalization on life chances, we begin to understand the subjectivity and ethnocentrism that governs our own Western analyses of social phenomena. Through these reflections we can also highlight the power of individual and collective agency (Davids & van Driel, 2005). Ultimately, women and men are not the "victims" of social processes. Instead, individuals on their own and as a group have the power to effect changes— sometimes albeit in minor and, at other times, significant ways.

It is important at this juncture, however, to point out that particularly in non-Western contexts the situation of low-income women is very much influenced by their gender. Obviously, not at all times and not in every place—however, there are still many places in the world where gender is one, if not the most, defining aspect of an individual's identity. In many communities, girls and women are often the group that is marginalized or suppressed in official discourses, policies, and actions. Even in their families, cultural values may dictate that girls receive less food than boys, are not allowed to continue their schooling, and are not given the right to movement after they reach puberty (Plan UK, 2009). The dynamics of unequal gender relations are closely linked to institutional and structural factors that affect the intra-household distribution of resources and the social construction of gender. Multiple studies illustrate that in certain contexts women may have access to material resources but are not guaranteed access to them (Darbinger, 2007). For instance, a popular contemporary development strategy is to encourage women to participate in microfinance ventures. While women are almost always the primary recipients of microcredit loans, it may ultimately be their husbands who subsequently utilize these funds to promote their own agendas.[11]

It is important to remember that traditions, norms, and gender constructions interact with access to resources and power relations. These processes, in turn, shape gender ideologies and behaviors. For example, in a study of lower-class women in West Bengal, India, Ganguly-Scrase (2003) illustrates that women do not necessarily seek to be autonomous beings, independent of their families. They view their financial contributions as important to the collective, which they, in turn, perceive as the support system that aids them in accomplishing their desires for greater opportunities. And in spite of an increasing global concern with improvements in the roles and positions of women, the truly disadvantaged are still being subjugated and exploited, particularly from an economic and social perspective. This brings us to the contentious topic of globalization, as globalization is often perceived as a contemporary form of economic domination. However, as we shall see in Chapter 2, globalization is a broad phenomenon, not just limited to economic processes, and is not easily classified as either oppressive or opportune.

From a mainstream perspective, globalization is associated with the economic restructuring of world markets. However, recent contributions from the social sciences also stress the significance of people and ideas being interconnected through global processes. Giddens describes globalization as a "two-way flow of images, information and influences … a 'decentered' and reflexive process characterized by links and cultural flows which work in a multidirectional way" and as "the product of numerous intertwined networks" (2001, p. 60). This conceptualization of globalization highlights this phenomenon as unique and dynamic, a process that is open to continuous changes and stimuli. Globalization opens up new options and horizons, and presents new risks. An integral aspect of the process is that information and communication are exchanged instantaneously through flexible networks. The implications of this social phenomenon are profound for individuals and, as I argue throughout this book, for women in particular. Globalization has opened up workplaces and educational opportunities for many women. Simultaneously, many women have taken on exploitive employment and increased responsibilities since their home obligations have not lessened. However, globalization has also allowed for the spread of information about women's rights, new opportunities for women, and the creation of female-centered local and transnational networks. Embedded in the process is the potential for new and different ways of relating and collaborating across national, racial-ethnic, class, and gender boundaries.

The complexities that accompany globalizing processes are perhaps best understood through a longitudinal example, such as what has happened with respect to gender representations and images in India.

Case Study: Working-Class Men in India and Gender Perceptions

The relationship between global restructuring, economics, and localized events and gender transformations are at time particularly complex in non-Western societies. Derne (2008) describes a process in India where in 1991 as the Indian government lifted restrictions on the economy in response to pressure by the International Monetary Fund (IMF), Western media and advertisers responded by flooding Indian markets with their messages. As individuals from a mix of social classes were exposed to Western styles of clothes, consumption goods, and new ideologies with respect to love, marriage, and diverse family styles, many Indian men did not embrace these new gender ideologies. Instead, many Indian men became enthralled by Western media depictions of pornography, violence, and female body ideals. In particular, the graphic images that objectify women took hold and were grafted onto traditional gender role ideals that privilege men over women. This phenomenon stands in stark contrast to the viewpoints of many globalization scholars who have advocated that exposure to Western gender ideals would lead to an improvement in the status of women. This hypothesis was based on a stereotypical notion that in non-Western societies there was little previous focus on gender and power relations and that through contact with new ideas, those concepts would now take hold. In order to understand why this progression has not necessarily played itself out, we need to examine the relationship between economics and cultural flows.

Up until the 1980s, India pursued an economic strategy that was primarily focused on internal development and not widely interconnected with the rest of the world. However, due to the rise in oil prices associated with the 1991 Gulf War, a crisis of foreign exchange reserves occurred and the government had to rely on the IMF for a bailout. In turn, the IMF set up a series of preconditions, including that the government end licensing for a majority of industries, reduce restrictions on multinational investments, and devalued the rupee. This lead to imports doubling, exports tripling, and foreign capital investment quintupling (Shurmer-Smith, 2000). Economic change was simultaneously accompanied by cultural flows, in particular with respect to media. For instance, in 1991 India had one state-run television channel which morphed exponentially to 70 cable channels by 1999. Simultaneously, individuals' access to televisions jumped from somewhat less than 10 percent of the population living in urban areas to about 65 percent in 1999. In 1991 about 300,000 homes received cable television. By 1999, this figure had multiplied to 24 million homes. As foreign exchange restrictions were lifted, contemporary Hollywood movies were dubbed into Hindi and were seen widely. These movies were accompanied by local language programing that drew in the majority of the audiences.

In order to understand the impact of this change in media access, Derne conducted two studies, one in 1991 and another one in 2001 comparing non-elite middle-class Indian men's responses to films with an emphasis on gender and family life. He emphasizes throughout his work that these were men who did not have access to cars, trips abroad, or global consumer goods but instead due to constraints in employment opportunities and money, as well as a lack in English skills, had to make do with local goods. This middle-class segment of men was a group that prides itself and identifies specifically with sustaining traditional gender arrangements. They were also the group that critiqued more affluent Indian groups for having abandoned these customs (Derne 2005).

When Derne first conducted his study in 1991, none of the men in his study had seen a Hollywood movie, but by 2001, 60 percent had watched such a film and about half reported that they regularly watched these movies. Most of the men had also acquired access to cable in some form by that time.

Interestingly, Derne found that while one of the primary media values that is being transferred from the West to the East is the notion of romantic love and finding the "right" one as the basis for marriage, the men in his study stayed as committed to the notion of arranged marriage in 2001 as they had been in 1991. Interviews revealed that young men adhered to this notion due to their belief in the "stability" and "security" of such marriages. Moreover, virtually all of the men expressed a strong belief in traditional gender roles and the importance of home life for women. These non-elite men while now aware of these new lifestyles did not feel any desire to emulate in their family lives these Western ideals. Derne explains these men's reactions by suggesting that "media celebration of unattainable lifestyle-standards may heighten men's attachment to existing gender arrangements that provide them a fictive measure of status in a world of limited opportunities" (p. 127).

Concerns about global media images in countries such as India are often orchestrated by political elites with singular agendas. However, these concerns resonate in particular with middle-class men who feel that cultural changes will not work in their favor and, thus, they would like to maintain traditional gender arrangements. Derne, for example, describes the public backlash in India with respect to Valentine's Day, which is perceived as a purely American export. In recent years there have been multiple Valentine's Day attacks against couples out at local restaurants in cities such as Delhi and Kanpur, with activists blackening their victims' faces and forcing them to leave, as well as demonstrations against stores selling Valentine's cards. Protesters believe that Western-style love matches threaten the very foundation of Indian society by destroying the concept of joint family living and arranged marriages (Shukla, 2003). While globalization has increased awareness among these men of a wider range of lifestyles, it has also wholeheartedly led them to embrace more traditional concepts of gender relations. In fact, if anything they now support customary male privilege even more resolutely than before.

Interestingly, while local Indian men may resist media representations that introduce new more equal gender arrangements, they have, however, embraced other notions introduced by Western media into their lives and imaginations. For example, most popular have been those beliefs that reinforce images of male privilege, in particular the association of maleness with violent aggression. The increased realism with respect to male violence in Western films in comparison to Hindi films is a favorite aspect of these movies for local men. What we find, then, is that instead of introducing new egalitarian cultural blueprints, globalization at the local level may actually bolster and *increase* the privileging of male hierarchies and notions of power over women.

Derne (2005) also discovered that the transmission of Western images is rapidly impinging on conceptualizations of beauty and attractiveness. Television, foreign films, and the Internet have introduced new standards of beauty in India that depart radically from more traditional trends. While previously females were admired for being voluptuous, newer beauty ideals stress ultra-thin models, similar to what is thought to be attractive in the United States and Europe. Derne describes how fan magazines now stress the diet and exercise regimens of Indian celebrities and are celebrating a completely different standard of beauty. Part of this new focus on transnational standards of beauty are driven by corporate interests that are attempting to instill more universal consumer cravings for clothes, make-up, and foods around the globe (Munshi, 2001). However, more importantly, the new standard for women emphasizes the idea that women are thin, fragile, vulnerable, and depend on the protection of men.

Transnational trends with respect to appearance are not limited to women alone. A new version of male attractiveness as muscled and large is also beginning to dominate the Indian media landscape. Jain (2001) points out that the characteristic iconography of traditional Hindu male deities depicted them as rounded, soft, and smooth bodied. A god's body was thought, ideally, to be gentle and beautiful. However, more contemporary representations now stress a muscled, strong look. From the perspective of certain analysts, the "new" bodies of men and women dangerously depict an increasing emphasis on female vulnerability and the need for protection, and an association with aggression for men (Derne, 2005).

In response to these trends, Indian feminist groups have targeted media portrayals that emphasize the sexuality of women and their commodification (Oza, 2001). The fact that these protests have been growing with vigor over the last several years indicates, in part, that this issue is becoming more significant in Indian culture. What we see with the Indian case example is that while transnational cultural flows may introduce new gender ideals and potential types of relationships, there is variation in how they are adopted in local settings. Aspects of these newly introduced representations may be integrated into the local culture and other facets may be employed to advance the status quo. As the case of Indian middle-class men illustrates, new cultural resources may even be incorporated in order to strengthen the traditional gender hierarchies that are already in place. As Connell (1998) suggests, the emerging global order is not necessarily associated with gender progressivism but may instead give men new tools with which to affirm old ideals. The Indian media example illustrates that the processes of globalization can distort existing social constructions of gender, strengthen them, or lead to an assimilation of traditional and new concepts into new unexpected combinations (Pyle & Ward, 2003).

Globalization as a Multifaceted Phenomenon

The Indian case study illustrates that the progression of globalization is multidirectional and may have contradictory effects. On the one hand, globalization can spread universal images around the world, as is indicated by the more standard conceptualization of beauty that is increasingly embraced worldwide. On the other hand, global flows can also serve to strengthen traditional beliefs with respect to gender and family roles, as is witnessed by the working-class Indian men's marital choices. This illustrates that conceptualizing globalization as a process separate from the lived experiences of individuals creates a false notion about the process and the effects of this phenomenon. Globalization is a dynamic process that has varying effects and is itself affected in a myriad of ways. As the case study about India illustrates, individuals in specific locales attach meanings to their day-to-day rhythms, values, and practices. Some of these meanings are bound in historical precedent, while others are created and/or negotiated through new stimuli. Globalization feeds this process as new images and beliefs are distributed widely and rapidly. In turn, various aspects of globalization are in turn transformed through these same processes.

Gender as an analytical tool allows us to gain more intimate insight into the dynamics and mechanisms of globalizing processes. Gender is a set of social relationships produced in specific institutional contexts (Jones, 2007). It cannot be reduced to purely being informed and driven through culture or economic relationships. Instead, as Fraser (2007) suggests, gender needs to be understood through a bifocal lens: one that correlates gender issues with the economic structures of society, that is, the division of labor and the fundamental split between paid productive labor and unpaid reproductive and domestic labor; and one that explicates how status is determined in different cultural contexts, specifically institutional-ized patterns of interacting that are culturally valued as masculine and femi-nine. By applying a two-dimensional approach to examining these activities and the institutions that sustain them, we begin to see how ideologies are formed and transformed into praxis. This type of investigation allows us to understand which activities and institutions in certain places support gender inequality, and how we can address injustices.

The examination of the relationship between gender constructions, work–family issues, and globalization throughout this book illustrates that globalization is not a top-down process that influences our behaviors and wreaks havoc with our lives. Instead, globalization is a dynamic pro-cess, constantly changing and, thus, has the potential to be used for the betterment of the human condition. However, in order to effect positive changes, we need to be conscious of how these processes work and the impact they are having. This entails detailed analyses of family and work lives as well as changing gender constructions. Moreover, these analyses need to situate their subjects in the socio-historical contexts in which they are occurring. In particular, cultural boundaries often create barriers to understanding social processes. For instance as Nussbaum (2001) points out, even some feminists may perceive cultures in non-Western societies as "backwards" or "reactionary" while ignoring the fact that until recently sexism played a major role in Western women's lives, and that actually other places in the world are also characterized by progressive traditions.

Ultimately, the incorporation of gender, cross-cultural comparisons, and globalization into our work will help us shape more effective policies and programs. For instance, we need to rethink our educational systems in order to make individuals become more successful in our new skills- and knowledge-based economies. We also need to re-consider current conceptualizations of work, the ideal worker, and productivity. All of these notions are tied not just to profitability and markets but also to quality of life issues. And most importantly we need to move away from dualistic analyses that juxtapose the market versus cultural beliefs.

At this point in our globalized world, everything is intertwined, inter-related, and interdependent. In order to move forward in a manner that will be beneficial and create the greatest good, we need to re-examine traditional concepts that were developed when societies had very differ-ent historical and economic foundations. For example, much of the theo-rizing that we look to today has its roots in the time of the Industrial Revolution when work moved out of the home and separate spheres became the dominant ideological framework for the distribution of gender roles. The incorporation of socio-historical moment is critical due to our tendency to subscribe to Bourdieu's (1991) concept of "habitus." We tend to rely on learned, fundamental, unconscious beliefs and values, which we take as self-evident universals and we act within certain envi-ronments, conditions, and constraints without examining what *may* be possible. For instance, we are currently immersed in a free-market ideol-ogy that presupposes that all individuals are rational agents seeking to maximize their utility (Nussbaum, 2001). This type of approach ignores that individuals in other cultures may hold very different values, shaped by their traditions and contexts. Globalization forces us to confront these cultural differences and to find mechanisms to overcome them.

Synopsis

As we have seen in this chapter, working outside of the home is becoming a central tenet of the female experience in both the industrialized and the developing world. However, female participation in the paid labor force is accompanied by a host of challenges and opportunities, primarily revolving around balancing work and home responsibilities. While, there is increased recognition that this phenomenon is changing households, communities, and societies in unforeseen ways, in particular the realm of the family has become extremely politicized as the site for restructuring processes. As will be discussed in the next chapter, in every region of the world, the global economy encourages and demands that a constantly growing number of women join the formal workforce. However, women in both high-income and low-income countries are then met with contradictory rhetoric and public policy. On the one hand, they are valued for their labor and devalued for their familial roles; and on the other hand, conservative viewpoints continue to stress the importance of women as mothers and caretakers. As Brodie (1994) suggests, when women simultaneously are expected to be in the workforce and to take on additional domestic and caretaking responsibilities, this leads to "a crisis in social reproduction" (p. 58).

An additional complex aspect in this situation is a primarily Western perspective that assumes, despite empirical evidence to the contrary, that families are increasingly losing their relevance as a foundational element of societies. Evidence for this assumption is often provided by pointing to the lack of formal family policies in many countries and a growing global reduction in family-centered programs and services. This perspective however, is the result of the lack of holistic analyses that link family life, research on women and gender, and global processes. Moreover, this perspective can be traced to a Western bias toward individualism.

As the post-World War II traditional breadwinner–homemaker family disappears, and new diverse family forms become the norm, there is an implicit assumption embedded in analyses of these changes that individuals do not "need" families in the same manner as in the past. Scholars and policy-makers point to the democratization of family life, dual career couples, the decreasing authority of men, the growing acceptance of alternative lifestyles such as cohabitation, single parenthood, divorce, and same-sex couples, and more varied life course trajectories as evidence of this point (see for instance the work of Beck-Gernsheim, 1998). Moreover, oftentimes, these changes in Western families are also assumed to be occurring in the non-Western world, leading policy-makers and scholars to assume that the family realm is losing its significance for individuals around the globe. This Western bias ignores the reality that for much of the world life chances are still determined by family affiliation and values, and that the connection between family well-being and the economic and political systems is very closely intertwined.

In the industrialized and developing world, concerns about changes to the labor force, rising inequalities, and increased poverty are increasing. In addition, massive rural–urban and transnational migrations as well as the increased labor force participation of women are effecting complex changes in family and community life. These changes indicate that there is a direct connection between transformations in the economic and political realms, gender roles, and the microcosm of families. Women are at the center of these changes from both an ideological and a role perspective. In the past, in many Western and non-Western societies, women were second-class citizens without initially the right to vote, and later with restricted access to paid work. Men earned rights to pensions, unemployment, and other economic benefits through paid work, and women accessed these rights by their relationship to their husbands. Now, women's lives have changed dramatically as they too have been able to attain material and symbolic resources (Orloff, 2002).

However, as we have seen, women's lives have not universally been improved and, in fact, their growing presence in paid employment has led to new debates and controversies about the nature of work, family life, and the programs and policies that would better their lives. In order to understand how some of these changes have come about, it is instructive to examine some of the processes of globalization and why neoliberalism and the spread of the women's movement have brought about these changes in women's lives.

Notes

1 See a very interesting report by the Families and Work Institute on the changing roles of men in U.S. society entitled "The new male mystique" (Aumann, Galinsky, & Matos, 2011).
2 I do not particularly care for the dichotomization of the world into the industrialized versus developing world, but as that is common terminology, I will employ these categories throughout this work. Some scholars like to use geographic categories such as the Global North versus the Global South, but I see that dichotomy as being even more problematic.
3 The statistics for sub-Saharan Africa in particular vary depending on how work is defined. Traditionally, a high percentage of women have participated in agriculture or in market work, accounting for the high figures. There are significant inconsistencies in how statistics are gathered.
4 Statistics for working mothers for developing parts of the world are not available—they are gathered by region pointing to some of the issues characteristic of analyses of the developing world. See for instance the United Nations report, *The world's women 2010: Trends and statistics* (2010).

Table 1.1 Employed mothers (Industrialized world)

Mothers that work outside of the home	Percentage
United States	61
Sweden	76
Denmark	74
Norway	73
Netherlands	66
Austria	66
France	59
United Kingdom	55
Germany	53
Italy	47
Australia	45
Japan	34
Czech Republic	32
Global Average	54.3
Satisfaction Survey (Statisticbrain.com)	
Working mothers who say they are "happy" or "pretty happy"	85
Working mothers who say they "sometimes/frequently" feel stressed	86

Source: Statisticbrain (2013); Nationmaster (2013).

5　I am here referring specifically to women joining the global market economy. However, there are places, for instance in West Africa, where women have traditionally participated in the market economies of their communities.

6　For instance, in the United States just 69.8 percent of all men over age 16 were in the labor force in August 2012, compared to a long-term average of 78.3 percent since the Labor Department began tracking these data in 1948 (Bureau of Labor Statistics, 2013).

7　See Dorothy Smith's article on SNAF—the Standard North American Family (1993)—for an explication of the in-grainedness of that model in US policy and life.

8　Reproductive labor refers to the labor that households need to care and maintain themselves and future generations. The main aspects of reproductive labor are child bearing and raising, and the daily survival and sustenance tasks that maintain household members.

9　See for example, Hakim (2000) for a strong proponent of the viewpoint that employment choices are based on values and not on structural constraints.

10　See the work by Margaret Mead in New Guinea (1939) for examples of how in some cultures males behave in ways that are thought of as intrinsically female in the West, such as body adornment.

11　See the discussion on microfinance and microcredit in Chapter 8.

2

GLOBALIZING FORCES

Neoliberalism, Economic Restructuring, and the Transformation of the Global Workforce

At a global conference organized by the Women's Forum for the Economy and Society in Deauville, France in 2009, Sandra Aguebor from Benin City, Nigeria described to an audience of 1,100 participants a dream she had had for a whole week at the age of 14: she dreamed of repairing cars and of working with oil and black machines. Her parents who farmed a small plot of land at first ignored her pleas to bring this dream to fruition. Sandra persisted, went to school in the mornings, and learned car repair skills with 33 boys in the afternoon. Her efforts paid off: she became Nigeria's first female auto mechanic, training other women in the process. She calls her project the "Lady Mechanic Initiative" (Supp, 2009). Also presenting at this conference were Diane von Fürstenberg, the U.S. fashion designer, Sandrine Devillard, a French executive with McKinsey & Company, and Irene Khan, from Bangladesh who was at that point the head of Amnesty International. Each of the female presenters had a unique take on globalization: they had benefited from the collaborations engendered by new opportunities and contacts, and they were aware of the tolls that the process had taken on some of their native citizens. The speakers described globalization as the collision of the top with the bottom: some individuals benefit from globalization and others are harmed by it. None of the presenters understood globalization to be just unidirectional. Instead, each of these women pointed out that globalization is simultaneously an economic and social force, with challenges and opportunities embedded in its processes. However, each woman also asked the same question: in the minds of many, globalization is synonymous with progress—but does progress just mean more opportunities for a select few, or does progress translate into the creation of a better, more just world (Supp, 2009)?

Our contemporary time is marked by the phenomenon of globalization which has brought with it unprecedented economic, political, and social changes. Globalization is a broad construct that encompasses a variety of

28

processes including an increasing flow of capital, goods, people, and ideas, as well as massive changes in information and communication exchanges. An integral aspect of globalization from the mid-1960s onwards has been the move of record numbers of women in both high-income and low-income countries into the paid labor force.

Women's economic participation has been marked by three trends: the global labor force is becoming increasingly female, more women are working in the informal or more perilous economy, and a greater number of women are migrating to the industrialized world to work in the service industry (Desai, 2010). These trends can be attributed to a number of inter-related factors, including the changing nature of the labor market, the increased popularity of neoliberal policies, and the spread of feminist ideas about women's emancipation through work. All of these changes have had wide-ranging social implications. For instance, as women have increasingly entered the workforce, there has been a parallel steady decline in men's employment (Standing, 1999). Moreover, the types of jobs that were traditionally held by men, jobs associated with lifetime employment and benefits, are being restructured and increasingly filled by women. Some analysts have characterized these changes as the "feminization" of the workforce (see Standing 1999; Wichterich, 2000; or Hawkesworth, 2006, for example), and have pointed out that this is not a positive phenomenon:

> The term "feminization" was intentionally ambiguous. Perhaps a better term could have been used. It was intended, however to capture the double meaning and the sense of irony that, after generations of efforts to integrate women into regular wage labor as equals, the convergence that was the essence of the original hypothesis has been toward the type of employment and labor force participation patterns associated with women. The era of flexibility is also an era of more generalized insecurity and precariousness, in which many more men as well as women have been pushed into precarious labor.
>
> (Standing, 1999, p. 583)

The feminization of jobs is problematic because traditional "masculine" jobs, jobs that offer full-time work, a family wage, and benefits are being eliminated in many employment sectors around the globe. These jobs are now being replaced by "newer" work arrangements that are often part time, without benefits, and lack the guarantee of permanence. It has not been uncommon in the past for women to take on part-time work and work without benefits in order to balance their familial responsibilities with employment options. However, in the new globalized labor market, these less steady jobs are becoming the principal form of employment, and strikingly in certain industries, they are almost always completely filled by women. For example, in the export-processing zones of many low-income countries, women comprise anywhere from 70 to 90 percent of the factory workers who produce microelectronics, textiles, leather goods, and toys (Wichterich, 2000). Even in northern Europe where there are many progressive work–family policies in place, part-time work is increasingly appealing to women. However, as is indicated by the range of speakers at the Women's Forum for the Economy and Society held in Deauville, France in 2009, globalization has also benefited certain women with respect to career chances and social success. Thus, from the start we need to understand that the global restructuring that is such an intrinsic aspect of our current time, is also a complex process with both challenges and opportunities embedded in its progression.

Massive transformations with respect to employment and the global labor force are a fundamental aspect of globalization, and have critical implications for changes in the roles of women and men, and family and community life. In order to understand why this transformation is occurring, it is instructive to examine some of the recent debates around globalization and the spread of neoliberalism.

Transformations Related to Globalization

While mainstream scholarship still primarily equates globalization with economics, broader conceptualizations increasingly also focus on the compression, intensification, and increased speed of time, space, and relationships due to advances in telecommunications and technology. Globalization is associated with a supra-territoriality where communications, capital, and relationships move in a space that is not necessarily dependent on national boundaries anymore. However, to completely disregard national boundaries does not adequately capture the true nature of globalization. In fact, under certain conditions (such as migration), territorial boundaries have become more important as states attempt to stem the movement of individuals from one society to another. Perhaps it is best to state that globalization is a broad concept that marks a new unique period in human history. However it is defined, there is a general recognition that the changes brought on through globalization provide mechanisms for individuals to form new relationships and collaborations across space and boundaries in a manner that was virtually unimaginable even just 20 or 30 years ago.[1]

An integral aspect of globalization is that it is constantly evolving and changing. Globalization is not a process that describes only one set of processes or a specific point in time; instead, it has multiple dimensions. Thus, while globalization is most commonly associated with the free movement of capital and rapidly changing communication technologies, it is also understood as a process that is bringing us together in new and often unexpected ways. Distant locales have become accessible in both a physical and a virtual sense. When a tsunami occurs in Indonesia, we immediately share in the plight of the local population through television images and the Internet. We are also able to connect, organize, and respond to these types of disasters in an unprecedented rapid fashion; for instance, in the aftermath of the earthquakes in Haiti, virtual organizations that raised relief money sprung up practically overnight. We are all also affected on a personal level by globalization in other ways: depending on inclination and interest, we are now able to enter into new relationships or maintain old ones with individuals who live in far away places. This is leading to a re-conceptualization of the notion of borders and citizenship. On the one hand, the globe is becoming a single space, and on the other hand, at the same time local places still matter. Where someone lives or where they are a citizen determines the opportunities they may have access to, the values that influence them, and which behaviors will be deemed as appropriate. Individuals may be exposed to new lifestyles and images, but this does not necessarily mean that they will emulate or adopt them. Moreover, nation-states are increasingly under pressure to conform to transnational standards and policies while trying to ensure national security and peace. Cerny and Evans (2004) suggest that:

> The central paradox of globalization, the displacement of a crucial range of economic, social and political activities from the national arena to a cross-cutting global/transnational/domestic structured field of action, is that rather than creating one economy or one polity, it also divides, fragments and polarizes. Convergence and divergence are two sides of the same process. Globalization remains a discourse of contestation that reflects national and regional antagonisms and struggles.
>
> (p. 63)

Globalization, in all its complexity, has reshaped many issues including concepts of human rights, poverty, development, and gender. It has also raised our awareness about the acute manner in which beliefs, policies and programs in one part of the world can influence the lives of individuals in another region.

The Gendered Nature of Globalization

A less obvious but integral aspect of globalization is its gendered nature at an ideological as well as a praxis or behavioral level. For instance, Freeman (2001) states:

> feminist critiques have begun to challenge the ways in which wittingly or not, accounts of globalization have frequently reproduced a model of locality and movements not unlike the public/private

31

formulation of social space long familiar and much debated within feminist social science. This model has depicted women and femininity as rooted, traditional and charged with maintaining domestic continuity in the face of flux and instability caused by global movements that, explicitly or not, embody a quality of masculinity.

(p. 1017)

And Ferguson, Merry, and Mironesco (2008) suggest: "Practices of masculinity and femininity, as well as homosexuality and heterosexuality, both produce and reflect global economic, political, military, and cultural webs of relations" (p. 2). These quotes highlight feminist concerns with the inherent gendered valuations that are embedded in globalizing processes and with the gendered hierarchies that "naturalize" certain aspects of the process. Specifically, feminists have pointed out that gender operates on an ideational level by at times promoting certain institutions, practices, and beliefs that are associated with men and masculinity. Those that are relegated to the female realm are devalued and often marginalized or even ignored.

Feminist critics of globalization suggest that gender symbolism is a fundamental aspect of globalization discourses and serves to privilege certain actors and processes over others. Particular concepts and practices are "feminized" in relation to those that are primarily described as masculine, and they are accorded varying degrees of status. In other words, we highlight those entities, beliefs, and practices that are associated with the masculine realm over the ones related to the feminine one (Freeman, 2001). From this analytical perspective, one can understand why, from a mainstream policy perspective, finance capital is considered more important than manufacturing, the market takes precedence over the state, and the global supersedes the local (Marchand & Runyan, 2000).

The gendered hierarchical nature of globalization is extended beyond the marketplace to other spheres. For instance, since economics and the marketplace are considered the most important aspect of globalization, families and households and the role they play in globalizing processes are usually invisible. The same holds true for dynamics within families and households: the gendered relations that characterize the work–family intersection are ignored in globalization discourses. Marchand and Runyan (2000) eloquently highlight that the language that is so commonly used to speak of globalizing processes privileges male discourses. They point out that men and women are often portrayed as playing out fixed gender scripts where the aggressors (capitalism which is associated with men) cannot control their behaviors as they penetrate their victims (weak non-capitalist economic systems—the women) who are incapable of stopping the violence that is being inflicted on them. Such a discourse privileges the economic side of globalization and makes globalizing processes that have undesirable consequences seem "natural." It also tends to negate debate about possible alternative social, economic, and political arrangements that might counteract some of the more damaging effects of globalization.

As insightful as many of these analyses about the gendered nature of globalization are, a serious problem underlies their basic conceptualization. Primarily, the Western feminist tradition has tended to highlight women's subordination as the result of their interactions with men. Men are understood to control the public realm—the state and the market—and women are customarily relegated to the "private" sphere of the home and family (for example, Okin, 1989). From this perspective, families are oppressive to women (as this is the arena where they are dominated by men), and this "private" realm is less important in the social hierarchy of societies. As will be seen, this traditional feminist dualism does not adequately reflect the realities of women's lives in non-Western societies in particular. Nor does this dichotomous approach to social life adequately account for current globalizing processes that are dissolving traditional conceptualization of the public and the private spheres, and linking Western and non-Western experiences.

Western feminist theorizing about the public and the private has been challenged and criticized by non-Western feminists. For example, they argue that unlike in the West, the home is not necessarily an essentially private space, because for women in many societies, the home may have very important public dimensions—it can embody an ethnic community that assists in shaping identities and roles while it protects women from outside repression and domination (for instance, racial oppression). The view of public and private being correlated with the state and the home is also challenged by scholars from the "transitional" or postcommunist states of Eastern Europe and the former Soviet Union. Historically, communist states sought to suppress private spaces and encouraged women to enter the labor force by providing access to child care, health care, abortion, and paid maternity leaves. Women who have participated in the postcommunist transitions during this period of globalization question the role of the state with respect to the so-called "liberation" of the private space. They are instead turning toward the arena of the market as a space that offers them opportunities for entrepreneurial careers, consumer goods, and a first taste of individual representation and expression (Runyan & Marchand, 2000).

This discussion allows us to understand that while globalization definitely has gendered dimensions, we need to be wary of descriptions that focus on binary categories and of ethnocentric Western perspectives on the inter-relations between the market, the state, and the family. Gendered relationships in all of their complexity as well as other social processes are not necessarily accurately captured through dichotomous descriptions when viewed through a global lens.

To better understand some of the underlying dynamics in contemporary social developments, it is useful to delineate some of the economic and ideological foundations associated with globalization. In particular, it is important to outline the basic tenets of neoliberalism which is a philosophical viewpoint about markets and the relationships of individuals to wealth accumulation. Neoliberalism is a concept that is spreading around the world, and increasingly determining government policies with respect to markets and social programing. At this juncture it has a significant number of adherents as well as detractors.

What is Neoliberalism?

The central assumption of neoliberalism is the equating of wealth accumulation with the betterment of the human condition (Keddie, 2010). From this perspective, the larger social good is negatively affected by state intervention. Neoliberalism is an ideology that is founded on the concepts of individualism, the accumulation of private wealth, and the stress on personal responsibility (O'Connell, 2007). Neoliberal ideology has fundamentally shifted Western ideas about what constitutes a functioning democracy. Basically we have moved from understanding that a democracy is a political entity to a new conceptualization of a democracy as one that privileges the economic nature of social life. The fundamental premise of neoliberalism is that a democracy is an entity "in which unattached individuals—supposedly making rational choices in an unfettered market—will ultimately lead to a better society" (Apple, 2005, p. 211). This concept has come under a great deal of criticism as social analysts point out that this transformation undermines social democracy and virtually ignores the concept of the "public good," by shifting away from issues of equity and justice (McLaren & Faramandpur, 2005). Moreover, from a neoliberal perspective, social inequality is understood to be the byproduct of personal choices, personal responsibility, and individual failure. It disconnects poverty, unemployment, and other social ills from broader structural problems and limits the possibility of collective social action (O'Connell, 2007). In other words, neoliberalism allows critics of social programs and government interventions to subsume their arguments under the rhetoric of individual enterprise and initiative, as the drivers of economic and social success.

Detractors of neoliberalism point out that in a quest for the highest profit margins, producers in the world market are intensifying the exploitation of labor. In order to boost profit margins, the costs of production need to be kept down by employing a low-wage workforce. Regions compete for business by offering an ever-cheaper labor force. This is accomplished by loosening regulations on labor practices and environmental safety concerns. Low-cost production, in turn, fuels customer demand for goods.

Neoliberal discourse has had a major influence on perspectives on the role of the state in regulating economic life. While previously the market was understood to be "public" and under the purview of the state, from a neoliberal perspective, the market is now construed as belonging in the "private" sphere, not to be regulated by the state. Increasingly, the market is even portrayed as in competition with the state, that is, the state (and the regulations that come with state control) do not serve in the best interest of the market. This reconceptualization of the marketplace as the driver of social, political, and environmental agendas was virtually inconceivable in the middle part of the twentieth century. For instance, in 1944 Karl Polanyi, one of the founding fathers of cultural economics, stated that "To allow the market mechanism to be sole director of the fate of human beings and their natural environment ... would result in the demolition of society" (p. 73).

In contrast, today a neoliberal agenda emphasizes a completely free market, bereft of government regulations, labor unions, and environmental laws, and suggests that this is the only course to achieving human prosperity and happiness. This single-minded perspective on the role of the marketplace obscures and marginalizes other social institutions, in particular families and households. Moreover, taking again a gendered perspective on this situation, the newly "privatized" state is now "feminized" in relation to the "public", that is, "masculine" vigorous market, which is considered more important to society at large. From this vantage point, relationally, the state becomes to the global economy what the state used to be to families, and thus should be subordinated and minimized.

Promoting Neoliberalism

Neoliberalism is very much associated with the intrinsic economic, political, and social transformations that have characterized the Western world in the post-World War II period since the mid-1960s. As the booming post-war U.S. economy became increasingly threatened by the economic success of Europe and Japan, by Third World nationalism (in particular the spikes in oil prices from OPEC in the 1970s), and by being weakened through the longevity of the war in Vietnam, the U.S. government responded with a series of strategies designed to solidify America's economic and political standing in the world (Pollin, 2003).

Initially, the U.S. economy "de-industrialized," which meant that manufacturers transferred aspects of production overseas, negating a post-World War II trend where industry was moved from the unionized North to the non-unionized South. By shifting production overseas, corporations were better able to take advantage of low-cost labor, anti-union policies, and the new creation of export processing or free trade zones (Freeman, 2000). Certain industries in particular became very

important in this trend. For example, in the electronics and textile industries, female labor became preferred over men's labor (Lim, 1990). In
various parts of the world, including China, Southeast Asia, Mexico and
Central and South America, women's more "nimble" fingers were adver-
tised as "ideal" for this kind of work. In reality, the dialogue around
"nimble" fingers referred to women's "cheaper" fingers, making them
the logical workforce choice for corporations that were trying to lower
costs of production and raise profit margins. This move to attract corporate business also allowed local governments to amass much-needed
foreign currency (Wichterich, 2000). Simultaneously, U.S.-based production cut costs by moving toward automated means of manufacturing or
increasingly employing immigrant, female labor.[2]

The next transformative phase was the growth of the service sector of
the economy. This includes transportation, wholesale and retail trade,
insurance, real estate, finance, government, business and personal
services. For example, from 1970 to 2010, service sector jobs more than
doubled from 49 million to 112 million while jobs in manufacturing
increased only by 15 percent (Bureau of Labor Statistics, 2012).
Simultaneously, the growth in the U.S. service sector was accompanied
by the rapid entrance of high numbers of women into the labor force. In the
period from 1970 to 2000, 60 percent of the 53 million new jobs were
taken on by women. Thus, what we find is a unique social and economic
phenomenon: the increase in women's labor force participation and a
disproportionate increase in the jobs in the service industry came about
almost concurrently. As Heidi Hartmann (1987) described it:

> The service sector grows because the availability of cheap female
> labor provides the supply and because the demand for replace-
> ment services (fast-food replacing home cooking, for example)
> … And the shift toward the commercialization of personal services
> is required by women's increased labor force participation.
>
> (p. 55)

Early feminists such as Hartmann supported these changes and saw them
as particularly beneficial for women. They predicted that these changes in
the labor market would eventually empower women not just in an economic but also in a social manner. Equally important is that during this
period the financial component of the service industry experienced significant growth. As the U.S. economy increasingly moved toward money and
securities management, derivatives trading, and other such types of financial services, women became progressively more incorporated into this
sector. Thus, an important transformative aspect of the U.S. economy was
the shift from post-World War II production of goods, construction, and
mining to finance, insurance, and real estate.[3] This enormous economic

transformation changed the nature and the participation of the labor force through a new emphasis, and by simultaneously rapidly incorporating female workers. The percentage of women employed outside of the home rose from approximately 34 percent in 1960 to more than 60 percent today.

While the 1950s had been characterized by government attempts to encourage particularly married women to stay at home and take care of their families, the 1960s witnessed an expansion of women's roles. The prevailing taboo of married women participating in the paid labor force was trounced by a combination of economic need for a dual-worker household due to the recession in the 1970s and the simultaneously growing ideology of the women's movement. In the United States, this pattern of white women's employment increasingly started to look like that of African American women who had historically worked outside of the home while balancing marriage and a family.

The radical societal shift was accompanied by ideological transformations as well. Commonly referred to as the move from a Fordist welfare state, characterized by well-paid breadwinner jobs with benefits, to a neoliberal market ideology, this transformation was to prove critical to a complete restructuring not just of the U.S. economy but also of the economies of the rest of the world (Carrington, 2001).

Early proponents of neoliberalism promoted a philosophy of limited government and a series of strategies that were thought to promote economic growth. This school of thought, introduced through the University of Chicago by the philosopher-economist Friedrich von Hayek, and then endorsed in the 1960s by a cadre of conservative economists led by Milton Friedman, basically advocated a return to a pre-New Deal arrangement that allowed economies and markets to self-regulate without government intervention.[4] From this perspective, any type of government interference was seen as a move toward totalitarianism. As the political landscape became more conservative in the 1980s with the ascendancy of Ronald Regan and Margaret Thatcher, and later in the 1990s with the election of George Bush, neoliberal ideas took root in both the United States and the UK. Neoliberalism became a mainstay of right-wing movements, and included attacks on unions and other movements that sought to organize labor, de-legitimizing the concept of the welfare state and progressive taxation, and attacks on the role of government in encouraging economic growth and employment. Simultaneously, a focus on deregulation sought to remove the constraints on business and corporations imposed by government policies (Eisenstein, 2005).

Neoliberal thought and policy was not constrained to the Western world. In particular, the Bretton Woods institutions (the International Monetary Fund (IMF) and the International Bank for Reconstruction and Development that eventually became the World Bank) that had been established after World War II used the international debt crisis of the 1980s to restructure the economies of those countries over which it held some influence.[5] By imposing what were called "Structural Adjustment Policies" or SAPs, the World Bank and IMF forced indebted governments to institutionalize a series of changes in their economies. Specifically, governments were forced to shrink the public sector, devalue their currencies, terminate fuel and food subsidies, realign domestic prices to the world market, liberalize trade, and privatize state enterprises (Chossudovsky, 2003). The first "rescue" package of Structural Adjustment Policies was introduced in 1982 in response to an announcement by Mexico that it would be unable to meet its debt payments. A series of other countries followed suit, and the IMF and World Bank, and including the participation of international commercial banks and with the aid of governments from high-income countries, supported the implementation of these neoliberal policies.

World political developments served as more fuel for this venture. As the Soviet Union and its Eastern European satellites collapsed in the period from 1989 to 1991, neoliberal policies became increasingly popular as formerly state-governed enterprises were privatized and national economies had to discard state-run development. While China and some other Southeast Asian nations experienced rapid economic growth and were able to maintain their state-run systems, from the 1980s onwards many other countries in Latin America, sub-Saharan Africa, and South Asia had to abide by the Structural Adjustment Policies of the World Bank and IMF. Changes to production and services resulted in lowered economic growth and a growth in poverty, malnourishment and disease for their populations. As Pyle and Ward (2003) point out, while global restructuring was associated with free markets and concepts such as liberalization, in order to perpetuate the false idea that economic outcomes result from free markets, minimal government interference, and equal opportunities for all, empirical evidence actually points to the opposite outcomes.

The 1990s witnessed growing criticism of the Structural Adjustment Policies, and, thus, the World Bank decided to institute new strategies in order to alleviate poverty reduction in highly indebted countries. Nevertheless, many of these changes were cosmetic in nature as governments were still expected to adhere to the macroeconomic policies that had induced the growing poverty in the first place.

> The privatization of essential services, like water and electricity, and the deterioration or privatization of public services, such as health and education, have never been in the interests of the poor. For instance, the imposition of user fees on health care or education has led to a sharp drop in hospital attendance and

school enrollment from poor or low-income families; it has also increased the gender gap, since girls and women are the main victims of those policies.

(Dembele, 2003 in Eisenstein, 2005)

Moreover, it became clear that the burden of Structural Adjustment Policies was unequally distributed throughout the populations of the various affected nations (Beneria, 2003). Many states saw a sharp growth in poverty, income distribution, and social divisions. In particular, countries in the global South were relegated to a form of servitude in a global trading system that advantaged well-to-do countries. On local levels, the absence of supportive social policies combined with cuts in social services pushed households into becoming the primary social welfare institution (Jaggar, 2002). In other words, families had to pick up new responsibilities, ones that had previously been provided through states.

When looked at from a global perspective, neoliberal policies over the last 30 years have served to destabilize many non-Western societies. In particular, poorer countries have been characterized by a deterioration of living conditions for much of their populations coupled with increased financial insecurity and concomitant social tensions. While global flows have allowed for new accumulations of wealth within and between societies, these same trends have also given rise to greater inequalities within and between countries. Study after study indicates that countries around the world are characterized by an increasing polarization between the haves and have-nots. This polarization is not confined just to the economic sphere but instead characterizes social life, technological access, and even the proliferation of ideas. Nonetheless, mainstream discourses continue to promote neoliberal policies that privilege the individual over the collective. From a neoliberal vantage point, financial responsibility and success ultimately lie in the hands of individuals. Conversely, poverty and the lack of opportunity are not perceived as a public responsibility.

Neoliberalism has increasingly become associated with the building of democracies and the increased "liberation" of people. In this process, not much attention is given to the concerns of those who cannot access resources or to a general more equitable redistribution of wealth. However, as is indicated throughout this book, neoliberalism and globalization are complex dynamic ideologies and processes that manifest themselves differently at various times and places. Importantly for this discussion, they have had specific social consequences, many of them affecting women in particular. Still, it is important to note that women are not necessarily always the casualties of these processes. Their experiences and responses are diverse and need to be understood in a relational context to men, their communities, and other environmental and ideological factors.

The Changing Role of Nation-States

The spread of neoliberalism and the ever-increasing power of markets and globalized capital has raised numerous debates around the role of the state as a source of collective identity and as a provider of the programs and services needed to support the shared interest of its populace (Bergeron, 2001). The extent to which this is truly a valid hypothesis is widely debated in the political and economic literature. However, there is agreement that our traditional models of economic and political space are being restructured and that the concept of the state is in a process of transformation. In particular, the decline of the Keynesian welfare state in the United States, Europe, and Australia is thought to symbolize this shift (Carrington, 2001). Comparatively in the developing world, the shift from state-controlled development policies to neoliberal, export policies (most commonly due to directives by the World Bank and the IMF with respect to Structural Adjustment Policies) signals the weakening of national sovereignty. A significant consequence of this shift has been the deterioration of services and programs, particularly for the less fortunate members of various nations' citizenries. In order to maintain economic stability, states have had to adjust their policies and programs toward inclusion in transnational markets and the mandates of transnational institutions, thus weakening their ability to take care of their populations.

Some analysts assume that this is indicative of a weakening of the power of nation-states, which are often predicted to have little influence in the future on the global economic system. Instead, it is forecast that the traditional functions of nation-states with respect to determining policies and laws will be replaced by transnational entities. Others maintain that the state will retain its responsibilities, particularly toward the less fortunate members of their societies, but will have to find new and more cost-effective, efficient ways to serve them (Bergeron, 2001). Feminist analyses of these debates lean toward highlighting the increasingly transnational processes and policies that seem to impact women primarily. They predict that globalization in combination with communication and information technologies will lead to the formation of a global identity for women from different parts of the world. From this perspective, nation-states and national subjectivities are not particularly meaningful anymore, and instead women will need to be engaged in transnational resistance strategies to global capitalistic ventures. For example, Sen (1997) suggests that "it is difficult if not impossible to challenge global actors if women are unwilling to act globally" (p. 23). In other words, in order to combat the implied negative tide of global capitalism, women need to leave behind national and local identities and now adopt transnational, global identities. By forming this global identity, women will be able to mobilize and receive support for determining policies that will better serve their lives.

From this perspective, the nation-state will not play a significant role in the process, and instead actually becomes superfluous. Simultaneously, as will be seen in Chapter 3, many feminists advocate that by gender mainstreaming, incorporating a gender dimension into institutional structures such as the United Nations, the World Bank and the International Labor Organization, greater strides will be made to assist the situation of women than anything that can be done at the state level (Bergeron, 2001). For the purposes of this discussion, in order to better explicate the intersection of markets, the state, and the position of women, we need to examine the substantial role that informal work is playing in the global economy and the lives of women.

The Growth of Informal Sector Work

The global spread of neoliberal ideologies and practices has been accompanied by changes to the actual labor market, in particular the growth of the informal work sector. Until relatively recently, policy analysts negatively contrasted the informal work sector with the formal sector. The formal work sector has traditionally been perceived as the contemporary solution to the low productivity and poor working conditions that characterized the informal sector. While in the 1970s and the early 1980s the informal sector was expected to shrink as economies grew, it was thought that as countries developed, their formal sector would eventually incorporate the informal activities and the workers from this part of the economy (Beneria, 2003). The informal and formal sectors were dichotomized despite a number of studies suggesting that there were actually strong linkages between the two and that the industrial sector (the formal sector) benefited through subcontracting work. In fact, the formal sector was able to increase its competitiveness and profits through linkages with the informal sector (Portes, Castells, & Benton, 1989).

Despite these early indicators, economists and policy-makers in particular ignored the warning signs that accompanied these market activities. However, the last two decades have witnessed a global growth in the informal sector, with an increasing reliance by both households and corporations on precarious forms of employment and a deterioration of the labor market for many individuals in the labor force. The informal sector grew in particular in those countries that came under the harsh auspices of the Structural Adjustment Policies. As countries attempted to mold their economies to these policies by shrinking their public assistance, hundreds of thousands of public servants lost their jobs. As health care and education fees increased, and food subsidies were reduced or removed, families were now forced to rely on themselves. In particular, women were expected to absorb these changes (Chang, 2000). Since it was often women working in these public sector jobs, they were the first ones to become unemployed. Some survival strategies exercised by women included taking on informal work (such as selling goods in urban markets), prostitution and sex trafficking, and emigrating to wealthier countries to sell their services as domestics, caretakers, and nurses (Ehrenreich & Hochschild, 2003). Thus, women entered risky forms of employment that lacked any kind of social protections or access to social benefits. While this is a trend that was particularly true in developing countries, increasingly we are witnessing the same phenomenon in high-income countries. Characterized by low marketable skills or other impediments such as child or elder care obligations, poor women engage in informal activities in order to generate whatever income is accessible to them.

Involvement in child and elder care responsibilities constrains the labor market choices of many low-income women in particular, and constrains their choices and ability to participate in paid work vis-à-vis men. Moreover, as states decrease their services, women's work responsibilities in and out of the home tend to grow. What we find is that for poor women to survive, an increasing global phenomenon is the growing reliance on precarious informal forms of income. Families subsist by combining low-wage labor with self-employment and temporary domestic and international migration. Beneria (2003) cites as an example the work of Bolivian sociologist Garcia-Linera (1999) who calls this type of work "nomad labor" as individuals move from one job to another, oftentimes as an aspect of international migration. Beneria also points out that unemployment rates often do not reflect the large number of individuals who are employed in unstable and precarious jobs. As these kinds of jobs become more common, questions about the "erosion of work" and the disappearance of mechanisms to enter the middle class are beginning to dominate in both high-income countries and the developing world. Nonetheless, the growth of the informal sector is not necessarily a purely negative phenomenon. In fact, the public sector is becoming less attractive in many countries as it is associated with stagnant wages and the loss of benefits. Informal and entrepreneurial forms of employment are instead on the rise in an increasingly global social environment that stresses individual agency, empowerment, and political rights (Beneria, 2003). That same tension, between discourses that advocate rights and citizenship and the erosion of a solid labor market that benefits its workers, is now found in both high-income and developing countries. High-income countries are witnessing the dissolution of the welfare state along with market deregulation and the erosion of workers' rights and labor unions leading to what some believe will be social unrest due to great economic inequalities (Standing, 1999).

In developing countries, the phenomena associated with globalization are playing themselves out somewhat differently. In most of these countries the welfare state has always been fragile or non-existent and while the global marketplace thrives on the low-cost labor of these areas, global processes have also introduced the greater recognition of individual rights. This is occurring without a necessary focus on democratic institutions and policies. What we find is that, for example, rural women may migrate to urban areas due to employment opportunities. While these jobs may be exploitative and marginalized, they also provide these women with increased autonomy and new exposure to other lifestyles and ideologies. Ultimately, this may serve to free them from the patriarchal constraints under which so many are currently living. Global links also foster relationships between workers, allowing them access to information about their rights and unfair labor practices. That said, economic insecurity, precarious jobs, and lack of benefits continue to plague large portions of the population in the developing world. With globalizing processes that include labor market deregulation and increased flexibility in production, many countries are unable to provide even minimum wages to their workers. This is leading to even more abject poverty and raising questions about the future viability of societies where there is an increasingly exacerbated divide between the haves and the have-nots.

Neoliberalism, Globalization, and "Victimized" Women

As has been noted, free trade, privatization, and greater integration of the global marketplace have had many unintended effects for women. Trade liberalization and privatization have led to an escalating number of part-time, temporary, and low-wage jobs in both the industrialized and the developing world. These jobs, for which employers typically prefer women, usually do not come with health or retirement benefits, and leave workers vulnerable and open to exploitation. Women's overrepresentation in this sector of the labor market also makes them vulnerable to job cuts. When the jobs move due to cost-cutting initiatives, women are the ones to be let go due to the "flexible" nature of the jobs. Similarly, the significant cuts in social services that are advocated by Structural Adjustment Policies have had a significant effect on low-income women in particular. Especially in the developing world, when social services are curtailed, girls' educations are often interrupted, women's domestic responsibilities intensify, and the nature and conditions of employment worsen. The impoverishment and marginalization of women, particularly those who were already burdened by poverty and racial, ethnic or class discrimination, stems in part from the disregard in neoliberal discourse "to acknowledge the feminized space of the private sphere" (Keddie, 2010, p. 140).

Feminist analysts have long highlighted how contemporary global economic transformations have disadvantaged women in other ways too. For example, women around the globe are the primary caretakers of children, the disabled, and the elderly. As social welfare provision continues to move from being the responsibility of the state to that of the household, women's unpaid care burden increases (Mohanty, 2003). Moreover, in many parts of Africa and Central America, traditional female industries such as basket weaving and food production have been eliminated as a result of economic restructuring. This leaves women involved in those industries with few economic options. We, thus, find that neoliberal initiatives "overlap and are often mutually reinforcing in their assault on many women's economic and social wellbeing" (Keddie, 2010, p. 141). However only focusing on the negative consequences of globalization for women paints a one-sided and potentially incorrect picture of this phenomenon.

The Women as "Victims" Approach Reconsidered

The necessity of incorporating gender into analyses of globalization cannot be overstated. However, a one-dimensional perspective that portrays women purely as the victims of globalization and men as the oppressors does not provide any more insight into the true nature of globalizing processes than does completely eliminating gender from the analysis. For instance, as Wichterich (2000) describes: "'globalized woman' is burnt up as a natural fuel: she is the piece-rate worker in export industries, the worker living abroad who sends back foreign currency, the prostitute or catalogue bride on the international body and marriage markets, and the voluntary worker who helps to absorb the shocks of social cutbacks and structural adjustment" (p. 167).

Davids and Driel (2005) point out that this perspective emphasizes the economic nature of globalization and does not account for the social, cultural, and political factors that also come into play. This viewpoint is also a reminder of a previous time in Western history when women were urged to rise against their oppressors and to resist the "system" despite an acknowledgment that they did not have the power to effect change. Such approaches are unidimensional and do not adequately address the complexity of the situation. Moreover, the women as "victims" perspective presents globalization purely as a monolithic phenomenon that is destructive to individuals and the social order, and, thus, cannot and should not be contained. This is an inaccurate assessment of globalization. Globalization is the product of human activity—and therefore, subject to change and control. Ultimately, markets, policies, and services can always be re-formulated and re-packaged. In order to successfully re-tool and re-direct the more disadvantageous aspects of globalization, we need analyses that incorporate and integrate the economic and social dimensions of the process. We also need to understand how these processes are impacted by the decisions and behaviors that are made in local contexts.

Incorporating a Relational Perspective

Recent scholarship on globalization and gender indicates that globalization is a complex multifaceted process that both excludes and includes women *and* men. Neither are just victims or oppressors. Instead, in order to advance feminist *and* globalization debates, and especially to incorporate this critical dialogue into the mainstream of scholarly analysis, we need to be incorporating a *relational* analysis into our discourses. Peterson suggests that relational thinking should contain three separate aspects, including "[t]his involves understanding the world 'out there' (practices, institutions, structures of social re/production), how we think (meaning systems, ideologies, paradigms), and who we are (subjectivity, agency, self and collective identities) as interacting dimensions of social reality" (1997, p. 185). By adopting this perspective, we can introduce human agency and subjective lenses into a dialogue that is generally an abstract debate about markets, economies, policies, nation-states, and processes. Importantly, a gendered relational perspective does not mean adding stories about women or the feminist movement to the current mainstream analyses of globalization. Instead, it incorporates an understanding that the participants of globalization—the practitioners, producers, and consumers—are not generic human beings, but gendered individuals who are situated within social, political, and economic power relations and processes (Freeman, 2001). This perspective supports the notion that women can be agents of change and that globalization gives them the tools to mobilize and resist the powers that may be subjugating them.

There are aspects of globalization that act as a counterforce to the more destructive or challenging aspects of this phenomenon. On the one level, globalization can become the symbol against which women mobilize on issues ranging from environmental change to poverty to reproductive and sexual rights (Davids & van Driel, 2005). However, as Davids and van Driel (2005) correctly point out, to portray women in a unidimensional manner, purely as victims or as collective saviors, oversimplifies the relationship between globalization and gender. A wide variety of factors including national origin, region, religion, and race and ethnicity intersect with the class issues that are embedded in the globalization debates. While some groups of women have been disadvantaged through aspects of globalization, not all women and not all poor women have had the same experiences. However, by equating globalization completely with the increasing poverty of women, "the impoverishment of women becomes a global orthodoxy that is not questioned anymore" (Davids & van Driel, 2005, p. 6). This depiction of globalization represents it as a homogeneous development with uniform outcomes.

Davids and van Driel (2005) also highlight that as part of this debate women have been replaced by the term "gender," and that "globalization" has become the stand in term for patriarchal capitalism. By delineating dualities such as the "male" oppressor and the "female" oppressed, decades of theoretical advances have been reduced back to dichotomized analyses. Globalization actually encourages exactly the opposite process: it allows us to realize that identities are not exclusive, categorical and fixed nor do they only exist in binary opposition. Instead, in a globalized world, identities are in constant flux—individuals have an increasing number of roles to choose from and may have fluctuating identities. As the landscape constantly shifts, so do our gender categories and our understandings of these conceptualizations. It is this fluidity that is so difficult for many to grasp, and yet, it is the defining paradigm of our time.

Challenging the Hegemony of Markets and Binary Categories

The increased fluidity that is associated with globalization entails a fundamental rethinking of customary boundaries such as between international and national spheres, the political and market arenas, the economic and domestic realms, and the global and local. This realignment, in turn, has raised questions about the role and prevalence of global capital. For instance, recent analyses have questioned if there is truly a unified, intentional economic logic to neoliberal policies and the emphasis on transnational markets, or if even the outcomes from these policies are truly only determined by complex processes governed in part by transnational organizations and interactions with states and corporate entities. From this perspective, globalized capitalism is a socially constructed process, subject to the same vagaries and dynamism that is an inherent feature of all social processes. This is an important transition from hegemonic conceptualizations of markets as unstoppable, transcending forces and has raised questions about the concept of a "global economy" (Beneria, 2003). Now it is understood that global corporations are decentered and fragmented and subject to the actions of a multitude of factors including national and transnational policies, laborers, consumers, sources of investments, and the language and cultures of the places where they are based (Afshar & Barrientos, 1999). Importantly, this approach challenges the dominant view of an all-encompassing, all-powerful economic globalization. In other words, this approach opens the black box of globalization. The power of the "oppressor" is brought into question and opens the way for a new discourse, one that can incorporate feminist interests including the vulnerable, the poor and the marginalized.

We need at all junctures to be careful about a discourse on "global feminism" that groups a supposedly unified voice against a purportedly unified capitalist global market. We cannot talk about a homogeneous identity of "women's interests" where local interpretations and experiences are collapsed into an allegedly unified whole. And yet, this often happens because Western feminist concerns while valuing individuality and self-expression, do not take into account the wide-ranging contexts, experiences, and belief systems of women around the world; this includes women's very varied experiences with the global economy. By clarifying the multiple and contested nature of global capitalism we can open up the debate and the possible strategies that would offer appropriate responses to the challenges raised by these global forces. Much of the feminist work on globalization is focused on women in the southern hemisphere, or the Third or developing world. This terminology complicates the literature on globalization because it does not adequately describe the true complexity of global relations.[6] Moreover, these types of descriptions again set up dualistic categories and downplay the true relational character of the flows and processes embedded in this process. For example, scholarship on gender, work and family, and the role of economics in the industrialized or "developed" part of the world is abundant, but has not clearly been linked to globalization or to globalizing processes. What we find is that when we examine the work on women in developing countries and women and work–family issues, they represent two distinct research directions with different dialogues and even different participants (Acker, 2004).

A primary problem with distinguishing the actual effects of globalization and neoliberalism on gender ideologies and practices, and specifically on women, is that different meanings are ascribed to similar phenomena depending on time and place. Thus, for instance, women's labor force participation is understood to have very different implications depending on region and context, and on whose opinion or analysis is being considered. In arguments focusing on high-income or the developed world, women's labor force participation is these days usually understood to be complex but empowering. In the initial example of the Women's Forum for the Economy and Society held in Deauville, France in 2009, both Diane Von Furstenberg, the U.S. fashion designer and Sandrine Devillard, the French banking executive, described how contemporary circumstances have allowed them to be as successful, if not more successful, than most men (Supp, 2009). However, as was stated above, when it comes to the developing world, women's employment is usually portrayed as exploitative despite empirical evidence chronicling a multiplicity of experiences (Ganguly-Scrase, 2003). Again, the example of Sandra Aguebor the auto mechanic from Nigeria who also spoke at the Women's Forum in Deauville provides an example that new opportunities have opened up for women—even in low-income countries and for women from rural areas. Moreover, it is important not to forget that no matter which area of the world we are examining, local values and beliefs act as a filter for interpreting phenomena, ideologies, and behaviors. Depending on our personal circumstances, we in the West may not necessarily believe that working on an assembly line or learning to be a car mechanic is a promising path. However, those engaged in the various activities may themselves perceive them differently depending on the socio-historical moment—as do those analyzing those experiences. Responses to a particular phenomenon need to be understood from this multicontextual perspective.

Contrasting Perspectives on Global Processes

In contrast to viewpoints that advocate that as a world we are becoming more homogeneous, sometimes referred to as the "convergence paradigm," and made popular through Fukuyama's (1992) *The End of History*, a contrasting scholarship indicates that local settings, customs, and individuals are engaged in constant dynamic interactions with global mechanisms (Davids & van Driel, 2005). This interface between the global and the local is transformative on each level: local values may incorporate global perspectives imported from other places, and global phenomena may be influenced by local practices or beliefs. Perhaps we can best understand this process if we use gender as an example. In different places gender serves as a boundary marker for ethnic differences, nationality, or even religion. In those places, customary clearly defined gender roles allow us to understand who is who, and what they are permitted or not permitted to do. However, globalization has introduced new challenges to these types of previously clearly delineated conceptualizations. For instance, as more women move into the public sphere through working outside of the home, traditional boundaries about public and private spaces are being altered. Responses to this transformation have been multifaceted, ranging from women in some Islamic communities around the world donning the face veil as a symbol of traditionalism and conservatism, to Western women demanding and achieving complete equality in the distribution of roles in workplaces and homes.

Feminist critiques of mainstream globalization in particular are challenging the local–global dichotomies that are so often posited as an integral aspect of the process. Specifically, they are questioning the model that links women and femininity as traditional, and predominantly associated with maintaining domestic calm in the face of the instability, and transformations that are caused by global restructuring, a quality that is associated with masculinity (Freeman, 2001). From a more mainstream vantage point, processes of globalization are associated with moving women into the previously masculine realms of the labor force and work migration. These phenomena, however, are often interpreted as an unfortunate consequence of global shifts and transformation. Much of this understanding relies on specific ethnographic studies (see, for example, Fernandez-Kelly, 1997) that depict young women being recruited from rural village communities and then incorporated into multinational factory and urban free trade zones. In these new settings, women are seen as losing the primacy of their "traditional" female virtues such as family-based domestic labor and motherhood and, instead, replacing those with physical independence and wage earning. These new features of their lives are regarded with suspicion, and are often associated with accusations of sexual promiscuity and a loss of "feminine" qualities. However, such interpretations do not capture the complex global and local changes and interconnections. The social environment is changing as identities are not fixed and nameable any more, and Western binary categories do not adequately describe the processes that are now influencing individuals' lives. There is no clear-cut masculine or feminine realm anymore, nor is there purely a global or local one. Individuals ascribe meaning to processes and phenomena, and in the contemporary environment these concepts can come from anywhere in the world. However, what gets adopted and the value that is ascribed to these concepts will vary depending on location and individual circumstances. In order to examine how some of these processes play themselves out, it is instructive to look at the case example of Bangladesh.

Case Study: Bangladesh

Pyle and Ward (2003) present an interesting example of neoliberal policies intersecting with gender issues with respect to the case of Bangladesh. The following summary is excerpted from their article and from development work conducted in the country by the Bangladesh Institute of Development Studies (Kabeer & Mahmud, 2004), as well as by Plan UK (2009).

Since attaining its independence in 1971, Bangladesh has remained one of the poorest nations in the world. It has survived primarily due to international donors and, thus, has been subject to Structural Adjustment Policies, privatization, and a wide variety of anti-poverty strategies. As part of the global neoliberal flow, Bangladesh has pursued the same strategy as most other developing nations of participating in export processing (in this case, ready-made clothes), encouraging the migration of both women and men in order to generate remittances that could be sent back home, promoting NGOs to create and maintain microfinance programs, and ignoring the trafficking of Bangladeshi women to other parts of Asia. Yet despite its adherence to this neoliberal agenda, Bangladesh has remained extremely poor in economic terms (Kabeer & Mahmud, 2004).

Bangladeshi workers provide a prime example of the ups and downs associated with global restructuring and changes in trade agreements between countries and multinationals. An integral part of Bangladesh's economy is the export processing of ready-made garments accounting for about 76 percent of its foreign revenues. In order for the economy to shift to export processing, millions of girls and women moved from agricultural areas to factories in urban centers. This migration resulted in changed marriage patterns as girls married later and were increasingly perceived as more valuable in terms of providing an income for their families (Plan UK, 2009). The average girl worked for approximately five years before leaving this type of employment due to the hazardous conditions in which they were expected to function (Pyle & Ward, 2003). Up until the year 2000, the United States received about 46 percent of its garments from Bangladesh. However, once the U.S. Trade Development Act was enacted in the year 2000, duty-free access and trade preferences were shifted to African and Caribbean countries. Due to the diverted garment orders from Bangladesh, the workers were fired and the factories closed. To mitigate some of these displacements, the Bangladeshi government began to encourage the migration of men to Middle Eastern and Southeast Asian countries to work in construction and other low-wage service sectors. As some of these industries dissipated after the first Gulf War and the men became unemployed, Bangladeshi women were encouraged to migrate to the Middle East and Asia to work in factories, obtain private employment, or work as domestics and nurses (Kabeer & Mahmud, 2004). Many of these women undertook these movements unofficially, leaving them vulnerable and open to exploitation.

In response to several unfortunate incidents, the Bangladeshi government put into place policies that restricted some of the most vulnerable women from migrating. However, this move created an unexpected new set of problems due to the fact that the nation depended on foreign remittances for about 25 percent of its foreign exchange. Meanwhile, the global recession took its toll by reducing the amount of work available abroad (Pyle & Ward, 2003). This was then compounded by the fact that returning migrants could not find employment back home. In response to these dire economic conditions, some women founded the Bangladesh Women Migrant Workers Association, an NGO that trains returning women for new types of jobs. However, for most girls there were and currently remain very few employment options (Kabeer & Mahmud, 2004). Girls and women are confined by the tradition of purdah (female seclusion), and across the country there are few places were they can find jobs (Plan UK, 2009). Thus, many girls now have become domestics where they have to endure harsh working conditions that often average 15–16 hours a day, and at times are characterized by physical and sexual abuse. In worst case scenarios, these girls are often trafficked into the sex trade in Pakistan and India. Thus, what we find is that while globalization can provide opportunities to women, these prospects can also disappear again. As is described in this example, women can at times become even more economically vulnerable, and after a period of positive change may be forced into even more complicated circumstances.

Even though the representations in this case study paint a rather dire picture of the effects of neoliberal policies, these analyses ignore some of the positive changes that have also accompanied the globalization process that Bangladeshi women and girls have been a part of. In Chapter 8 we will revisit some of the challenges that Bangladeshi women have faced and some of the other opportunities that have arisen for them. What each discussion does indicate, however, is that global restructuring is multidimensional and can simultaneously enhance individuals' prospects as well as curtail them. The example of Bangladesh illustrates that despite the popular appeal of simplistic denouncements of globalization, the situation is much more complex than is often reported. Global restructuring brings with it both opportunities as well as challenges to women in the developing world, and we need to take care not to characterize the process as purely destructive or opportunistic.

The Complexity of Globalizing Processes

The gendered nature of globalization is not just an intrinsic aspect of ideology or culture but is also deeply embedded in social institutions (Chow, 2003). However, Bhagwati (2004) provocatively suggests that globalization cannot be discussed only by referring to the problematic of women's status. Instead, in pursuing the gendered nature of social change, societies need to consider the ways

in which women in that society and economy may be more vulnerable to the consequences of policy changes such as trade liberalization, projects such as the building of roads and railways or the provision of irrigation or drinking water, and indeed the myriad ways in which change comes. Rather than setting up roadblocks on every policy change, big and small, and demanding that each policy change be made conditional on an examination

of its impact on women ... it is more useful to think of policies
that alleviate the totality of distress to women from the multitude
of policy changes.

(Bhagwati, 2004, p. 87)

Globalization processes are affecting men also. Especially with respect to
job security and entitlement benefits, men in high-income and low-income
countries are increasingly at a great disadvantage. The kind of work and
labor force involvement that has until recently been primarily associated
with women (low paid and 'flexible') is spreading to jobs that in the past
were associated with men (steady and unionized). In fact, some argue
that we are seeing a convergence in labor market experiences of men and
women (Standing, 1999).

The global restructuring that we have examined in this chapter has
serious implications for both women and men. However, as we have seen,
numerous feminist scholars have highlighted that the inherent vulnerability
of so many women, particularly poor, low-income and minority women
in both industrialized and developing countries, makes them particularly
susceptible to market fluctuations, labor force demands, and other social
factors that are out of their control (Freeman, 2001). Rodrik (1997),
however, illustrates that places which emphasize strong social safety nets,
such as the Scandinavian countries, are in a better position to deal with
the social impacts of globalization. Since societies, communities, families,
and individuals are becoming increasingly destabilized in our current
social, economic, and political environments due to unemployment and
underemployment, we are seeing a growing need for the institutionaliza-
tion of social policies and safety nets that most states are not interested
or in the position to provide. Incorporating gender into the globalization
debate will begin to move us in a direction that makes us think about
what we value and how we want to promote and support those values.
Gendering globalization studies and policies introduces a social justice
perspective that questions if we should ignore the reality that an increasing
number of women, men, and children are living without steady streams
of income and without adequate means for providing shelter and sustenance for their families. This type of analysis also highlights the impacts
of globalization as inequalities between groups continue to grow instead
of to lessen.

Globalization is now a part of all of our lives. It challenges us to rethink
our values, our identities, our lifestyles. The boundaries of our beliefs are
no longer just governed by territorial, familial, ethnic, or national borders.
There is a constant influx of new ideas, new categories, new ways of relating.
And symptomatic of globalization, these changes are reaching the farthest
corners of the earth—albeit with varied responses and depending on a
multitude of markers including gender, class, sexual identity, nationality,

age, religion, and region just to name a few. Moreover, this is not a unidirectional flow with all ideas flowing from the West to other parts of the world. Nor is this a top-down process where the global influences the local and rearranges and transforms it. Instead, these are multidimensional flows characterized by dynamic transformations. It is this dialectic that is most symptomatic of the process. It is also the reason that globalization is so difficult to characterize, to analyze, and to predict. As Davids and van Driel (2005) so eloquently state: "we not only have to identify the different elements that shape the landscape, but we also have to realize that we see different landscapes according to the different perspectives and scripts attached to these different elements" (p. 11).

Simultaneously, an expanding global consciousness is transforming everyone's sense of connectedness and belonging. As individuals are increasingly exposed to new and rapidly changing images, representations, commodities, and styles of life, they are struggling to understand what their roles and futures in this new world order will be.

Globalization is the paradigm of our time and we need to understand that its causation and realization are created through a continuous dynamic struggle and negotiation between images, ideas, flows, and individuals on both local and global levels. This is also the context in which we need to understand the rapid transformations in workplaces, families, gender ideologies, and lived experiences of individuals.

Synopsis

The neoliberal policies and programs that have spread globally have resulted in contradictory experiences for women. While, as we have seen, the effects of global restructuring of work has been uneven across the globe and within societies, the effects are not clearly delineated or understood. Both benefits and challenges have accrued through the process of globalizing flows. For example, interestingly, as part of this transformation, gender gaps in education are rapidly decreasing across various regions. One case in point is that in the Arab countries, women's literacy rates have more than doubled between 1970 and 2000 (Fennell & Arnot, 2008). It is important to note, however, that while there has been a general improvement in women's educational status, this has not always translated into labor market gains, let alone to improvements in their private lives.

There are also clear indicators that as women's educational levels increase globally, they begin to enter into managerial and professional occupations. Three out of the four main presenters described in the initial example of the Women's Forum for the Economy and Society held in Deauville, France in 2009 exemplify this trend: they have achieved power, status, and wealth. But this phenomenon has also led to a widening of the gap between highly educated women and those at the bottom of the economic and educational ladder. This polarization is reflected in growing income inequalities among women within the same society, creating further complexity with respect to gender dynamics. In later chapters we will examine these phenomena in greater depth. For right now, suffice it to say that we cannot argue that neoliberal ideologies and policies combined with the restructuring that is an integral aspect of the process are either detrimental or beneficial for women. Both positive and negative elements are part of this transformation. Likewise, the fact that large numbers of women are entering the global labor force due in part to these changes does not necessarily mean, as so many Western feminists imagine, that there is increased gender equality in the global world of work or that women are universally empowered through their participation. Nor are the aspects of family life, like caring work that so many women remain accountable for, incorporated into this picture. Importantly, however, it would also be incorrect to just assume that women the world over are working outside of the home purely for economic benefits. The immense transformation in the global workforce is part of an even more expansive phenomenon that has strong ideological underpinnings. We examine some of these developments in the next chapter.

Notes

1 In particular, social networking stands out as a form of newly collectivized action that is redesigning social spaces.
2 This trend is continuing as increasingly white collar jobs such as advertising, web design and programing, and even legal services are outsourced to other "cheaper" parts of the world where women tend to predominate those sectors.
3 This sector of the economy is sometimes referred to as FIRE: finance, insurance, and real estate.
4 While von Hayek is most commonly associated with this school of thought, what is little known about him is that he also believed that it was the obligation of the state to create in some form, a social safety net. He wrote: "There is no reason why, in a society which has reached the general level of wealth ours has, the first kind of security should not be guaranteed to all without endangering general freedom; that is: some minimum of food, shelter and clothing, sufficient to preserve health. Nor is there any reason why the state should not help to organize a comprehensive system of social insurance in providing for those common hazards of life against which few can make adequate provision."
5 The chief purpose of the system was an obligation for each of the 44 allied nations that convened and signed the Bretton Woods agreements in 1944 to adopt a monetary policy that maintained the exchange rate by tying their currencies to the U.S. dollar. The IMF was then obligated to bridge temporary imbalances of payments. In 1971, the United States terminated the convertibility of the dollar to gold, creating a situation where the U.S. dollar became the sole backing of currencies and a reserve currency for all the member states.
6 In this work I tend to rely on the terms high-income and low-income countries, even though these are not ideal for describing the various societies either.

3

THE GLOBAL SPREAD OF FEMINIST PRINCIPLES

The Expansion of the International Women's Rights Movement and Concepts of Gender Equality

In December 2012, in view of her male companion, a 23-year-old young woman was beaten and gang raped on a bus in New Delhi by five men including the bus driver. She died from her injuries 13 days later. News about this incident spread immediately both in India and abroad, and was condemned by women's groups everywhere. Subsequently, multiple public protests against the Indian government and the government of New Delhi focused on the lack of protection for women and the rampant discrimination that particularly poor women face (Kassim, 2013). Thousands of people joined in and demanded that stronger laws be put in place against rape, sexual harassment, and child abuse. This most recent case of female victimization in India has become a rallying cause for women's groups worldwide, as they increasingly cooperate and collaborate in order to address complicated topics such as child marriage, sexual slavery, and violence against women.

As women's issues globalize, celebrities and activists have joined forces in an effort to make a worldwide impact. For instance, the first Trust Women conference was held in London in December 2012, and included speakers such as the model Christy Turlington and Queen Noor of Jordan. In a similar vein, the Women in the World Foundation sponsored its fourth annual conference in New York City in April 2013. In order to draw attention to women's issues, they are highlighting the shooting of Malala Yousafzai, the Pakistani student who was attacked by Taliban men after she advocated for the education of girls. Their fund-raising appeal has already successfully garnered $100,000, which will be used to improve the access to education for girls in Pakistan and Afghanistan (Torregrosa, 2013). The gathering of these women symbolize a new phase in the international women's rights movement: the joining together of women from high- and low-income countries and from various segments of their respective societies, working together to solve what are increasingly being understood not just as women's issues, but as global issues.

As these initial examples indicate, while global restructuring and neo-liberalism have had many unintended and often oppressive features, especially with respect to a range of issues affecting women, these same processes have also been accompanied by the creation and expansion of new spaces for pursuing gender equality and collectivized women's move-ments. As global human insecurity has risen to the forefront of state and transnational agendas, gender-focused initiatives and programs have become an integral aspect of development policies and are simultane-ously increasingly garnering international attention. In particular the spread of core principles of the Western feminist movement in conjunc-tion with United Nations initiatives, and in particular the Millennium Development Goals (MDGs), have helped propel women's rights to a new transnational level. These same forces have, however, also engen-dered a counter response. Particularly in non-Western settings, a focus on the universal oppression of women by men (a mainstay of the 1960s and 1970s Western women's movement) has led to some criticism of gener-alizations about the universal situation of women and the policies and programs that are supposed to benefit them.

In order to understand how these processes have come together, it is instructive to examine aspects of the Western women's movement, its global spread and influence on development polices, and specifically the Millennium Development Goals. We then turn to the capabilities approach that has been advocated by Amartya Sen (1999) and expanded by Martha Nussbaum (2001), as a blueprint for re-thinking the situation and prospects of women and marginalized individuals in general.

The Spread of the Women's Rights Movement and Notions of Gender Equality

In the United States, from the early twentieth century onwards, the first roots of feminism focused primarily on gaining access to political and economic power. The early beginnings of feminism began as part of women's struggles to attain the right to vote. At that point, women were also engaged in the transformation of social policy, anti-fascist and national liberation movements (Unterhalter, 2008). In what is often termed as "the second wave of feminism," traced back to the 1960s, feminism shifted to a focus on political action that included but was not exclusive to violence against women, the politics of sexuality, the role of the family in women's lives, and the representations of women in art and media. During this period, two strands of gender equality became increasingly important to adherents of this movement. The first, with roots in the first wave of twentieth-century feminism, focused on the general social inclusion of women and girls and the restructuring of policies that had stopped them from gaining access to certain schools, educational opportunities, careers, or political participation. Here gender equality referred to the idea of achieving sameness between men and women in relation to the prospects that were available in society. A second strand of feminism became much more associated with a diffuse conceptualization of gender equality. For instance, one area of emphasis highlighted the differences between women and men and stressed their varied approaches to talking and interacting in social life. Another focus was on the complexity and multiplicity of gendered experiences, stressing the fact that women's and men's lives could only be understood by also accounting for factors such as race, ethnicity, and class. This approach advocated that wider social structures limited the prospects of individuals and, thus, needed to be reorganized.

As the women's movement grew, multiple foci and purposes also arose, specifically in the United States. On the one hand, the radical women's liberation activists amassed followers (Freeman, 1975). Meanwhile, as other social movements of this period such as the Black Panthers and opponents to the Vietnam war died out, the women's movement continued to grow and increasingly focused on issues such as reproductive rights, domestic violence, and pornography. These topics rose to the forefront of activist concerns and became increasingly integrated into mainstream American conceptualizations and critiques of social life. However, the main thrust of the movement focused on incorporating women into the paid labor force and ensuring equity in the workplace. From the early 1970s onwards, feminists fought for government regulation of issues such as equal pay for equal work for women, the recognition and negation of sexual harassment in places of employment, and the use of affirmative action to allow women entrance to traditionally male professions (Eisenstein, 2005).

Most of the debates on these topics took place in the United States and to a certain extent in Europe, and occurred within the bounded confines of nation-states. However, increasingly during this period women started to reach out across borders to form social connections, share concerns, and learn from one another. As a byproduct of the globalizing forces that were rapidly transforming the world, Western ideologies with respect to values such as individualism and the rights of women entered the discourse of other societies. Thus, the burgeoning women's movement of the mid-1960s gained momentum during the same time frame that witnessed the radical restructuring of the world economy. As the global service sector expanded and women, particularly married women, poured into the paid labor force, a complex synergy of ideology, need, and labor coincided. As Beneria (2003) explains:

> The links between gender and globalization should not be seen as responding only to structural and economic forces. They are also shaped by the interaction between these forces and the different ways through which gender constructions have been reconstituted during the past three decades. The feminist movement, in its quest for gender equality, has contributed to this trend on the supply side by emphasizing the need for women to search for greater financial autonomy, bargaining power, and control over their lives. But other tendencies have been at work, both on the supply and the demand side.
>
> (p. 77)

What we find is that the feminist movement of the 1960s and 1970s that primarily emphasized the shift of married women into the paid labor force collided simultaneously with a new global demand for labor and set about a reconceptualization of the work and home intersection.

New Conceptualizations of Women's Roles

On an ideological plane, the women's movement set about to reverse the gender rules that had characterized the 1950s. Feminists from various orientations dismissed the notion that there was a "natural" order to families with men functioning as breadwinners and providers, and women adhering to a standard of femininity that focused on mothering, nurturance, and homemaking. While this was a model that in reality only white suburban couples were able to adhere to, it was one that quickly became the gold standard of American ideological depictions of gender roles and family life. This highly gendered ideal was undergirded by a consumption culture that stressed the importance of attaining material goods for the home and setting up the conditions that would allow families to attain a certain standard of living. Basically this perspective stressed that it was by abiding by gender norms that families would be able to attain the style of life that symbolized "middle-class" status. During the 1950s and early 1960s, middle-class status was primarily characterized by a gendered division of labor, life in the suburbs, and the acquisition of a wide variety of consumer goods. This view took hold despite the reality that African American, immigrant, and working-class women and men were not able to observe such stringent gender conceptualizations. Nonetheless, their experiences were marginalized and ignored, and highlighted as "deviant" from the contemporary norm (Hill Collins, 1994).

Feminists of the 1960s, 1970s, and 1980s were primarily concerned with the access of white married middle-class women to paid employment and disregarded the experiences of other women in society. These activists achieved their initial goals. Within a relatively short period of time, legislation was passed that began to ensure that under the law women were treated as full citizens with rights equivalent to men. Some of this legislation included *Roe v. Wade*, allowing women the right to determine if they wanted to carry a child or not, the right for women to access credit in their own name, and Title IX of the education act which ensured funding for women's sports (Eisenstein, 2005).[1]

Even though the U.S. women's movement included a variety of different ideological leanings and activist programs, including over time feminist critiques by women of color and Third World women's agendas, the primary focus remained the representation of women as self-empowered and self-realized individuals. The American version of feminism at its core stressed individualism and identified the ability to be economically self-sufficient and to partake in the paid labor force, separate from a woman's role as wife and mother as the primary goal of women. Instead of becoming stay at home mothers after marriage, it became normative for women to spend most of their adult lives in the workforce. In fact, one of the earliest proponents of this view, Heidi Hartmann, suggested that the increase in divorced and single parent households should be viewed as a positive societal development and could be interpreted to mean that the achievement of women's economic independence was paramount (1987).

Women's New Roles Become Incorporated into Social Policy Formulations

Through their vigilant efforts, American feminists achieved success. The "new" mainstream conceptualizations of women's roles began to be incorporated into corporate and political policy decisions. Married women and women with young children became more dominant in the labor force and businesses began to abandon the concept of a family wage that would serve to support a spouse and children. While a family wage had been a primary goal of nineteenth-century unions, many of the early 1970s feminists viewed the family wage as means for keeping women dependent on their husbands. However, Brenner (2000, as cited in Eisenstein, 2005) points out that this was an inaccurate interpretation of the historical evidence as the family wage had been a victory for working-class families in the nineteenth century. The well-intentioned efforts of 1970s feminists, thus, set the stage for the decline of the family wage. This phenomenon was accompanied by a recession and subsequent wage stagnation for workers, leading to an increased necessity for dual-income households. In the United States, this resulted in a massive entrance of women into the labor force, but at low wages and with little or no benefits—a trend that has grown over time.

By the 1990s, the concepts of "personal responsibility" and that women needed to be in the paid labor force became so dominant that the welfare reform legislation enacted in 1996, the Personal Responsibility and Work Opportunity Act, dismantled the New Deal welfare legislation that had provided support for the poor mothers of young children and replaced it with mandatory work regulations. The weak safety net that had been a cornerstone of American society since 1935 when it was first enacted as part of Social Security legislation, and when the idea of single mothers with children working outside of the home was virtually unimaginable, was replaced. In part, this shift also occurred through a reframing by right-wing ideological groups of who welfare recipients were. While in 1935 the primary beneficiaries were thought to be young white widows with children, by the 1990s that image was replaced with black single women with children through media representations. Both policy-makers and the public became eager to see these women in the workforce, and a conflicting dialogue about "families" ensued.

As has been noted by many family scholars (see, for instance, the extensive work by Patricia Hill Collins, 1994, 1998), a dialogue ensued that suggested that it was the primary responsibility of low-income and poor women to work outside of the home and not be dependent on the social welfare system. Concurrently, mainstream discourses emphasized the importance of middle-class women maintaining a strong family presence even should they take on an economic role in their families (Marchand & Runyan, 2000). These dialogues, based on white middle-class-based feminist conceptions, gave policy-makers the tools to reorganize the welfare system around values that were now considered mainstream, and which were also extremely beneficial to employers. For instance, Temporary Assistance for Needy Families, as the reformed welfare legislation became titled, was devolved to the state level and a five-year receipt limit was implemented. As Chang (2000) points out, this was also extremely advantageous to employers as they were now able to have illegal immigrants and women who were no longer on welfare compete for the same jobs, thereby keeping wages low. These occurrences highlight how ideological transformations can be used, manipulated, and translated into unforeseen policy consequences.

Feminism and Development Initiatives

While the 1970s and 1980s witnessed an upsurge in feminist concerns with the role of women in Western societies, critiques by feminists of color raised awareness of the lack of understanding about gender issues in non-Western low-income countries. Socio-political developments, such as the fall of the Soviet Union and the dissolution of the Iron Curtain coupled with Western-led development initiatives, also highlighted cross-cultural differences with respect to gender arrangements and priorities. These events helped set the stage for a global consciousness raising with respect to incorporating gender equality into national and transnational agendas as well as a backlash against these movements.

International development as a field can be traced back to the post-World War II period of reconstruction. Western economists bolstered by the success of the Marshall Plan became convinced that the gap between the industrialized and developing world could be bridged through aid-based strategic planning (Visvanathan, 2011). This resulted in a complex strategy of disseminating money and technical aid through United Nations agencies. Principally, development was linked to economic growth, with the hallmarks being the expansion of industrialization, an increase in trade, the growing income of nations, and the reduction of poverty among respective populaces. Significantly, development was understood as a state-led, top-down process characterized by market-led economic growth (Pieterse, 2000).

As the Western feminist movement spread and infiltrated policy analyses, questions arose about the role of women in development work and non-Western contexts. Feminist critiques in particular pointed to the invisibility of women in development initiatives, and how this omission led to policy imbalances. These critiques also raised awareness that women's domestic work was not accounted for in development indicators (Boserup, 1970). Thus, as global concerns about growing inequalities within and between societies arose, women's rights increasingly moved to the forefront of development agendas.

The Role of the United Nations

In particular, the United Nations has played a significant historical role in acknowledging the marginalization of women's rights both institutionally and conceptually, and then setting into motion development initiatives that promoted the global equality and empowerment of women. From a legal perspective, probably the most important innovation has been the adoption of the Declaration on the Elimination of All Forms of Discrimination Against Women (United Nations, 1967) which culminated in the Convention on the Elimination of All Forms of Discrimination Against Women (CEDAW) in 1979. CEDAW placed the concept of women's rights in a global framework and founded a supervisory body that was similar to those that existed for human rights concerns.

The importance of the UN Women's Convention grew out of the recognition that ineffective strategies were being employed to advance the rights of women. The fact that the UN General Assembly adopted it in 1979 symbolizes the international obligation to the commitment and spread of women's rights. Tang and Peters (2006) point out that women's problems are often ignored because women do not have powerful advocates that can stand up for them and enforce their rights. The convention solved this problem by creating the Committee on the Elimination of Discrimination against Women. The role of this committee has been to oversee the actions of states with respect to implementing the suggestions of the Women's Convention that include social and economic rights such as health care, equality in marriage, the elimination of sexual and gender-based violence, and the right to education and protection when employed. By ratifying the convention, states commit themselves under international law to uphold these rights through their national laws and policies and to "condemn discrimination against women in all its forms." Within one year of ratification, each state must submit an initial report on the status of women in their society. The Committee on the Elimination of Discrimination against Women also asks governments to include the perspectives of non-governmental organizations on actual women's concerns. This forces those organizations that are involved with women to play an important role as brokers between women's concerns and the government.

Case Study: Canada

There are multiple documented incidences when the perspectives outlined by women's groups have proven to be an invaluable tool for the committee's analysis of states' compliance with United Nations standards. For example, Tang and Peters (2006) present the example of Canada which ratified the convention in 1980 and submitted a positive fifth report to the UN committee in 2002. However, simultaneously Canadian NGOs submitted four reports to the CEDAW Committee detailing violations to women's rights on both national and provincial levels. In particular, a report highlighting a wide variety of dramatic changes in the province of British Columbia drew the attention of the UN CEDAW: "It expressed its concern about 'recent changes in British Columbia which have a disproportionately negative impact on women' and it recommended that 'British Columbia ... analyse[s] its recent legal and other measures as to their negative impact on women and ... amend the measures, when necessary" (CEDAW, 2003, p. 6 in Tang & Peters, 2006, p. 577). Moreover, CEDAW addressed a variety of issues in British Columbia with respect to the levels of poverty found among women, retaining legal aid for women, and establishing more women's and transitions centers. They then issued a broader recommendation to the government to better regulate poverty among vulnerable groups of women such as the Aboriginals.

Tang and Peters (2006) illustrate through the Canadian example that without the oversight and pressure provided through NGOs, state and provincial governments lack incentives to properly enforce the convention. When funding is cut to women's groups, these same entities lose the resources to make their concerns public, thus, further eliminating their ability to advocate for reinstating certain types of programs. Pressure is exerted on states to recognize and enforce women's rights through the intersection of local non-governmental entities with international bodies such as the United Nations. For example, in most countries today, in the process of creating domestic laws, the courts now need to take into account international conventions and norms. The value of the convention then lies in its role as a broker between local concerns and advocacy groups. Governments, backed by a neoliberal agenda, tend to be quick to deviate from stated goals and in particular to dismiss women's rights. The convention acts as a buffer and as an intermediary on behalf of the rights of women. The Canadian example illustrates that international advocacy will only grow in the future and that it has the potential to force governments to halt or at least lessen discriminatory practices and policies against women.

The Canadian case provides a clear example of how, in the current amorphous global environment, non-governmental organizations can play a critical role in promoting a feminist consciousness and agenda. Their capacity to mobilize on failures of public policy and to monitor state deviations from stated goals has brought about new social policies and greater protections for women in areas such as exploitive labor and environmental practices (Bandy, 2004).[2] By adopting the convention, the United Nations created the foundation for an international women's law of human rights that now crosses the boundaries of national, religious, and customary laws (Hellum, 1999).

The United Nations Women's Conferences

The most visible public action on the part of the United Nations has been the coordination of transnational women's conferences that have been held around the world beginning in 1975 in Mexico and culminating in the Fourth World Conference on Women in 1995 in Beijing. At the Beijing conference approximately 40,000 women came together and a declaration was issued that women's autonomy and rights to an education were also a human right. This marked a major turning point for feminists the world over as it moved concerns that had been perceived as "women's issues" to center stage. The initial conferences also resulted in the United Nations Decade for the Advancement of Women (1976–85), the World Plan of Action and the First World Survey on the Role of Women in Development (Tikly, 2004). Moreover, the United Nations has played a critical role in supporting and implementing a focus on women's issues by creating units that deal specifically with the concerns of women, such as the Division for the Advancement of Women (DAW), and the United Nations Development Fund for Women (UNIFEM).

The United Nations-sponsored conferences have served as powerful forums to focus and discuss women's concerns while setting global agendas and milestones. Part of the agenda and emphasis of each of these conferences has been the notion of patriarchy as a central reason for underdevelopment, especially as it relates to women. This consciousness has led in part to the modernization of states becoming equated with the role of women and their rights in relation to development and underdevelopment. These conferences have had a broader effect than expected. Feminist thinking has infused national and international agendas and led to the rapid dissemination of an emphasis on gender equality.

The focus on gender equality became popular in part due to efforts during the period known as the United Nations Decade for the Advancement of Women. Initially, this effort was termed the "Women in Development" (WID) approach and centered on the understanding that there had been a significant deficit in development theory and practice by not taking into account women's contributions to national economic activities. Mainstream economic assessments had focused on industrial production and market-based activity. By employing the new WID approach, however, women were now understood to be an untapped resource that could further development in countries that were perceived as lagging behind. WID approaches identified women's lack of access to resources as the reason for their secondary position in societies but did not raise questions about the role of gender relations in this lack of access (Razavi & Miller, 1995).

By the late 1970s, WID advocates questioned the sufficiency of only focusing on women. They also began to adhere to the sociological perspective that gender relations were not a physiological fact but predicated on relationships, as well as the rules and practices of different institutions in a society such as the household, community, and state. During this time, what became known as the gender roles framework was taking hold. This approach was based on the foundational insight that households are not undifferentiated groupings of individuals. Instead households or families were now understood to be systems where different individuals had varied levels of power depending on resource allocation (Razavi & Miller, 1995). This perspective led to the notion of gender equity being defined as equal access to, and power over, resources.

Gender equity became a critical aspect of development approaches. For instance, the United Nations Development Programme in 1995 stated: "Human development is a process of enlarging the choices of all people, not just for one part of society. Such a process becomes unjust and discriminatory if most women are excluded from its benefits" (p. 1). However, supporters quickly discovered that they would be more successful if calls for social justice and equality for women were purposefully linked to mainstream development enterprises. In other words, notions of equality resonated more when a larger group of individuals could profit from the venture. In part, due to the influence of Amartya Sen, the first Human Development Report in 1990 advocated a shift from development economics to people-centered policies (Fukuda-Parr, 2003). This bold project promoted a much more ambitious goal for development work than had previously been the case. The new approach included measurement, tools for analysis, and policy objectives. Fukuda-Parr (2003) quotes Jolly's (2003) description: "[The] Human Development (HD) approach embodies a robust paradigm, which may be contrasted with the neoliberal (NL) paradigm of the Washington consensus. There are points of overlap, but also important points of difference in objectives, assumptions, constraints and in the main areas for policy and in the indicators for assessing results" (p. 302).

In order to sway their opponents, proponents of this approach created different measurement tools for evaluating human achievements, based on the concept that in today's world many individuals are more likely to accept policy arguments that are based on "hard" numbers. In order to capture some of the complexities advocated by the new focus on individuals and human capacity, the Human Development Index (HDI) was instituted. While there is dispute if it is truly possible to capture the complexity of human activity through "numbers," the development of the HDI has had significant policy impacts.

The ranking of countries by HDI raised awareness and concerns about why countries that have similar GDPs differ with respect to their HDIs. In other words, why do countries with similar economic levels exhibit stark differences with respect to individuals being able to survive, be knowledgeable, and achieve a decent standard of living—the three cornerstones of the HDI approach. One of the most valuable aspects of the HDI approach turned out to be that it incorporates gender disparities in its evaluations. In fact, the 1995 Human Development Report ends with the statement that "human development is endangered unless it is engendered." The emphasis on gender is noteworthy because besides including education, health, and income outcomes, it also focuses on the participation of women in political and professional life, their ability to participate in decision making, and the distribution of unpaid work between women and men.

The HDI became a powerful tool in the arsenal to promote women's rights, and ultimately let to the adoption of the "Gender and Development" (GAD) approach. This perspective highlights power relations and the social conditions and beliefs that subordinate women to men in many societies (Razavi & Miller, 1995). This new concept stressed the importance of understanding the historical place of men and women in particular societies and their relationship to their own history. Gender differences were now understood as shaped by various factors including history, religion, ethnicity, economics, and culture—and as socially constructed by, and through, development processes and experiences. The GAD also promoted the idea that in order for women to attain equality and access and control of resources, their relationships to men must be incorporated into programming and policies.

The GAD is fundamentally a human development approach that suggests that investing in education and health is fundamental to achieving economic and social progress in a society. However, its truly distinctive feature is that it highlights the importance of human agency in effecting changes to social policy through collective action and attention to human rights (Fukuda-Parr, 2003). The GAD approach is specifically apparent in the emphasis of several of the Millennium Development Goals.

The Millennium Development Goals and Female Empowerment

The Millennium Development Goals are the result of the Millennium Declaration, signed by 189 countries at the September 2000 Millennium Summit of the United Nations. The declaration states that there are essential values and non-negotiable rights that are shared by all individuals: the right not to be hungry and afraid, the right to equality, solidarity, and tolerance, the right to ensure the sustainability of the environment, and the right that the international community needs to join in a global partnership for development (United Nations, 2009). The Millennium Declaration validated a long-coming shift in the conceptualization of what is meant by "development" from a focus on purely economic progress to a so-called "rights-approach" that emphasizes wider human capacities and capabilities. This emphasis highlights individuals' potential "to be" and "to do" (Beneria, 2007b, p. 9). In other words, there is now a dual emphasis in development approaches: removing obstacles in people's lives is combined with a focus on what they want to achieve. The Millennium Development Goals embody this goal by emphasizing human capabilities and functioning.

New interactions and collaborations in global spaces have spurred the advancement toward universal goals such as the Millennium Development

Goal of promoting gender equality and empowering women (UNESCO, 2005), and the formalization and mainstreaming of feminist concerns. This has been accompanied by understandings of gender justice and equity, and growing agreement that the Western conceptualizations of markets and capitalism are rooted in androcentric, individualistic notions of human nature and behavior (Keddie, 2010). In other words, there is an increased realization that analyses of markets are not "objective" and rational, nor are they neutral as was claimed previously.

The acknowledgment of the privileging of markets has highlighted the fact that emphasizing technical and quantitative aspects of economics and human development over human and social factors yields inaccurate analyses of phenomena. For example, feminist economists have long pointed out that women's well-being cannot be equated with a nation's GNP nor that their economic participation necessarily yields a higher standard of living or better life for them.

Despite the progress indicated by the success of various United Nations initiatives, the events of September 2001 marked a turning point for the advancement of women's rights (Desai, 2010). A renewed focus on military armament, a resurgence of fundamentalism in various regions in the world, and a continued emphasis on market-driven development strategies deflected mainstream interest in women's empowerment. Moreover, questions have arisen about what exactly is meant by Western concepts of empowerment and development. In fact, various critics have highlighted the fact that in certain parts of the world, such as sub-Saharan Africa or the Caribbean, women have now taken on a triple burden with respect to participating in production, reproduction, and care work. Women have also lost some of their traditional economic safety nets (such as local markets), while being the victims of discriminatory labor practices:

> Despite its promise to put people at the centre of development in order to realize their choices and freedom, human development has been in many ways co-opted by the dominant mainstream that in the end put economic growth ahead of people's choices. Human development has been whittled down to competitive indexes and measurements of nations in the Human Development Index (HDI) and ultimately in the measurable goals of the Millennium Development Goals (MDGs).
>
> (Harcourt, 2010, p. 1)

Analysts who adhere to the GAD approach to development point out that we cannot and should not just speak of markets and economics when millions of individuals are living in great poverty, without access to health care and education, and in decaying social environments. These critiques suggest that the focus of human development should not be modernization and economic growth, nor should they be linked to one another (Harcourt, 2010). Instead, contemporary approaches need to emphasize building healthy communities and promoting individual well-being, functioning, and capacities.

Gender Equity in Non-Western Contexts

Over the last 30 years or so, we have witnessed a strong focus by Western feminists on the global subjugation of women due to patriarchal gender norms and practices (Fennell & Arnot, 2008). Non-Western feminists have criticized this stance by pointing out that the Western experience may not necessarily reflect the situation of women across the globe. They have highlighted the fact that singling out gender relations and patriarchy over other types of power and control such as those that come with access to wealth, or age, caste, race, ethnicity or region may not always be a valid basis for understanding the subjugation of individuals when compared across cultures (Momsen & Kinnaird, 1993). These same critics also challenge the negative focus of Western feminists on the role of family life for women and the dichotomization of private and public space, pointing out that there is a great deal of global variety with respect to these institutions and arrangements. Fennell and Arnot (2008) point out that the greatest contribution of these feminist debates is in "the valorization of the contribution of women beyond the quantitative world of economics" (p. 7). They explain that these debates have moved policy makers from measuring the contribution of women purely to economic development, to a greater understanding of the social construction of gender inequality and gender dynamics in local contexts. When viewed from a non-Western perspective, we find that the challenges facing women and how they overcome them may provide new ways of thinking about gender equality. For example, increasingly development work has focused on capacity building and the role of education as a means of building and supplementing the inadequate skills and resources that women may be constrained by (Sen, 1999).

The focus on women and their rights has served to move the development agenda at the United Nations and subsequently, at the World Bank, to one that has not just focused on the reduction of poverty but also on gender equity. Tikly (2004), however, points out that Western forms of female empowerment which were rapidly incorporated around the globe by elites in both high- and low-income countries stressed gender equality, individual rights, self-realization, and the importance of a global sisterhood, while in reality not mirroring the concerns of so many poor and marginalized women. These women tend to experience various forms of oppression and a fundamental lack of power in their relationships, making Western-based concerns inapplicable to them. Moreover, since they are most often part of collectively oriented cultures, their struggles are less concerned with individualized ideals of self and more with improving the collective well-being of groups, be it their families, communities, or even nations.

Tikly (2004) interestingly argues that the transformation of World Bank policies with respect to women was primarily governed by economic rationales. In keeping with the spirit of the times, the discourse around women was spearheaded by the notion that women's productivity was "wasted" as it flowed through informal channels, instead of being properly incorporated into the formal labor force and the global marketplace. For example, the World Bank proclaimed that "no country can afford to under-utilize and under-equip more than half of its resources" (Simmons, 1997, p. 245 in Tikly, 2004, p. 185). Thus, the primary rationale behind gender equity was to better integrate women into national and international markets.

Beneria (2003) has succinctly described this phenomenon as the "demand" sector growing concurrently with the "supply" sector. This reframing of the capabilities of women and the restructuring of the global marketplace was accompanied by "a recasting of the liberal *Homo economicus*" as a free economic agent invested with basic rights and civic duties. "What emerged was a valorization of entrepreneurialism as the basis for growth along with the notion that these qualities could be actively formed through the actions of individuals themselves rather than on the basis of state intervention" (Tikly, 2004, p. 185). Women, thus, became imbued with a number of "new" characteristics: they were to become an integral part of the marketplace, this was to empower them, and they could take over the services that previously had been provided by the state. Women could also now be counted on to provide limitless, cheap labor. One of the first places to implement this program was South Korea, where women were encouraged to leave agriculture and enter factory work, allowing the nation to industrialize with an unlimited supply of available labor. According to some analysts, one of the primary reasons for the Korean "economic miracle" was the significant gender wage disparities. Labor-intensive industries were able to draw on cheap female labor, increasing the international competitiveness of their manufactured goods (Amsden, 1989).

As state-run development declined, and economies re-oriented themselves toward the global marketplace, indebted Third World countries allowed multinational corporations to manufacture their goods in "free trade zones" where taxes and tariffs were either extremely low or completely eliminated, and legislation forbade the formation of trade unions. Starting with the electronics industry in the 1960s, multinationals increasingly sought out these free trade zones in order to produce a wide selection of goods ranging from garments to toys and shoes, in ever more cost-effective environments. Simultaneously, the service industry also began to move to Third World environments. For example, data entry shifted to parts of the Caribbean (Freeman, 2000) and programming and sales work to Asia (Kelkar & Nathan, 2002). As was noted previously, multinationals preferred female workers for these jobs as they thought them unlikely to organize or to resist unfavorable working environments. It is important to note that particularly in export-processing economies, low-paid females now make up approximately 80 percent of the workforce (Rosen, 2002).

While many feminist analysts have criticized this move to a feminized labor force due to the exploitive conditions and the vulnerability of the employees and their families (see Pyle and Ward, 2003 for example), others have expressed a more ambivalent opinion and have pointed out that for many of these women, employment by multinational corporations, no matter how oppressive the conditions, is better than their other even bleaker options (Beek, 2001).

It is important to remember that the move to free trade zones and subsequently to ever-cheaper labor environments was not the only economic restructuring taking place over the last 30 years. In the quest for cheaper production costs, multinationals have instituted other strategies as well, including automating some aspects of production and establishing subcontracting networks with local manufacturers who employed cheaply paid workers who could also be terminated at a moment's notice. This employment practice was termed as more "flexible" work arrangements, and advantaged the employer. Women in particular were affected by these practices. As they were the main source of labor, should a manufacturer move to a new location or automate production, these women subsequently were the first ones to lose their jobs. Women who are involved in subcontracted work do not fare any better. Most often economically impoverished women undertake this informal sector work as it allows them to work at home and still earn wages. However, this kind of work is extremely underpaid and since typically these women are not connected with others, they are unable to organize and form any kind of collective action against unfair labor practices. These women are often very vulnerable as this type of employment is usually not steady. It is not uncommon for women who then lose these wages to subsequently seek work as domestics, both at home or abroad, or in the sex industry (Parrenas, 2001).

Beneria (2003) points out that despite all of the global progress with respect to the dialogue around the rights and the empowerment of women, significant concerns remain. Aggregate data from the United Nations indicates that, in reality, the situation of some groups of women has worsened over the last ten years or so (United Nations, 2009). Beneria (2003) also suggests that there is a tendency to instrumentalize some of the issues with respect to women, that is, women are incorporated into larger national and transnational agendas that do not necessarily serve their goals—or may even impair them. For example, programs curtailing population growth may really be much more focused on demographic goals than on the actual well-being of girls and women; or women may be used for temporary work to deflect from the negative effects of male unemployment. What we find is that while empowering women has definitely become a global policy priority, especially in the development arena, the more insidious and critical aspects of gender inequality persist, and dialogue and policy responses remain marginalized. Beneria (2003) points as one problem to the disconnect between academics' analysis and policy-makers. While academics may stress the importance of gender approaches, they are often unaware of the successes, challenges, and failures of international organizations, advocates, and activists that concern themselves with these issues. In order to overcome this deficiency, we need greater dialogue between policy-makers, academics, NGOs, and service providers. This will lead to a multipronged analysis of how the different levels of social and economic life intersect with gender concerns from both a theoretical and a practical perspective.

What we find is that a strange paradox is inherent in global neoliberal processes: on the one hand, inequalities within groups and between groups have been exacerbated; on the other hand, a new global space has opened up where transnational feminist networks and coalitions have been able to emerge, unite, and engage in cooperative action. This new landscape has encouraged the promotion of a gender justice movement at both a local and a global level through the work of non-government organizations (NGOs) and civil society organizations (CSOs) (O'Connell, 2007). These kinds of movements indicate the complexity of understanding globalization processes, as this phenomenon is at work simultaneously both in a transcendental supra space and in local contexts.

The Human Capacity and Capabilities Approach

The worldwide women's movement, which I again want to emphasize, has multiple agendas and strands and has served to create a new vision that focuses less on the growth and development of capital and more on individual and collective well-being. In this new model, issues of care and unpaid work rise to the forefront as aspects of women's lives that are to be incorporated into analyses of markets, work, and paid labor. Nussbaum (2001), in particular, has elaborated a ten-point elucidation of how we may want to think about universal women's rights in a framework that is both comprehensive and yet remains true to local concerns. She suggests that there *are* universal moral imperatives and that we cannot just argue that everything is culturally relative. She suggests that there are ten capabilities that women and, in fact, all individuals have the right to develop.[3] They include the development of knowledge accompanied by agency and freedom in the arenas of human rights, bodily health and integrity, and the intellectual and emotional affiliation and well-being with others. She states:

> The capabilities approach is fully universal: the capabilities in question are important for each and every citizen in each and every nation, and each is to be treated as an end. Women in developing nations are important to the project in two ways: as people who suffer pervasively from acute capability failure, and also as people whose situation provides an interesting test of this and other approaches, showing us the problems they solve or fail to solve. Defects in standard GNP and utility-based approaches can be well understood by keeping the problems of such women in view; but of course women's problems are urgent in their own right, and it may be hoped that a focus on them will help compensate for earlier neglect of sex equality in development economics and in the international human rights movement.
>
> (pp. 6–7)

Nussbaum's reasoning is in part founded on the writings of Amartya Sen (1999). Sen defined human development as the process of expanding the capabilities of individuals to give them a broader range of choices of what to do with their lives.[4] He advocated that development needed to focus on improving individuals' lives by removing obstacles to what people can achieve. Obstacles can include but are not limited to lack of resources, or civil and political freedoms. From this perspective improvements in individuals' lives and human achievements are key aspects of social progress, and women and men need equal access to those opportunities (Fukuda-Parr, 2003). Sen's philosophical work is integral to key aspects of contemporary development agendas which now make gender parity a primary component of this social justice perspective.

Sen and Nussbaum's positions with respect to policy formation stand in stark contrast to supporters of neoliberal agendas which advocate that well-being be translated as "utility maximization" and point to economic markers as signs of success. This neoliberal perspective focuses on profit and efficiency: maximizing the total value achieved from the available money and evaluating people's well-being based on their access to commodities. Sen has pointed out that the problem with the neoliberal perspective is that it neglects context: that there are places where individuals are not free to make their own choices, nor can they even access basic rights. Moreover, the neoliberal approach emphasizes commodities rather than capabilities as the basis for achieving greater human fulfillment. It leads to policy formation that targets institutional efficiency and meeting individuals' material needs as goals, rather than emphasizing human rights or freedoms.

Nussbaum's framing of these issues through a capabilities lens moves the discourse from understanding women's well-being through economic productivity, to one that links agency, autonomy, and local circumstances. It highlights the fact that there are both economic and sociocultural aspects of well-being that need to be accounted for and addressed with respect to women. It links the gendered experiences of women in the market sphere with a recognition that certain cultural practices marginalize and silence women (Keddie, 2010).

Nussbaum's primary contribution to the literature on feminist economics is her philosophical stance that improving the lives of women in a holistic sense is a moral imperative. This position has been further elaborated from a scholarly perspective by Beneria (2003), and Kuiper and Barker (2006) among others, and through the development agenda of the World Bank and the United Nations. The Gender-related Development Index and the Gender Empowerment Measure which the United Nations added to its Human Development Index has expanded global interest in health, health care, literacy, education, income, poverty, and the professional representation of women. These indices have also led to recognition and analysis around effective economic strategies that include gender disparities, and social and environmental factors.

Depressingly, however, despite revised development agendas and transnational initiatives, the situation of women in the poorest region of the world remains unchanged, and in certain cases has actually worsened. According to recent UNESCO (2005) and United Nations (2009) reports, the situation for women continues to be dire in sub-Saharan Africa and parts of Asia and China. This of course raises the question: Why is this happening? With such stringent development efforts, an increased global focus, and intensive work on gender issues, equity, and mainstreaming, why do so many women still live under such impoverished conditions?

Why Gender Parity is Not Enough

As we have seen, a strong feminist scholarship has highlighted the fact that understanding and addressing issues of gender inequities cannot be solved through relying purely on economic indicators. Unterhalter (2008) suggests that increasingly even the developing world understands that gender equity can only be addressed by reframing programs of action to include equal gender relations with equal access to resources. Thus, the shift that needs to occur is a cultural one, not just an economic transformation. Colclough (2007), moreover, highlights the relational aspect of a gender focus. He suggests that the traditional development approaches on "women only" ignore the relationship between men and women and how those add to female subordination and that a simplistic focus on quantitative measures of gender parity does not solve the problems. Keddie (2010) states that:

> These conventional approaches tend to understand and address women's issues in instrumentalist or functionalist ways that do not necessarily reflect, and indeed can be counter to, feminist goals. For example, much feminist critique has surrounded the ways in which various initiatives aimed at controlling women's fertility in low-income contexts (instituted by organizations such as the World Bank), continue to reflect agendas of economic rationality, rather than the best interests of women.
>
> (p. 145)

Colclough (2007) highlights gender and development approaches that explicitly focus on the social construction of gender and how in certain cultural contexts males are privileged and females marginalized. This focal point allows us to understand that while economics are an integral aspect to changing women's lives, transforming social and cultural relations is equally important. Gender disparities exist due to norms and contexts that privilege one group over another. Any kind of real economic progress can only occur when each side of the equation—the economic and the social ones—are addressed.

Moreover, the prospect and potential for collective action is often neglected in analysis of globalization. This occurs because of the strong relationship in so many analysts' and policy-makers' minds between globalization and neoliberalism and its emphasis on individualistic empowerment. However, while individual action is empowering on a private level, social change requires collective agency in the public sphere. In order to effect policy changes with respect to issues such as safe working conditions or access to health care, collective action is necessary. Individuals are often most effective by forming associations, creating alliances, and becoming involved in public debates. Thus, collective action requires political participation that gives people voice and ensures the accountability of those who are in charge.

Global restructuring actually provides an ideal springboard for such activity. The initial examples in this chapter of the coming together of women, and increasingly also men, around crimes against women that are now also understood as human rights violations, illustrates the power of collective transnational movements. Constantly improving communication technologies and the ability to organize across borders allows marginalized individuals to unite around a common purpose or goal and utilize collective agency. Collective agency can also be exercised through the collaboration and partnering of various entities and individuals across local, national, and transnational domains. It is, thus, not necessarily accurate to exclusively focus on the individualistic, entrepreneurial aspects of globalization and neoliberalism, when the potential for collective action is also embedded in these processes.

As new global spaces have opened up, we are increasingly witnessing transnational coalition-building feminist activists with agendas that are sensitive to local issues. In particular, individuals are creating cross-border alliances that encompass economic, political, and social concerns while being "relatively autonomous from both government and market actors" (Bandy, 2004, p. 410). As states continue to limit their regulatory and redistributive capabilities, concerns about individual rights and obligations and their access to resources have moved from the nation-state to the international level (Bandy, 2004). In part this has occurred because as new organizations for global decision-making such as the G8 and the OECD gained power, they have furthered more connections between states, non-governmental organizations, and regional institutions.[5] These new interconnections are simultaneously opening up new visions and pathways to global participation in various realms. Moreover, these networks and coalitions have created the possibility and the mechanisms for the diversification and strengthening of feminist activities and for the monitoring of equity policies and programs. From a contemporary perspective, these global spaces allow for the inclusion of a more representative and democratic citizenry. They provide a new mechanism for counteracting some of the more negative injustices that have characterized neoliberal flows and have highlighted the social structures and practices that in particular disadvantage women. These same mechanisms have also encouraged collective civil responsibility and social agency toward stopping and redressing some of these injustices (Keddie, 2010).

The Contentious Relationship Between Women's Rights and Capitalism

In some circles, the women's rights movement is very much associated with the adoption of capitalism in the developing world. According to Eisenstein (2005), mainstream thought often links democracy, free markets, and the attainment of women's rights together: "Indeed, the equation is that 'modern' equals women's rights, the Judeo-Christian heritage, and democracy, while 'traditional' equals patriarchal suppression of women's rights, the Islamic heritage, and terrorism" (p. 509). From this perspective, on the global stage, Western-style feminism has become a symbol for and an expression of Western thought and its emphasis on individualism. This perspective stands in direct opposition to many non-Western cultures where a strong collectivistic sentiment intertwined with an emphasis on nationalism and "traditions" rejects that notion. Feminism, as an ideology, encourages women to be individuals, to be self-empowered, and to realize their own desires and talents. Women are to be individuals first, and members of a family or community second. Globalization is spreading this concept, even as it is rejected and/or negotiated in local contexts.

Part of global development has been the inclusion of women into the market economy, and as will be seen in subsequent chapters, part of this package, the education of women, has become a prerequisite to economic development. In places like the Middle East, women are often pointed to as an underutilized commodity that could move economies and societies forward. As countries increasingly need to rely on private-sector exports in order to compete in the global market, women are perceived as providing the necessary labor. However, as Eisenstein (2005) suggests, this is a paradoxical situation as other aspects of neoliberalism require states to reduce the services that are most needed by women who work outside of the home. She points out that neoliberal global forces, on the one hand, "liberate" women by promoting a feminist ideology and incorporating women into the global market economy. On the other, they tear apart the traditional structures and social supports that protect women and their children, including family life, education, affordable housing, and health care.

Synopsis

As this discussion has highlighted, when viewed from a more transnational perspective, it becomes increasingly complicated to defend and advocate for just one set of global women's rights, to uniformly partake in a dynamic global justice movement, or to create a unique distinctive voice that reflects the uniform concerns of local women in a context of neoliberal globalization. Moreover, the simultaneous rise of religious and nationalistic fundamentalisms, the constantly evolving multiplicity of foci about the nature of feminism and what its goals and strategies should be, and the divide between those who advocate for the right of women to control their social lives versus those who are most concerned with women's economic justice has created a situation where it is unclear which aspects of the women's movements can be universally enacted from a global perspective (Barton, 2004). Despite these complications, global restructuring is creating new spaces for women and men from high- and low-income countries to come together to collectively examine complex topics such as crimes against women, which are increasingly understood as human right's violations. The various women's conferences, including the original ones that were initiated by the United Nations, as well as the more recent transnational ones, such as the Trust Women conference or the Women in the World one, indicate that new collaborations are possible and are likely to effect changes that will fundamentally effect women's lives for the better.

Increasingly, through public attention to some of the more horrific crimes committed against women as well as through publicity about general women's issues in high- and low-income countries, it is understood that a particularly productive path to empowering women is to examine primarily the power relations between men and women, and how these are deeply entrenched in different social institutions. There is an increased recognition through these transnational dialogues that by altering these relationships we will be working toward a greater social justice system for *both* women and men.

It is important to remember that despite increased collaborations, from both a local and a global perspective, women's rights movements are not one homogeneous front. They are often characterized by very different agendas such as in some places women wanting greater control over their own bodies, while in other regions women advocating for their rights primarily for economic reasons. Thus, we cannot really speak of a global women's movement. These are many movements spearheaded by one unifying term. Various groups, issues, and identities are converging in a global arena where different and, at times, conflicting agendas collide. Moreover, many of these projects have now been taken over by nongovernmental organizations or NGOs, instead of being part of larger societal institutions such as the peasant movements of former times. As Barton (2004) points out, this is not necessarily a good or bad phenomenon. This shift does raise the question of how these NGOs will function in arenas that are increasingly cost competitive and where funding is the highest priority. Instead of necessarily being able to align themselves with an ideology, most NGOs are forced to follow the directives set by their funders.

As neoliberal policies shift the functions of the state to the private sector, many groups have had to professionalize and are at times coopted by other agendas. That said, in terms of implementation, many NGOs are leading the way with respect to gender equity projects. For instance, each of the UN agencies has incorporated a focus on women into their work, and they have worked toward what is sometimes referred to as "gender mainstreaming," the representation of women at all levels of management and the incorporation of gender issues into every aspect of their work. Mainstreaming involves making sure that gender perspectives and an emphasis on gender equity is fundamental to all endeavors. This may include but is not limited to policy development, advocacy, implementation and monitoring of programs, and research. A commitment to gender mainstreaming is understood as one of the most effective mechanisms for ensuring that the promotion of gender equality at all levels of work and policy formation is upheld (United Nations, 2013). This focus on gender mainstreaming has also spread to the organizational and practical aspects of other internationally focused NGOs.[6] Those NGOs that have made gender mainstreaming an important aspect of their mission are rapidly becoming part of a global network of activity, information sharing, and activism, and are themselves an advantageous outgrowth of globalization.

Notes

1 Interestingly, in the United States the main beneficiaries of affirmative action have been white women not minorities.
2 See Bandy (2004) on how creative coalition building has mobilized reforms against exploitation in the export processing sectors of the Maquiladoras.
3 Nussbaum builds on the ideas of Amartya Sen's concept of capabilities which refers to a space within which comparisons of quality of life or standards of living are made. Sen suggests that instead of asking about resources or life satisfaction, analyses should examine about what people are actually able to do or to be. He also insists that a capabilities approach is the arena within which questions about social equality and inequality are best brought to the forefront.
4 For a more explicit discussion of Sen's work to development policies, see Fukuda-Parr, 2003.
5 The G8 stands for the Group of Eight which represent the governments of eight of the world's wealthiest countries. The forum began in 1975. Founded in 1961, partially as a result of the Marshall plan, the OECD is currently composed of 30 of the world's most developed countries including those of the European Union, Japan, Australia, New Zealand, Turkey, Canada, and the United States.
6 See, for instance, the World Health Organization for their gender mainstreaming strategies. http://www.un.org/womenwatch/osagi/gendermainstreaming.htm.

Part II

WOMEN'S UNIQUE EXPERIENCES IN THE GLOBAL ECONOMY

4

GENDER ROLE SOCIALIZATION
Setting the Stage

Consider the following two scenarios.

Christine and John are 14-year-old twins, excited that they are about to start their last year of middle school. Christine is already talking about the science fair in the spring that is always an important part of the graduation process and her brother is excited about playing lacrosse. Sister and brother are very close and plan to attend the same college one day. Their comfortable middle-class lives are filled with school activities, homework, extracurricular activities, and friends. They love their house that is located in a tree-filled suburb of a major metropolitan area, they each have their own bedroom, and they are looking forward to the day when they have their drivers' licenses. Their worries include peer pressure at school, raising their GPAs in math, and saving up for a new computer.

Contrast the lives of Christine and John with that of the life of Fawzeia, a 14-year-old girl growing up in a village in Upper Egypt. Fawzeia lives with her eight-member family in a clay mud house right next to an embankment along the Nile. She has four brothers, one sister, and her parents. Until last year her remaining grandmother was living with them, but she died at age 64 of a parasitic infection. Fawzeia is smart, ambitious, and was always recognized as the best student in her class. Her parents understand that she is better at schoolwork than her brothers. However, her mother recently became ill after giving birth and cannot do the work that needs to be done around their house anymore. Fawzeia's parents decided to pull her out of school, with her father arguing that helping her mother in the home would prepare her to be a better wife. In his mind, Fawzeia has been in school long enough and since she will have to marry in the next two or three years, there is no reason to further inconvenience the family by not having a female perform the much-needed domestic duties. Initially, Fawzeia came up with a series of reasons why she should stay in school, including the fact that once she finishes she can earn money to support the family. Her father was not pleased, however, that his daughter would oppose his opinion, and he scoffed at the idea that she would eventually become the primary breadwinner. Fawzeia's uncles on both sides of the family agreed with him and encouraged him to set an example not only for his family but also for the village about how a father knows what is better for his daughter. The resulting decision was predictable in this cultural climate: at the end of the school year, Fawzeia was taken out of school and now spends her days preparing food, carrying water, making bread, cleaning, looking after her younger siblings, and nursing her somewhat disabled mother.

The lives of Christine and John will be familiar to those who have grown up in the West, or even in other societies as part of the middle or upper class. However, just like Fawzeia, in many areas of the world girls and young women continue to be disadvantaged despite increasing globalizing influences that are spreading democratic and egalitarian ideals. Specifically in the developing world, for many young girls gender inequality and discrimination begins early and is characterized by a lack of gender parity with respect to economic, social, educational, health, and employment opportunities. In these cases, girls often have a lack of access to resources and limited decision-making ability within the family, the household, and the community. In parts of sub-Saharan Africa and rural areas of the Middle East and Southeast Asia, girls are encouraged or even forced to marry at a young age. They immediately begin bearing children, further limiting their economic and educational opportunities and, often, perpetuating the cycle of poverty into which they were born. Girls' lack of power to make decisions about their own lives, coupled with limited economic resources, makes their position in the global economy perilous at best.

The Persistence of Gender Discrimination

Gender discrimination is embedded into the social norms of many cultures and communities. Particularly in the developing world, this often results in young girls being burdened by unpaid care work. In some cases they are taken out of school at puberty due to cultural beliefs pertaining to their family roles and modesty issues. Thus, social and cultural factors can increase girls' vulnerabilities with respect to their future prospects, health issues, and educational attainment. Girls and women currently account for two-thirds of the world's approximately 774 million adults who are illiterate. This proportion remains unchanged over the last 20 years despite global efforts to decrease gender disparities with respect to adult literacy (United Nations, 2010). Out of the 72 million children of primary school age who are not attending school, over 39 million (54 percent) are girls. On the positive side of the equation, the gender gap with respect to primary education is declining for younger girls in East Asia and the Pacific.

However, in sub-Saharan Africa where the population is still growing exponentially, many young girls are not in school, and an increase in the number of illiterate girls is actually projected for the future. Further, recent data illustrate that in sub-Saharan Africa, North Africa, and the Middle East, women comprise more than half of all individuals living with HIV/AIDS. Girls and women, thus, face specific risks that need to be acknowledged in policy and programmatic planning.

Cultural beliefs that devalue the roles of girls and young women are often coupled with legal challenges such as the inability for girls to own property or to have their own legal identity. Changing the course of girls' lives depends on solving some of the challenges that they face in their homes and communities. It also depends on providing them with the foundation to build the personal, social, and economic assets they need in their future lives. Intervention efforts that ensure that girls acquire the same nutrition, health, and education as boys are an integral aspect of this process and depend on re-conceptualizing gender differences right from girls' birth.

In this chapter, we examine some of the gendered socialization experiences of girls and young women, specifically in the developing world. The main focus is on the cultural constraints that so often limit the potential of girls and hinder their development. For instance, as a response to the one-child policy that was instituted in China beginning in 1979, some rural parents never registered the birth of their daughters, thereby depriving them from a legal identity, educational opportunities, and health care (Chen & Rao, 2011). The focus on girls in this chapter does not imply that boys in many developing countries are not also bound by strict cultural conventions and the lack of economic and social opportunities. In fact, when families are living under severe economic constraints, boys are often just as disadvantaged as girls due to the heavy responsibilities they have to bear for the group. However, given the cultural valuing of boys in so many places, this chapter seeks to give voice to the many girls who are forgotten and unheard, and whose lives could be improved, often through some relatively simple initiatives. In particular in our contemporary context in which gender equality is increasingly assumed to be a foundational aspect of Western children's upbringing, the contrasting circumstances of girls and young women in non-Western low-income contexts tend to be marginalized or overlooked. That these girls and women so often face very different life chances because of their sex is in fact one of the main points of this book: we cannot speak of a universal female experience. Instead, the many opportunities that middle- and upper-class women now take for granted in the West are still often not available to many girls and women in other places. Moreover, exploring how gender is intertwined with particular vulnerabilities for poor girls and young women allows us to create a plan of action that involves families, their societies, and the larger global community. It allows us to encourage, protect, and create new opportunities for girls and women. By examining the cultural underpinnings that regulate so many vulnerable girls' lives, we also provide more evidence for Risman's proposition that gender is fundamentally a social construction and thus, is susceptible to change: "Even though gender structure is powerful, it is not determinative … as individuals and families develop new ways to live, the gender structure itself evolves" (1998, p. 5).

Understanding the lives of poor girls and young women, and the economic and societal restrictions they face, is the first step in creating interventions that will lead to them having brighter, more successful, and productive futures. By examining the cultural aspects of gender socialization and the dynamic qualities of gender role construction, we can make the case that what are considered appropriate gender behaviors can change over time. In other words, gender conceptualizations do not need to be static and can respond to changing norms (Deutsch, 2007). These changes can occur in Western and non-Western contexts. This is an important observation since in so many parts of the world girls and boys are socialized into what are often perceived as fixed gender roles. With globalization introducing new images and lifestyles to even the most remote parts of the world, different gender conceptions and opportunities are also spreading. In fact, there is evidence that some positive transformations in the lives of girls and women in different regions are already taking place. As Deutsch (2007, p. 108) states, "Gendered institutions can be changed, and the social interactions that support them can be undone."

Setting the Scene: The Impact of Socialization

Many of the problems associated with the lives of girls and women stem from the fact that, in certain parts of the world, parents continue to believe in innate sex differences between boys and girls. These differences are thought to influence abilities and the future potential of children. Within this framework, boys are usually culturally valued and privileged with respect to access to nutrition, health care, and education. In the worlds that their parents grew up in, boys traditionally were the ones who had better future employment opportunities and were able to provide for their parents in old age. From this perspective, if low-income parents are going to invest what little resources they have, they usually feel that providing health, educational, and skills-based opportunities for their sons instead of their daughters makes more sense. Contemporary cultural favoring of sons over daughters in many societies is primarily predicated on intrinsic beliefs that sex differences in behavior are biologically based and that the behavior of males and females can be further defined through socialization mechanisms "that are culturally approved and parentally preferred" (Udry, 2000, p. 443).

In order to understand the interactional nature of gender, we need to first be clear about what is meant by the terms sex and gender. While they are often used interchangeably, they actually have distinct meanings. Sex can be understood as the biological or physical attributes of an individual that are defined by chromosomes, anatomical, hormonal, and other physiological characteristics. Gender refers to the socially constructed characteristics, and learned roles, behaviors, and attributes usually associated with an individual's sex (Eliot, 2009). Nowadays in academic circles, gender is understood as being shaped by social and cultural expectations.

From a purely biological perspective, there are distinct differences between males and females. However, over the last 40 years in particular, the exact nature of these differences and the extent to which they are influenced by social and environmental factors has led to vast discussions and disagreements among academicians and others, especially in the Western world.[1] For example, in the United States, Canada, and northern Europe, it has become common for parents to believe that they are raising their children in a gender-neutral manner despite the recognition that there are some sex differences that are rooted in biology. For instance, the maturation rate of boys and girls, activity levels, and play focus are all associated with biological differences. However, other characteristics such as speaking, aggression, risk taking, and empathy are closely linked to environmental influences. Yet the question as to how best to understand the interaction effects of biological traits and the physical and social environment remains complex and contested.

While we may not be sure about the degree to which developmental trajectories are influenced by environmental versus inherited characteristics, we do know that the human brain is malleable and responds to environmental cues throughout an individual's lifetime. This plasticity and the brain's ability to continually change are at the basis of every human being's ability to learn. We also know that from a life-course perspective children's brains are the most malleable when they are very young and that it is in the period from birth through adolescence that much of the brain's permanent hard wiring takes place. Children's early experiences thus critically influence their physical and social development. Eliot (2009) suggests that while sex differences, biases, and traits originate from basic physical differences in the brain, "each of these traits is massively amplified by the different sorts of practices, role models, and reinforcements that boys and girls are exposed to from birth onward" (p. 7).

Case Study: New Guinea

Some of the most persuasive evidence that supports the notion of gender as a social rather than a purely physical attribute is found in cross-cultural notions of masculine versus feminine behaviors. For example, in a classic study conducted by the anthropologist Margaret Mead (1935), she identified various combinations of gender roles among neighboring tribes in New Guinea. In one tribe, the Arapesh, the men and the women raised and nurtured the children. Meanwhile, the men and women of the Mundugumor tribe who resided nearby were competitive and aggressive. In contrast, Mead also described the neighboring Tchumbuli whose female residents were the primary economic providers and the men functioned as the main nurturers of children. Moreover, among the Tchumbuli women were perceived as rational and dominant, and men as passive, submissive, and emotional. Mead concluded from her observations that characteristics and behaviors long identified in Western cultures as masculine or feminine were, in reality, culturally determined. Other evidence from anthropological studies illustrates that a number of cultures identify more than two genders and/or recognize gender as changing across the life span.[2]

Changing Perspectives on Gender Roles

Even just a cursory overview of gender roles from a historical perspective in the United States reveals that notions about what is "appropriate" with respect to behavior and roles for men and women have changed dramatically over the last several hundred years. Or when examining American sub-cultures, we find that women who participate in orthodox American religious groups express their femininity in a very different manner from those external to their communities (Rose, 2001). This empirical evidence substantiates the observation that gender roles and norms are learned and differ based on time, place, and expectation. It is therefore instructive to examine gender socialization in greater depth. As Risman (2004) states:

> When we are concerned with the means by which individuals come to have a preference to do gender, we should focus on how identities are constructed through early childhood development, explicit socialization, modeling, and adult experiences, paying close attention to the internalization of social mores. To the

extent that women and men choose to do gender-typical behavior cross-situationally and over time, we must focus on such individual explanations. Indeed, much attention has already been given to gender socialization and the individualist presumptions for gender. The earliest and perhaps most commonly referred to explanations in popular culture depend on sex-role training, teaching boys and girls their culturally appropriate roles. But when trying to understand gender on the interactional/cultural dimension, the means by which status differences shape expectations and the ways in which in-group and out-group membership influence behavior need to be at the center of attention. Too little attention has been paid to how inequality is shaped by such cultural expectations during interaction.

(p. 436)

If we are to understand how to affect more universal changes with respect to gender identities and gender roles and relations, it is imperative that we begin by examining childhood socialization and how from birth onwards individuals "learn" gender. However, gender socialization does not stand on its own, as an independent entity. Instead, it is an institution rooted in the social processes of daily life (Lorber, 1994). And as Risman (2004) explains, agency and choice are an integral aspect of this process. Women and men choose "gendered paths" because social structure indirectly shapes individual's perceptions of their interests and constrains their choices. From the West and Zimmerman (1987) "doing gender" perspective, gender is an achievement and a process that involves activity, agency, and the possibility of resistance. While "undoing gender" approaches have been debated since those early deliberations took place (see Deutsch, 2007, for example), the "doing gender" approach still very much applies when thinking about socialization, specifically in cross-cultural contexts. In those preliminary discussions, West and Zimmerman proposed that an individual "achieves" gender by following the socially accepted norms, roles, and behaviors. People are understood to be expressing their masculine or feminine natures in this manner (1987, p. 126). Children learn this mode of expression from birth onwards and it is a process that continues to unfold throughout their lives.

The Role of Families Around Gender Socialization

Around the world, families are the primary mechanism of socialization for children, and virtually every aspect of their future lives is affected by these initial experiences (Karoly, Kilburn, & Cannon, 2005). Socialization is usually understood to involve learning the roles, norms, and values of a specific culture at a certain point in time. For example, Baumrind in an address to the Society for Research in Child Development explained:

> Socialization is an adult-initiated process by which developing children, through insight, training, and imitation acquire the habits and values congruent with adaptation to their culture. At birth, a child may be viewed as a range of possibilities whose discrete potentialities are realized in interaction with the training contexts in which the child develops. Individuals become what they are in reciprocal interaction with the environment and the crucial environmental context for young children is the family.
>
> (1980, p. 640)

A wide body of scholarship indicates that initial experiences in families are particularly formative and influence the trajectory of individual development. Young children attain their first concepts of self, of others, and of social relationships through their associations with their primary caregivers. While in the United States the importance of the mother in early socialization and development has been emphasized often in exclusion to all other primary relationships, there is an increasing scholarly and popular realization that fathers, siblings, and other involved kin and non-kin are also extremely important role models. These individuals also provide nurturance and influence the attachment of infants to caregivers (Palkovitz, 2002).

Due to a burgeoning scholarly interest in parenting, an extensive literature has arisen around child socialization, intensive mothering, and involved fathering. The most controversial aspect of this scholarship has centered around the issue of gender socialization. Gender socialization is conceptualized as the development of cultural roles according to the sex of the child and is assumed to start at birth. However, growing cross-cultural evidence indicates that even pre-birth the fetus may be treated differently depending on whether it is a boy or a girl (McHale, Crouter & Tucker, 2003).[3]

From a foundational perspective, gender can be conceptualized as the meanings, practices, and relations of masculinity and femininity that individuals create in social situations on a daily basis (Spade & Valentine, 2004). Feminist social scientists in particular recognize "gender as a multilevel structure, system or institution of social practices that involves mutually reinforcing processes at the macro-structural/institutional level, the interactional level, and the individual level" (Ridgeway, 2009, p. 146). They also emphasize that these multilevel processes interact and support each other. Employing this perspective allows us to understand that the relationship between microinteractional and institutional levels of analysis is critical to understanding gender norms and how to go about effecting changes.

Empirical research indicates that parents, caregivers, siblings, and other individuals react to the young infant girl or boy differently. They thus teach the infant that there are significant gender differences and that societal expectations for girls and boys are quite dissimilar. Adherents to this position point out that children are quickly grouped into specific gender roles that impact their daily activities and development. Feminists in particular feel that through this emphasis on gender distinctions children's future potential may be limited (in the case of girls) or furthered (in the case of boys). Contemporary research findings indicate that despite the many changes that characterize Western societies, socialization based on gender remains intact and, in fact, intensifies as young people enter adolescence (McHale, Crouter, & Tucker, 2003). However, there are indications that some change is also in the process of occurring. For instance, some studies examining contemporary American parents' perceptions of their babies illustrate that parents today are much less likely to gender stereotype their newborns with respect to physical and behavioral traits than even just 20 or 30 years ago (Karraker, Vogel, & Lake, 1995).

From these varied perspectives, we can deduce that while gender socialization continues to play a dominant role in life-course development, the potential for at least subtle change coexists. It is this potential for change that is mirrored in the upbringing of our initial case study example of Christine and John. They have been raised with similar gender norms resulting in equivalent expectations of what the future holds for them. While they may not represent the experiences of every Western adolescent (and their example is not meant to), they do, however, help us understand that under the appropriate circumstances gender parity can be achieved. This leads us to examine the contrasting experience of young women like Fawzeia, a girl whose life experiences are also inextricably interwoven with the cultural expectations of the family and the community in which she is being raised.

The Tie Between Gender Socialization and Cultural Norms

Examples from around the world indicate that gender socialization is intimately connected with religious, ethnic, and cultural values. Hannum and Adams (2007) strongly suggest that cultural norms need to be understood with respect to the socialization of girls and boys. While economic explanations about gender investments in families abound, Hannum and Adams cite research from the United States as an example of how socialization and culture are intertwined. For instance, they point out that unlike in other parts of the world most American parents do not expect their children to take care of them in old age. Thus, these parents do not necessarily have economic reasons to socialize their children into different gender roles, and they may be more open to the concept of gender parity. Using the Wisconsin model of status attainment as their foundational starting point, Hannum and Adams emphasize the critical role of parents as socializing agents (2007).[4] Within this framework, perspectives on the employment chances of girls versus boys play a more significant role in parents' socialization practices than do expectations of future support. As they state, "One explanation for gender gaps is that culture leads directly to parents' discriminatory attitudes and practices, regardless of rationality. Moreover, varying forms of investment and socialization decisions made by parents, and even the choices of children, are influenced by cultural perspectives about essential gender abilities, rights and roles. These cultural perspectives become reified in different educational choices" (2007, p. 75).

While in the American contemporary middle- and upper-middle class, gender parity with respect to education and occupational access is more or less accepted as the norm these days, the same is not true amongst rural and ethnically diverse populations. For example, research on rural Appalachian populations indicates that socialization into specific gender roles continues to influence parental attitudes with respect to providing educational chances for their daughters. This, in turn, diminishes the life chances of these young women. In fact, while many younger middle- and upper-class Americans tend to believe that we have achieved complete gender equality, cross-cultural research indicates that the United States has not been as successful as some other countries in adopting gender neutral practices. Empirical evidence from the north European countries indicates that gender inequality is far less frequent in employment, family, and state policies and programs than it is in the United States and Canada (Baxter & Kane, 1995). Moreover, studies that examine the intersection between parents' ethnic–racial socialization practices and gender roles find that there are distinct variations with respect to how boys versus girls are socialized in diverse settings. For instance, Bowman and Howard (1985) reported that in African American families girls were likely to have been taught ethnic pride while boys were more likely to have been socialized to issues of egalitarianism and racial barriers. Thomas and Speight (1999) found that African American parents tended to alert boys about negative stereotypes and strategies for coping with racism, while girls were encouraged to strive toward the achievement of their goals and racial pride. Problematizing this discussion, however, is that other studies indicate that there are no significant gender differences in ethnic–racial socialization (see, for example, Caughy et al., 2002; or Scott, 2003). It is possible that, as Hughes et al. (2006) suggest, the discrepancy in these findings may have less to do with actual socialization practices than with the types of measures used and the type of ethnic–racial socialization that is assessed. Also, few studies examine ethnic–racial–gender socialization practices across multiple groups and, in fact, most studies in the United States are limited to African American families.

The Socialization of Culturally Diverse Adolescent Girls

While we know that families are the primary vehicle of socialization for children, and that virtually every aspect of their future lives is affected by these initial experiences, there is surprisingly little research on that aspect of culturally diverse girls' lives. Nor is there much known about how the socialization of these girls may impact their future opportunities or roles. We also know very little about the socialization of girls in low-income contexts in the developing world. This serious omission is reflected in programming: very few organizations and programs around the world specifically focus on the multiple issues that young girls face as they embark on the path to adulthood. It should also be noted that the socialization of ethnically diverse boys in Western and non-Western contexts has not been studied to any notable extent. Instead, studies that focus on socialization most commonly group "youth" together and do not break down their experiences by gender (Barber & Olson, 1997). The limited scholarship on youth in other parts of the world focuses on development in younger children, and more recently on the effects of immigration experiences.

From a cross-cultural perspective, gender socialization has intended and unintended consequences specifically for girls: at times girls are "protected" in order to ensure their modesty and chastity and at other times they are intentionally treated differently due to cultural norms. However, the results of gender differentiation tend to be similar. As both sexes mature, girls' opportunities become more constricted than those of boys in every sphere of their lives. Research indicates that as girls enter adolescence their mobility and free time decreases and their home responsibilities increase. For example, a survey of Egyptian girls aged 16–19 indicated that 68 percent of girls were involved in domestic work in comparison to 26 percent of boys (Mensch et al., 2000). This cultural differentiation tends also to be mirrored in their personal socialization. In many places, from birth onwards, girls are taught to be more submissive, modest, and have lower aspirations than boys. They are raised to believe that their primary role is in the home and as a caretaker to a husband, children, and the elderly. As was illustrated by the case of Fawzeia at the beginning of this chapter, despite a recognition by many parents that girls have equal or at times even superior scholastic abilities when compared to boys (see, for example, the findings of United Nations, 2010), traditional, gender-specific norms and beliefs dominate in many areas of the world and force girls to be socialized into very explicit roles.[5] The girls themselves do not have much say in the matter and must succumb to the wishes of their families. In keeping with theoretical analyses of gender socialization, both parents and their daughters cannot imagine another possible scenario or array of choices. Thus, an emphasis on marriage and becoming a mother are so inscribed into the fabric of the culture that any deviation from this norm is virtually unimaginable. And yet, as will be seen in succeeding chapters, even very ingrained beliefs can be transformed through relatively simple interventions. These initiatives can have enormous benefits for girls—and interestingly enough—for the boys and men in their families too.

While research on gender socialization in the developing world is quite limited, there is a growing interest in the United States in the study of Latino adolescents, and in Europe on immigrant young people. In both cases, much of this focus is driven by concerns around the integration of immigrants into "main stream" society and the potential issues these young people may face. For example, youth born to Mexican immigrants today represent the largest group of US immigrant children (Updegraff, Delgado, & Wheeler, 2009). Of all children born to immigrants, 39 percent are to parents that originate from Mexico. In contrast, no other country represents more than 4 percent (Hernandez et al., 2007). Most studies that focus on the children of immigrants emphasize the acculturation aspect of their experiences, in particular with respect to their relationships to their families as well as their romantic attachments. What makes the study of immigrant youths particularly challenging from a scholarly perspective is that these children are often exposed to norms and values in their host societies that differ from those that they are raised with within their families. This leads to a form of biculturalism but at times also to confusion around appropriate values and behaviors. The cultural negotiations that are characteristic of the lives of immigrant children are still poorly understood. Strikingly, the gendered aspect of these socialization processes is often ignored in these studies, and yet, it is precisely the differences in how boys and girls in immigrant families are socialized that can give valuable insight into issues of life-course development and acculturation.

Gender Socialization in Latino Families and Shared Similarities with Other Cultural Groups

The little that is known about gender socialization in immigrant groups stems primarily from empirical work conducted among Latinos in the United States. Dominating this research is a focus on *familismo* and how this concept deviates from "mainstream" contemporary American norms. *Familismo* refers to an individual's emphasis on family relationships, childbearing, and female gender roles. Ideally, women are supposed to be submissive, obedient to men, virginal, and dependent on the males in their families. Men are raised to be strong, virile, and the main breadwinner/provider in their families (Raffaelli & Ontai, 2004). While this generalization has been criticized as not applicable to all Latino groups, empirical evidence indicates that these values continue to dominate among many

Latino families and that similar ideals are found in non-Latino cultures as well, including in the Middle East, South and Southeast Asia, and Africa. This emphasis on family and appropriate roles in the family is in part linked to very strict conceptualizations of gender socialization once children enter into adolescence.

Among Latinos and also many other groups, gender norms become more strictly enforced around the time of the onset of puberty. Adolescent girls are often pulled out of school due to worries about preserving their chastity, maintaining the reputation of the family, or just meeting the demands of the household. Their mobility is often also restricted at this point (Mensch et al., 2003). For example, in many cultures, ensuring that a girl remains a virgin is considered critical to preparing her for her eventual marriage. The difference in the upbringing of girls versus boys becomes striking at this juncture. Girls experience limitations on their movements in public and lose out on opportunities for further schooling, while boys often continue with their previous activities (Villaruel, 1998). Studies of Muslim immigrant adolescents in France and Germany indicate similar patterns: young adolescent women are usually forced to conform to very strict rules with respect to gender segregation and behaviors while their brothers are allowed to participate in the adolescent activities of their new host societies (Pels, 2003). This leads to distinctly gendered experiences for both young women and men, despite the fact that they are growing up in societies that emphasize gender equality.

While a number of contemporary studies on immigrant groups focus on issues of gender and sexuality, very few explore what families actually teach their daughters and sons with respect to gender socialization and what it means to be either female or male. Moreover, most of this work does not take into account that Latino, Muslim, and other immigrant groups are not homogeneous. In other words, there is intra-group variability with adherence to cultural norms pertaining to gender and gender-related socialization. Immigrant youths provide a fertile ground for the exploration of what it means to raise children according to strict gender norms in environments that actually promote very divergent behaviors. As our world becomes increasingly globalized, the dilemmas that we are witnessing in immigrant families will move to the forefront in other types of families as well. As the case study of working-class Indian young men in Chapter 1 of this book illustrated, new images of gender roles and behaviors are pervading areas of the world where such beliefs were unimaginable even just ten years ago. The intensity and spread of new communication technologies alone will foster yet unforeseen changes. But this raises a question—despite the influx of new ideas and representations with respect to women and men, why do so many individuals and families cling to traditional gender conceptualizations in so many parts of the world? And why is it so difficult to specifically change gender socialization and beliefs in these areas?

Why Does Gender Socialization Remain Prevalent?

In part, these questions can be answered by examining the relationship between aging, economics, and families. In many communities, individuals and families tend to believe that investing greater resources in boys will serve as insurance for their old age. Girls are perceived as having fewer income-generating capabilities and may even be thought of as being a drain on household finances due to the costs associated with their marriages (Hallman & Roca, 2007). In societies where there is no social security system and where senior citizen communities and facilities are alien, families still provide the best form of care for the elderly. Moreover, since boys have traditionally been the economic providers and girls marry and move out of the home, an investment in boys is more advantageous in terms of ensuring the future well-being of parents. A strict adherence to traditional gender norms and socialization is thought to guarantee this outcome.

The world, however, is changing. Even in very traditional rural contexts, a growing number of young people are leaving their villages to seek employment. While this was historically a male phenomenon, globalizing forces have opened up opportunities for women. As young people increasingly move from rural to urban areas, neither sex is returning home to take care of aging parents (Zhan & Montgomery, 2003). This phenomenon has dramatic implications for the elderly in societies where caretaking has been completely under the purview of women.[6] Empirical data coming out of China, for instance, indicates that an increasing number of villages are inhabited only by children and the elderly, as all able-bodied young men and women have moved away to other areas with increased employment opportunities (Zhan & Montgomery, 2003). We are only at the beginning of understanding this enormous social rearrangement whose full force has not been felt yet in many places.

Despite these deeply rooted social transformations, in many developing societies young girls and women continue to face severe restrictions. Their movements are restricted when they enter puberty, decreasing the opportunities available to them for training and education outside of the home. These limitations also minimize their friendship and networking abilities, and can lead to negative feelings of self-worth and a lack of empowerment. While an increasing number of initiatives are attempting to assist rural and low-income women overcome some of the obstacles in their lives, many of these programs suffer from inherent flaws. As an example, Western programmatic initiatives often do not account for the cross-cultural context in which they are being implemented. For instance, in certain areas of the world, research indicates that in mixed gender classes that may address skills building, girls are often seated in the back of classrooms. This discourages them from raising their hands and participating (Plan UK, 2009). Or it may be the case that intervention programs only address the health and sexuality components of girls' lives and ignore the complex environments in which these girls live. It is important to note, however, that there are also effective new initiatives and programs. In Chapter 8, we will examine some of the most successful policies and programs that have been effectively implemented and that are actually improving girls' and women's lives.

How is Girls' Labor Accounted For? The Gendered Division of Labor at Home and the Implications for Girls

For girls, their future educational and economic opportunities are impacted by family decisions with respect to the allocation of their labor and their access to educational opportunities. However, sadly, many girls around the world are not acknowledged or are even forgotten in major human rights campaigns that emphasize equal work opportunities for women and equal rights for children. Much contemporary research and dialogue has centered on the importance of incorporating women into the paid labor force. But most of this discourse has ignored the fact that women often enter the labor force, particularly in the developing world, at the expense of their daughters. It is these girls who now take over the domestic responsibilities of childrearing, cooking, and housekeeping roles in order to maintain the family. Programs and campaigns that focus on children and/or adolescents also often do not take into account that boys are culturally privileged in many cultures. Thus, when having to choose between children, educational opportunities may be provided to the boys in a family rather than the girls.

Due to a concern with the rise of HIV/AIDS and early childbearing, much of the research and programming for young adolescent girls in the developing world has centered on issues surrounding sexuality and contraceptive use among unmarried girls (Singh et al., 2000). However, this focus on risk-taking behaviors does not take into account the full picture of adolescence and its role in preparing young people for the tasks of adulthood (Mensch et al., 2000). It has also served to ignore the many girls and young women who are not necessarily engaged in these behaviors but whose lives are impacted principally by their gender.

Around the globe, most societies are characterized by a strictly gendered division of labor in the family. This division of labor consists of men and boys working outside of the home, while women and girls are responsible for reproduction and the household. Today, in our globalized economy, many women and girls are often also engaged in market or production work (Cunningham, 2008). However, the heavy dual workload that the contemporary situation creates for girls and women is often not recognized, as females are still ascribed primarily to the sphere of the household. For young girls in particular, the result of a societal privileging of strict traditional gender roles is that their household responsibilities often take priority in every aspect of their lives. In poor families in the developing world, many families will choose not to educate girls because they are dependent on their labor. For example, educational programs and opportunities for girls are often bypassed by families as they prioritize allocating their daughters' time to caring for younger siblings and household chores (Bosch, 2001). When there is a limited household income, the family will also usually not be inclined to bear the indirect costs of sending their daughters to school. Girls' essential role in the family and the accompanying tasks they perform may prevent them from being able to physically attend school or may severely curtail how much time they spend at school and/or doing homework. Further, traveling to and from school can be extremely time consuming and can make school attendance unattractive to families.

In particular, care work and household work burdens girls in a dramatic manner, the results of which are often not understood. By placing a continuous routine of domestic work on girls in and around the home, they become limited in their movements. Also, their other talents do not get furthered or employed. This situation is often quite different for their brothers who are encouraged to stay in school and seek employment opportunities. The domestic, gender-based expectations of families not only reduce girls' quality of life and opportunities in adolescence but also have long-lasting effects into adulthood. By participating in an unequal amount of domestic labor and primarily care work, girls pay an enormous price. They are unable to develop their talents and increase the skills and knowledge they need to participate in an ever-more competitive, skills-based global economy.

Investments in boys versus girls usually result in differing outcomes and payoffs for families. Decisions about which children to educate are most often based on the family perception of the likelihood of a return on its investment. Given that in many places men are still more likely to attain more lucrative types of employment, parents will choose to privilege boys with respect to access to education, health care, and nutrition. In particular, evidence from South Asia indicates that boys receive more resources than their sisters. And as was noted previously, in many parts of Asia and Africa boys are perceived as old-age insurance for their parents. Thus, investing in sons is seen as preferential to investing in daughters. The short-term value of females is outweighed by the long-term value of sons. Boys need to be fed, nurtured, schooled, and kept healthy because they are an economic investment, while girls can be an economic drain due to their marriage costs (Moghadam, 2005). For example, Li and Tsang (2005) describe a common situation in rural China where sons expect to live with their parents when they become old. It is, thus, prudent from the parents' point of view to invest in their sons rather than their daughters. Li and Tsang also point out that parents often feel that the marriageability of their daughters should be their primary focus, as that will ensure the long-term well-being of the girls more than labor market readiness. These parents then concentrate on those assets that will assist their daughters in making a successful match rather than investing in an education. Li and Tsang conclude by warning that not all family decisions should be based on family economic resource models because for many parents their foremost concern is the long-term happiness of their children and not necessarily simply based on conceptualizations of children as old-age insurance.

These cultural patterns may in part be understood as stemming from conditions of scarcity, but they also serve to perpetuate patterns of poverty and deny girls basic human rights. An often-ignored basic fact is that girls give birth to the next generation. Ensuring their physical and psychological health is just as imperative as sustaining the well-being of their brothers. Further, from a basic human rights' perspective, girls must be allocated equal opportunities in every sphere of their lives.

As we have seen, the consequences of a gendered division of labor that conforms to traditional, stereotypical roles is detrimental to the long-term development of girls' potential and education. Interestingly, it is often the women in poor households that may exacerbate this division. As was mentioned above, when mothers find paying work outside the home, they allocate their domestic duties to their daughters. This leads to an increased workload for girls despite the external perspective that now "women are working outside of the home." This allocation of work is not ill intentioned or perceived as exploitative in nature by their mothers. In many places in the world, cultural norms dictate that boys work outside of the house and girls work in the house. Thus, when domestic labor is needed, the family immediately turns to the young females in the family. In this manner, girls are introduced to care labor and home responsibilities at a very young age. While formal labor statistics indicate that more boys are in the global workforce (54%) than girls (46%), their domestic labor is usually not taken into account in statistical analyses. For instance, a variety of recent studies on educational issues in India indicate that approximately 50 percent of school-age girls are primarily occupied with domestic labor (Fennell & Arnot, 2008).

From a long-term economic and social perspective, the inability of girls to access an education has both individual and societal consequences. Most countries around the world have affirmed the universal right to primary education for more than 50 years (Population Council, 2005). However, of the currently more than 130 million children who are not in school, two-thirds are girls. In developing countries, about 10 percent of boys and 40 percent of girls between the ages of 6 and 11 are never enrolled in schools. This is particularly true in rural areas where employment prospects for girls and women are few and where girls are thought to be more useful working in the household (Population Council, 2005). Without even a basic education, it is difficult for girls to access the rights and opportunities that may be available in their respective societies. Girls are not able, for the most part, to earn an adequate living, exercise power in their relationships, participate in the political decision-making of their communities and societies, and pass on a decent standard of living to their children. Denying girls access to an education perpetuates the cycle of poverty that has globally become a female phenomenon. And yet, research indicates that education is the primary vehicle for girls and women to improve their social and economic lives and their self-esteem. However, before turning to a more nuanced discussion of the interrelationship between education and girls' lives, it is important to examine the issue of social exclusion which is another complex social issue that often has consequences on their lives.

Social Exclusion and its Impacts on Girls' Lives

Increasingly, we are witnessing a more refined and nuanced understanding of the situation of marginalized groups in both high-income and developing countries. Especially when it comes to the lives of young girls and women, social exclusion is understood as a pivotal, defining factor in their experiences. Social exclusion is thought to stem from multiple sources including some immutable factors, such as race, ethnicity, and gender as well as more malleable factors such as poverty, religion, and class. As a societal characteristic, social exclusion tends to be much more common in heterogeneous societies characterized by multiple ethnic groups, languages, and customs. Lewis and Lockheed (2007) point out that foundational to exclusion is the social evaluation. In other words, one dominant social group passes judgment in terms of prestige and honor on another group. This judgment subsequently influences the opportunities and expectations of the marginalized group. A discussion of social exclusion is particularly important with respect to the situation of young girls and women. Girls from socially excluded groups are faced by two problems: 1) they belong to a socially marginalized group; and 2) they are female. Multiple studies now indicate that those girls most at risk for not receiving or continuing with their education are those that come from poor families, those from ethnic, tribal, or linguistically separate groups, those living in remote rural settings, and those from low social castes. When compounded with race, ethnicity, or caste, poverty is the single most determining factor that limits girls chances (Lewis & Lockheed, 2007).

While both in high-income and developing countries, gender equality with respect to schooling and the education of girls is increasingly understood as critical to social progress, there are still approximately 30 countries where girls lag well behind boys in terms of access to education. For example, in Nigeria, tribal Hausa girls are 35.4 percent less likely to attend school than Yoruba boys (Lewis & Lockheed, 2007). Especially, after primary school, cultural issues separate girls from boys with respect to continuing their education. In certain places, cultural norms with respect to gender mixing come into play. For instance, in some areas of Guatemala, parents do not want their adolescent girls interacting with boys in school, and, thus, keep them home. Noteworthy, however, is that this trend can be reversed. For example, studies in Bangladesh indicate that gender norms have been transformed over the last two decades. The establishment of co-educational schools has made education more widely available and cultural norms have shifted. Girls that have attained a secondary school education have recently become more desirable marriage partners due to their perceived ability to earn an income. The fact that they are now an economic asset has decreased the necessity of bringing a large dowry into marriage. Their economic worth has also been shown to be positively correlated with a decrease in abuse by the women's mothers-in-law (Schuler, 2007).

Another marker of social exclusion in certain places is religion. Girls that belong to a certain group may be discriminated against and stigmatized. However, empirical work indicates that how religious affiliation is perceived differs markedly from place to place. A specific religious affiliation is also sometimes understood as limiting girls' chances. But again, empirical data disproves this as a universally relevant notion. For instance, in Pakistan, Muslim girls are forced to attend single-sex schools but this does not hold true in Indonesia and Malaysia. In both countries, gender parity has been reached at both the primary and the secondary levels. In Tunisia and Bangladesh, also Muslim countries, girls are now more highly represented in secondary education than boys (Fennell & Arnot, 2008). These examples suggest that it is not Islam that limits girls' opportunities but the cultural beliefs and practices associated with gender that dominate in certain societies.

Understanding Intra-Cultural Variations

While there are obviously significant differences between societies with respect to beliefs about gender norms and socialization, within countries disparities are often ignored. For example, Lloyd, Mete, and Grant (2007) suggest that an examination of a specific society will consistently reveal that not all girls, even in low-income countries, face the same disadvantaged life chances. They point out that girls who live in urban areas, and are from high-wealth families, will be just as likely to attend school as their male counterparts. However, within the same society approximately one-third of the girls whose families belong to the lowest quartile of the income distribution may never receive any form of education. Thus, gender is not necessarily always predictive of the lack of future opportunities. Instead, gender is often interrelated with economic factors. As was mentioned previously, poverty in combination with other characteristics such as gender, race and ethnicity, and social marginalization can severely limit the life chances of an individual.

Context also plays a critical role in understanding gender disparities with respect to educational attainment. For instance, a limited number of rural girls attend Pakistani primary schools. Initially this situation was understood as a byproduct of cultural norms that encourage parents to withdraw their daughters from school in order to preserve their modesty and to protect them. However, more recent work has illustrated that school attendance is influenced by other factors as well. For instance, government officials are often reluctant to build schools in rural areas and face difficulties in finding teachers to staff them. Moreover, a preference for single-sex schooling has created further obstacles as there is a shortage of available, qualified female teachers in Pakistan. Other factors also come into play with respect to schooling decisions. For instance, the poor quality of government schools, the lack of access to secondary schools, and the hidden costs to parents when their children are not working, influence schooling decisions. While there is currently a dramatic increase in primary school availability in Pakistan, most of these schools are built in urban areas and in richer communities. They also indicate that this is an area where the private sector is *not* meeting the needs of the society at large, with respect to schooling for poor rural girls. The need for government girls' schools remains very high and is unlikely to be easily resolved as it is just too costly to build educational facilities in remote villages that only cater to one sex. Lloyd, Mete, and Grant (2007) suggest that this is an area where program experimentation and evaluation could make a significant difference. Innovations such as creating schools that can educate both girls and boys in culturally responsive ways would lead to an enormous transformation with respect to girls' access to education, especially if these initiatives were coupled with financial incentives for parents.

Synopsis

As has been argued in this chapter, young girls and women are particularly vulnerable to being poor. They are socialized into gender-specific roles and consequently are often denied access to educational opportunities, resources, and decision-making capabilities at the household and community level. In addition, they may also be barred from certain legal rights such owning property or inheriting money or possessions from their families. For instance, approximately 1–2 percent of all titled land around is world is owned by women (USAID, 2003). By not being able to inherit, women cannot acquire wealth and this increases their dependence on a partner. The vulnerable situation of girls and women is further exacerbated in areas that have been plagued by extreme poverty, HIV/ AIDS epidemics, or war and conflict situations. Moreover, girls and women who are from socially marginalized groups within their societies are at even greater risk. Poverty and a lack of rights coupled with discrimination based on race, ethnicity, or even just being from the "wrong" area of town, can lead to a sense of powerlessness in girls that has the potential to be highly destructive.

For many girls in the developing world today, marriage is the only socially acceptable way to leave home, and girls, thus, anticipate their marriages eagerly. However, young marriage is plagued by a whole series of new problems. Often, girls do not have any say over their choice of marriage partner, and are extremely young at age of marriage. Recent statistics indicate that approximately 100 million girls from around the globe will marry before the age of 18, and some are as young as eight years of age (Haberland, 2007; Plan UK, 2009). Programs concerned with adolescent issues often overlook this group due to their marital status. However, arranged marriages, coupled with young age at marriage, can be major constraints on girls achieving a more successful economic future. Young married girls tend to have little if any knowledge about reproductive health and often are forced to engage in unwanted sexual relations, with a partner who is at times much older. They are likely to bear children before they are physically and psychologically ready to do so, and usually become limited in their community and societal participation. For example, in Burkina Faso, one of the poorest countries in Africa (ranked 175 out of 177 on the United Nations Human Development Factors), almost two-thirds of young women from rural areas reported that they had been married by the time they were 18. Six percent of girls from rural areas reported that they had been married before their fifteenth birthday (Brady, Salouco, & Chong, 2007).

There is a very strong relationship between age of marriage and educational attainment. Girls who had had less than three years of education were nine times as likely to be married before the age of 18 than girls who had had eight or more years of education (Brady, Salouco, & Chong, 2007). A girl's marriage fate is compounded by her status in a polygamous marriage. Her situation is affected by her age at marriage, educational attainment, and family status. Thus, by marrying young she ends up in a highly perilous context vis-à-vis her co-wives. In these situations, girls have virtually no opportunity to make economic gains or ensure the livelihoods of themselves and their children. In areas where HIV and AIDS have spread and lifespans are unnaturally shortened, investments in long-term human capital has also decreased. Families may feel that it is not worthwhile to invest in training and education for girls, when their return seems minimal.

Marrying young can also be accompanied by an increasing risk of being exposed to HIV/AIDS. This happens for a variety of reasons including the fact that the spouses of very young brides are often considerably older and may have a greater risk of carrying sexually transmitted infections such HIV, there may be a strongly disproportional power imbalance in these relationships that impedes any sort of discussion of safe sex, and marriage to a young girl almost always is accompanied by active sexual relations and the lack of condoms due to cultural pressures to bear children (Brady, Salouco, & Chon, 2007).

What we see cross-culturally is that for many girls who live in poverty, their future is primarily determined by the interrelationship of their gender with social conditions. They are taught from a very young age to sublimate their individual desires and needs for the benefit of their birth families and later for their husbands and children. But especially for girls living in poverty, this puts them in a perilous position right from the start. Their chances are limited or non-existent and they have little opportunity to build an economic or social foundation for themselves. Further, their communities and societies do not benefit from their talents and abilities.

We now have an increased dialogue on internationalization, homogenization, and globalization. This discourse commonly highlights societal changes around the world and often focuses on a supposedly growing uniform youth culture. From this perspective young people the world over are increasingly sharing similar norms, beliefs, practices, and aspirations. An implicit aspect of these discussions is that family structures, values, and relationships are also changing, and conforming to a more Westernized model that emphasizes democratic gender ideals within the household. While certain trends are spreading such as the rising age of marriage and a general growing democratization of family life, these trends are not uniform in nature nor do they characterize every society. In many part of the world, girls do not have the choices and opportunities that are increasingly associated with contemporary social life for middle- and upper-class women in the West. And, increasingly, girls that grow up in poverty, particularly in non-Western contexts, are at risk in a global economy that values education, skills, and access to resources. The future of many young girls is conscribed by a very limited set of prospects. Far from participating in a global youth-oriented consumer culture, these young women are often barely surviving. Globalizing forces make them increasingly vulnerable to exploitation. We turn to some of these issues in the next chapter.

Notes

1 The nature–nurture debate remains one of the most contested areas of the social and biological sciences. See Eliot (2009) for an easily accessible discussion.
2 Most commonly cited is the example of the berdache among Native American tribes.
3 Adherents of this position point to the high abortion rates in China and India of female fetuses in their arguments.
4 The Wisconsin model of status attainment refers to a model that describes and explains how individuals move between classes and what the economic, social, and psychological determinants are that allow them to do this.
5 According the United Nations Development Programme (2001), in the industrialized world and some other countries, girls are now achieving greater educational success than boys at both elementary and secondary school levels.
6 Even in Western societies where there is much greater gender parity, empirical studies indicate that it is still primarily women who become the caretakers of the elderly.

5

VULNERABLE GIRLS AND WOMEN
Sexual Exploitation and Trafficking

Consider the following scenario.

Fourteen-year-old Akinyi wakes up hungry and tired. It is only six in the morning and she has barely slept five hours. But her grumbling stomach won't let her get back to sleep. She thinks about her brothers and sisters back in her native village two hours outside of Nairobi. Akinyi misses them terribly but also knows that for the foreseeable future she cannot go back there. She is still hoping to find work here in Nairobi so that she can send money back home to them. She came to Nairobi because an uncle arranged for her to clean the houses of two foreign families but when she arrived Akinyi found out that her uncle expected her to have sex with him before making any further arrangements. She refused despite knowing that he would be extremely angry and that she was defying what some others girls would have done in the same situation. After a big fight, her uncle told her to leave his house and that she was now on her own. So, in order to support herself, Akinyi has begun to sell bottles she finds in the trash. Every morning she gets up, locates a specific corner on a nearby street and sits there all day trying to persuade people to buy her bottles. In the evenings she picks through the trash looking for glass. Akinyi dreams of going back to school one day and becoming a nurse— she has seen much illness in her village and she knows that nurses can help people get better again. Now contrast the previous example with the following scenario.

Twenty-one-year-old Irina dances in the bar slowly. A couple of drunk Finnish men are watching her, but for the most part she is not attracting much attention. As she removes her clothes, a bored look crosses her face. After she is finished she goes around smiling trying to elicit tips from the customers. At the end of the evening she is disappointed by how little money she has made. She and the other dancers discuss the frugality of Finnish men and how men of other nationalities are much more generous. However, she also knows that despite the lackluster evening she is making

104

enough money that in six months she will be able to return to her native Ukraine and continue her studies as a teacher. She considers herself fortunate to have found this job and to have come over to Finland with a reputable agency. Irina knows of other girls from the Ukraine who signed up for similar types of employment but have instead ended up in brothels in Germany and Denmark. Interviews with her and her colleagues indicate that they do not define themselves by their current employment. Instead, they see the dancing in the Finnish bars as a type of leave of absence from their regular lives. The income they earn over this period of time will help them finance their families back home and their future education. They see the erotic dancing as a form of investment in their futures.[1]

Akinyi and Irina represent a new reality: the increased vulnerability of economically disadvantaged young girls and women in both low- and high-income countries. As a result of abject poverty and the lack of opportunities, some young girls like Akinyi are leaving their villages and families and migrating to urban areas where they hope to find more opportunities. Others like Irina leave their home societies for high-income countries where they hope to make money in whatever manner possible in order to create a better future for themselves. These young women are just two examples of the new risks and challenges that are faced by economically at-risk females in a globalizing world.

In the last chapter, we examined how gender socialization, particularly for girls and young women in the developing world, plays a critical role in their access to future opportunities and possibilities. Now we turn to some of the other disturbing challenges that young girls and women face in the new global economy. Globalization has introduced new opportunities for work and education for a multitude of women in high- and low-income countries. But Structural Adjustment Policies and neoliberal agendas have also severely curtailed social services and government-based programs in many poor countries in Asia, Latin America, and sub-Saharan Africa. In particular, many poor women in these countries have lost their jobs and been forced to find new means to support themselves. Moreover, as manufacturing has become cheaper through competition from Asia, unemployment rates in the former countries of the Soviet Union have risen. These occurrences have led to an increase in poverty among young girls and women and this has amplified their risk of being sexually exploited and trafficked. Some call this phenomenon "the shadow side" of globalization (Penttinen, 2008). It is an aspect of globalization that is not openly discussed and yet it is closely related to the changes that have been brought about through economic and technological changes. What is particularly disturbing about the widespread increase in sexual exploitation and trafficking is the highly gendered nature of this activity.[2]

The Increasing Recognition of Ties Between Economic Vulnerability and Sexual Exploitation

While the trafficking of girls and women for the purposes of sex work has been documented for several decades now, it has only recently risen to the forefront on the international agenda. The United Nations, UNESCO, and a variety of women's rights organizations have focused on drawing attention to this disturbing topic because of its connections with human rights violations and the ties to the spread of HIV/AIDS. However, mainstream interest in the United States about the exploitation of poor girls and women in the developing world has actually been brought more into the limelight by the publication of the book *Half the Sky* (2009) by Nicholas Kristof and Sheryl WuDunn. In this descriptive, ethnographic-style book, which spent many months on the national bestseller list, Kristof and WuDunn describe conditions of young poor girls who are sold or coerced into contemporary slave-like situations. These girls are taken as children into brothels, beaten brutally, and forced to submit to the sexual biddings of older men. In return they receive little if any money and live under constant threats of violence and abuse. Kristof and WuDunn point out that it is the exacerbated poverty brought on through globalizing conditions that has contributed to an environment where such abuses have been allowed to flourish. However, they also note that globalization provides new means of communication and mobilization that allow us to educate people about these occurrences and to provide safer conditions and environments for the poor.

Poor young women and girls are particularly susceptible to being sexually trafficked and exploited. Numerous studies and reports describe how poverty, war, and refugee conditions create circumstances that put young women at risk (Ferris, 2007). The United Nations' Office on Drugs and Crime (2005) has cited trafficking as having reached "epidemic proportions" and projections only indicate that this is a crime that is growing instead of diminishing. Complicating the matter is that trafficking and the sexual exploitation of young girls and women is now occurring in every part of the world, instead of just being limited primarily to Asia as was the case up until the 1990s. Globalization has contributed to this phenomenon in a multitude of ways. Poverty in various regions of the world has risen forcing or creating conditions that encourage young girls and women to migrate to other areas. Concurrently, growing economic and social linkages have allowed for transnational criminal networks to form that take advantage of collaborations with others in far away locales to make arrangements for identifying victims and luring them into their organizations. Simultaneously, the technological and financial aspects of globalization have allowed for money gained through illegal activities such as sexual trafficking to be easily transferred and laundered.

Compounding this problem is that contemporary communication technologies allow traffickers to interact and make their arrangements to sell their "commodities" in a relatively private manner.

Defining Sexual Trafficking and Exploitation

As with other such sensitive topics, there is much debate about how to define sexual trafficking. Currently, the most accepted definition is supplied by the United Nations' 2000 *Protocol to Prevent, Suppress and Punish Trafficking in Persons, Especially Women and Children*:

> "Trafficking in persons" shall mean the recruitment, transportation, transfer, harbouring or receipt of persons, by means of the threat or use of force or other forms of coercion, of abduction, of fraud, of deception, of the abuse of power or of a position of vulnerability or of the giving or receiving of payments or benefits to achieve the consent of a person having control over another person, for the purpose of exploitation. Exploitation shall include, at a minimum, the exploitation of the prostitution of others or other forms of sexual exploitation, forced labour or services, slavery or practices similar to slavery, servitude or the removal of organs.

While statistics are unreliable due to the sensitive and hidden nature of this topic, it is estimated that around 700,000 girls and young women are trafficked across international borders every year (U.S. Department of State, 2004). Domestic trafficking, which is even more difficult to trace, is estimated at approximately 2 to 4 million people per year. While there are many types of trafficking, such as young men who may be trafficked and forced into indentured servitude, the scale of sexual trafficking which involves primarily young girls and women indicates its gendered nature and the unique vulnerability of women and children. Among those who are trafficked, about 70–80 percent are female and about 70 percent are trafficked for prostitution or some type of sexual exploitation (U.S. Department of State, 2004).

There are multiple forms of trafficking, including situations that are associated with a limited form of independence, all the way to situations where girls and women are held in complete bondage situations. While some girls are forcibly kidnapped, raped, beaten, and imprisoned, many more initially choose to exchange sexual services for some kind of payment (Kelly & Regan, 2000). For instance, young women from the former Soviet block countries or Southeast Asia may exchange sexual services for passage out of their country and the opportunity to earn a livelihood in a well-to-do Western society. It is often only once they embark on their journey that they discover that they will have little if any independence and that they have placed themselves in a vulnerable situation from which there may be no escape (Long, 2002). Based on an understanding of the complexity of this issue, the United Nations Protocol specifically states that it is irrelevant if a victim of trafficking consents as trafficking entails acts of fraud and deception. The Protocol also makes the state responsible for assisting trafficked victims, taking the focus away from the victims and shifting it to the traffickers and their exploitation of children and women. The Protocol is an addendum to the United Nations' convention against transnational organized crime which has played a critical part in the globalization of sexual trafficking (Hodge & Lietz, 2007).

Case Study: Sexual Trafficking Goes Global

Globalization has played a significant role in the spread of sexual trafficking and exploitation. Prior to the 1990s, sexual trafficking was largely confined to non-Western parts of the world. However, with the breakdown of the Soviet Union and the increasing facility of movement and communication between borders, sexual trafficking has spread to every corner of the globe and has become the fastest growing area of organized crime (Erez, Ibarra, & McDonald, 2004). The process of trafficking itself has become more transnational and fluid. For instance, individuals may be recruited in one country, sold and "trained" in another, and then forced to "work" in a third one. The United Nations has mapped these patterns according to nations of origin, transit, and destination. Most trafficked victims are recruited in Asia, the countries of the former Soviet Union, Eastern Europe, Africa, and, to a much lesser extent, Latin America. They are then transited through Eastern Europe, Asia, and Africa with the end point being the industrialized countries of the world. The main destination countries are Italy, the United States, Germany, the Netherlands, and Japan (Monzini, 2004). The pattern indicates that originating countries are consistently extremely low-income countries with few employment opportunities, and destination countries are almost always high-income countries with legal or quasi-legal thriving sex industries. It is important to note that from a micro-perspective it is the poorest, most marginalized individuals in these originating countries that are the most vulnerable and who are most likely to be trafficked and exploited.

Factors Associated With Sexual Trafficking and Exploitation

The reasons for the growth of sexual trafficking are many and complex. On the one hand, poor economic conditions, wars, and the absence of future opportunities help fuel discontent and encourage individuals to want to leave their home societies. On the other hand, media representation of life in Westernized, high-income countries tends to glamorize life in these places, encouraging individuals to want to seek opportunities in new locales. Curtol et al. (2004) refer to this pattern as the push-and-pull factors. Individuals are pushed out of their circumstances because of poverty and the perceived lack of future prospects and they are pulled toward places that at the very least offer them the hope of employment or a better life. An increasing demand for younger children and virgins can be attributed, at least in part, to fears surrounding HIV/AIDS and the emergence of new sources and destinations for trafficked individuals (Joffres et al., 2008).

The Role of Criminal Networks

Others have suggested, however, that the main element in the growth of sexual trafficking has been the growth of international criminal networks. It is these criminal organizations that exploit the push–pull factors to recruit and traffick young girls and women. This is a highly lucrative business for these criminal networks preceded only by narcotics and arms sales (U.S. Department of State, 2004). Most trafficked women initially pay for their own voyage (or are forced later on to pay for their passage) and, further on, do not retain any or very little of the money they earn. The high profits and relatively low legal risks associated with this enterprise are understood as one of the primary reasons that sexual trafficking is on the increase. For example, Interpol has estimated that women who are prostituted in Europe earn approximately $124,000 for their pimps. In Israel, a Russian woman brings in somewhere in the vicinity of $50,000 to $100,000 for her owners (Hughes, 2000). Thus, a prostitute can make anywhere from 5 to 20 times as much for her owners as they may have paid for her. This high-profit margin is compounded by the relatively low risk that traffickers incur.

The Lack of Regulations and Misunderstanding of the Issues

Prostitution is legal or quasi legal in many places and there are not many punishments that are sustained by the perpetrators should they be caught. Instead, legal sanctions in most countries tend to criminalize the actions of the prostitutes instead of the traffickers. This forces the women who are engaged in these activities to attempt to stay under the legal radar. Since they often do not speak the language of the host country, have no social support networks, and live in great fear of their perpetrators, they are unlikely to call on the authorities for assistance.

Long (2004) points out that while there is an increasingly more visible dialogue about this issue, much of it centers on instituting controls on women's work opportunities, on limiting their mobility between societies, or on targeting organized crime. However, the underlying conditions that have led to the massive increase in trafficking, such as limited economic opportunities in home regions, and the social position and conditions of young women in their communities, have not been addressed. She also points out that while mainstream media and NGOs may highlight particularly troublesome examples and scenarios, they often exploit a form of societal voyeurism that distances the audience from the actual experiences of these women. By focusing on migration, public health, and crime, the family and community relationships and conditions that lead to this form of exploitation are hidden from view. For instance, many women are already caught in webs of servitude in their home communities due to poverty and cultural norms. They may be attempting to leave sexually exploitative situations or they may be immersed in oppressive kin relationships that do not allow them any autonomy and provide little if any opportunities for self-empowerment. As in the case of young sub-Saharan rural women, they may be forced to marry young and begin bearing children before the age of 18. Young women with limited opportunities may thus imagine that by fleeing these oppressive conditions they will improve their lives, even if there is a sexual cost attached to their escape. These young women, and often their families, do not realize that once they leave their home communities they become susceptible to sexual exploitation by a variety of individuals— including the very people who they may have turned to to facilitate their leaving.

In part, the international gender segmentation of the labor markets contributes to the sexual exploitation of young girls and women. For example, the International Organization for Migration (2000) has shown that the labor prospects for migrating men and women are sharply differentiated: young men that are smuggled from locales in the Middle East or South Asia tend to land in jobs that involve construction, electronics, or information technologies. However, young women who are smuggled from South Asia, Southeast Asia, and Eastern Europe usually end up in the service sector and work as domestics, dancers, and sex workers. The IOM studies also indicate that even when women are smuggled to work in specific industries, such as a group of Chinese women who expected to work in clothing factories in northern Italy, these migrants ended up being vulnerable to sexual exploitation.

Migration, Economic Opportunities, and Sex Work

The increased migration of women is thus, at times, tied to an increase of foreign-born women engaged in prostitution. Some girls decide to become migrating prostitutes as they are already working in the sex services industry in their native locales and they figure they can make more money abroad. However, many other young women are influenced by the perception that they can earn more money by dancing or selling sexual services in the West than they can by working in government, nursing, or education in their home countries. In a quasi-ethnographic study, Penttinen (2008) describes how young Russian teachers, fashion designers, and nurses migrate to Finland, often for short periods of time, in order to earn money as erotic dancers. As is described in the initial scenario of this chapter, these young women are able to amass more income during those short work stints than they would be able to earn in their home countries over the course of a whole year. The women then use their profits to go back to school, support their families, or take care of their parents. They view their time participating in the sex industry as of limited duration and not as defining of their future selves. They also perceive their work as an opportunistic adaptation to globalization as they are now able to move between countries and earn money in different places and through new means. As will be seen, however, the sex industry is far from benign and not all young women benefit in the same financial manner as the Ukrainian erotic dancers described in the initial case study.

Trafficking is driven by demand and by the availability of vulnerable populations. It is tied to social exclusion and marginality, ethnicity, and gender in complicated little-understood ways. However, we do know that this industry is thriving in part because globalizing conditions have created an inter-related set of economic, social, and political factors that have put more individuals at risk. This has created the supply necessitated by traffickers to meet the demands of the clients. Commonly, trafficking results from the interface of risk factors such as poverty, civil unrest, and other forms of illegal activities such as drug trafficking (Joffres et al., 2008).

The Secretive Nature of Sexual Trafficking and Exploitation

The clandestine nature of sexual trafficking and exploitation makes it difficult to assess the magnitude of the problem and the conditions that facilitate it. What makes this situation particularly complex is that, depending on social context, different factors and paths can lead to sexual exploitation. For example, in the poor communities of South and Southeast Asia, brokers may be community members who target poor parents to sell their children or to marry them off to clear debts through the promise of a dowry. Once these girls are married, they may be directly forced into prostitution by their husbands, or they may be divorced or abandoned and then sold to a broker who sells them to a brothel in the same locale, in a different region of the country, or even across national borders.

Customary Prostitution

In places like India, customary prostitution is also part of the cultural make-up. Thus there are socially accepted forms of prostitution where young pre-pubescent girls from certain castes are "given" over to specific deities. They are expected to have sexual relations with temple priests and then after a couple of years are sold or auctioned off to traffickers. Estimates indicate that such cultural practices account for approximately 16 percent of girls in the Indian sex trade (Joffres et al., 2008).

Sexual Tourism

The growth of sex tourism also contributes to the increase in sexual exploitation of vulnerable populations. For instance, access to very young girls and boys by international and national tourists is increasingly common. Specifically, street children in South Asia, Southeast Asia and parts of Latin America are vulnerable to this type of exploitation. Sex tourism is a difficult phenomenon to monitor and control. To a certain extent, it is public in nature as it is promoted by travel agencies, hotels, and tour operators. With the growing capabilities of the Internet, advertisers are able to spread their message about the "goods" they have available, and even set a price in advance. Clients can seek services from the privacy of their computers with little if any monitoring of any of these activities. It is important to note that much of sex tourism is very open. For instance, in Brazil prostitution is legal and easily available while in Thailand it is illegal but very public. Attitudes in sex tourism destination countries often assume that this is an unfortunate but necessary aspect of life and should not be heavily regulated.

HIV/AIDS

Also associated with the increase in trafficking, especially of younger girls, is the growing spread of HIV/AIDS. Because in many places cultural mores and government attitudes do not acknowledge the prevalence of homosexual relationships, men who engage in these relations have to hide their behaviors. Homosexual men are often legally married and then have clandestine relationships with other women and men. Thus, if they are infected with HIV/AIDS, they spread the disease. A study on prostitution in India found that HIV prevalence among prostitutes ranged from about

45 percent to 26 percent, depending on the state in which the girls lived, if they were in brothels or not, and how old they were when they had their first sexual contacts (Joffres et al., 2008). There is, thus, a growing demand for "clean" girls who have not yet been tainted by other sexual experiences.[3] In areas of South Asia, having sex with a virgin is believed to cure men of AIDS and other sexual diseases. This has led to a higher demand for the sexual services of children. Younger girls are also perceived to be free of sexually transmitted infections making it less risky for men to have sex with them. A preference for young girls can also be explained by the fact that it is usually easier for men to force younger girls to have unprotected sex. Many clients often do not want to use condoms and under certain circumstances (for example, the client is drunk, an official, a pimp) the girls have little if any negotiating power. Other factors that negate condom use include the lack of access to condoms, the lack of money to buy condoms, and the social stigma that is associated with the buying of condoms.

Case Study: Child Sexual Abuse in Sub-Saharan Africa

As we have noted, there is a clear tie between sexual exploitation and poverty. It is thus not surprising that in some of the poorest societies of the world, specifically in sub-Saharan Africa, issues around sexual exploitation and HIV are rampant. However, awareness, discussion, and prevention approaches about these topics are minimal. And, disturbingly, child sexual abuse is on the increase. For example, Lalor (2008) reports that in a study of 11,735 South African women, a high proportion of younger women reported having been raped before the age of 15. Nearly 3 percent of 15–19 year olds stated that they had been raped before the age of 15 in comparison to 1.3 percent of 20–23 year olds. Similar to the situation in India, the rise in child sexual abuse is connected to the spread of HIV/AIDS. Younger children are thought to be less likely to have HIV/AIDS and, again, it is often believed by men that having sexual intercourse with virgins may cure them of this ailment and other sexually transmitted diseases. Lalor also reports that a number of research studies have found that many African women's first encounters with sexual intercourse involve force. For example, in a study of Kenyan females, 3,400 had had sexual intercourse and approximately 23.8 percent or 809 reported having been forced to have sex the first time. In another study conducted in South Africa of 269,705 adolescents, 27.7 percent of boys and 27.4 percent of girls between the ages of 10 and 14 indicated that they believed that "girls enjoy rape." Virtually the same percentage of teenagers in the next age tier of 15–19 held similar views.

Lalor (2008) also points to what is sometimes referred to as the "sugar daddy" phenomenon. In sub-Saharan Africa it is not unusual for poor girls to exchange sexual services for basic life necessities such as shelter, food, or even safety. For instance, a survey conducted in Soweto, South Africa among 1,395 pregnant women aged 16–44 found that 21 percent of the group had engaged in transactional sex. In exchange for sex, the women received anything from cash, to money for school fees, or items for their children (Dunkle et al., 2004). The authors of the report point out that these women were primarily motivated to engage in these exchange behaviors because of their dire poverty. So, for instance, girls in Liberia received the equivalent of ten cents (U.S.) with which they could buy a handful of peanuts.

The Problem of HIV/AIDS in Sub-Saharan Africa

Childhood sexual exploitation is closely related to the spread of HIV/AIDS in sub-Saharan Africa. Currently approximately 39.5 million individuals worldwide are infected with HIV/AIDS. Of those about 24.7 million live in sub-Saharan Africa—which means that about two-thirds of all individuals living with HIV/AIDS live in sub-Saharan Africa (Lalor, 2008). Disturbingly, the widest spread of HIV/AIDS is among female adolescents in comparison to males. One study found that the risk of HIV infection among young women between 15 and 24 was more than double that of same age for men (Delius & Walker, 2002). And the UNAIDS update of 2004 reports that 78 percent of those individuals with HIV/AIDS are young girls. However, solid data about the connection between child sexual abuse and HIV transmission is difficult to come by due to a series of methodological obstacles.[4] Most of what we know about this topic comes from interviews and case studies by organizations such as the Human Rights Watch. In its reports, it details case studies of girls who are sexually abused, often by close relatives, some of whom are HIV positive (2002). As other studies have also noted, young girls are easy victims because of cultural expectations that require them to be obedient and subservient to men. For instance, Mabala (2006) reports the following quotes:

When I was 14, the house owner always followed me when I went to have a shower. I told my mother but she just said: "my daughter, what can we do? Where can we go if he kicks us out? Just do your best." In the end he raped me.
(Girl in Dar es Salaam, quoted in workshop for young people out of school)

Here you are not allowed to say "no". If you refuse, you are raped.
(Girls from Mukuru, Nairobi, to Edwina Orowe,
a UNICEF youth intern, who was asking why
they all had babies by the age of 16)

The problems surrounding HIV/AIDS are compounded by the fact that as an increasing number of children become orphans, they become even more vulnerable to contracting sexually transmitted diseases. In several countries in sub-Saharan Africa, HIV/AIDS has become the primary source of orphanhood for children. In Lesotho 13 percent of children and in Swaziland and Zambia 11 percent of children have now been orphaned by HIV/AIDS. Many of these children take care of their younger siblings under very trying circumstances. In contexts of great social and economic pressure, these children are often mistreated by adult caregivers or acquaintances and are vulnerable to sexual abuse. Studies conducted by the Population Council in Ethiopia and Kenya found that female orphans are three times as likely to have exchanged sex for food, money, or goods than girls who had a living parent. Young orphaned girls find themselves in positions where they have to support their siblings, at times ill or aged relatives, and take care of domestic duties. They migrate to urban areas where they believe there will be more economic opportunities, but it is there that they actually become more susceptible to contracting HIV/AIDS. These children end up in a vicious cycle of vulnerability and infection that is not easily broken and threatens to perpetuate itself and grow.

Other Risk Factors for Young Girls

Mabala (2006) points out that while most human rights organizations and organizations such as UNICEF and the World Bank often point to education as the key for lifting these girls out of the dire conditions that they find themselves in, schools and even the transportation to schools are often unsafe arenas for young girls. He reports the following from Human Rights Watch, Zambia:

> The length of the girls' commute to school is an important factor, since their risk of sexual abuse by minibus drivers or conductors, if they take transportation, or abuse by others along the road, if they walk, can be significant. The long distance to school makes some girls stay in insecure, unsafe structures nearer to school during the week, which then exposes them to abuse by men who can walk in at will. ...
>
> Even school environments are not always safe, with sexual abuse or exploitation all too frequent. Teachers themselves (also other workers in the school and fellow students) may prey on vulnerable

girls. … Most abuse is not reported and few teachers are penalized. "The laws are strict but there's no real attempt to find out what goes on", said Cosmas Musamali of ZIHP. The more likely outcome is that a teacher would be cautioned and possibly transferred.

Reports such as this indicate that even education as it is currently structured in certain places is not always the solution for assisting vulnerable young women. As the example above indicates, there can be physical dangers for girls associated with attending school. Moreover, when cultural norms that expect young women to be subordinate to males are coupled with poverty, refusing or negotiating safe sex becomes almost impossible for girls. As was noted before, the dire poverty that characterizes the lives of most of these girls also forces them into what is sometimes referred to as survival sex.

Survival sex also comes into play in situations of domestic employment. For example, in Kenya about one-third of all young women aged 15–19 who work are employed as domestic workers. Most commonly, poor rural families send their daughters to urban areas to work in other people's households. They then become dependent on the income that the girls send back home. A study conducted in Ethiopia indicated that young girls aged 10–14 worked on average 62 hours a week for less than $8 per month (Mabala, 2006). These girls tend to suffer from social isolation which puts them at risk of financial and sexual exploitation. They have no alternative but to accept their situations. If these girls lose their employment, it is most likely that they will end up living on the street and be exploited even further. One estimate, for example, puts the number of sex workers in Cape Town who are aged 10–14, at 25 percent (Mabala, 2006).

Can Some Forms of Sexual Transactions be Explained by Culture?

While it is easy from a Western perspective to label all forms transactional sex as exploitative, some anthropologists caution that the situation is actually more complex than is sometimes indicated by the statistics. For instance, a variety of ethnographies have long noted that in societies where there is a cultural precedent of "bride price," the longer-term exchange of sexual services for goods is not perceived as a negative phenomenon by certain cultural groups.[5] Lalor (2008) suggests that this makes it difficult to label all of these exchanges as prostitution. Instead, these relationships need to be understood as a complicated transaction that is often longer-term and more akin to "benefactor" relationships. Wamoyi et al. (2011) also support Lalor's suggestions that transactional sex is embedded in the norms of certain African societies, making it difficult to disentangle transactional sexual behavior from sexual exploitation and prostitution. In a study conducted in Tanzania, she and her colleagues found that some young women continued to engage in transactional sex even when they were not living in abject poverty. In fact, the absence of an exchange was perceived as demeaning to the young women. By examining both the parents and the children's views on exchange relationships and sexuality, Wamoyi and her colleagues found that even the parents of the males felt that men should "pay" for access to women's bodies. They state:

> One view was that prohibition of this practice would lead to rape because no woman would agree to have sex for free, without something in return. Since it was usually men who approached women for sex, they believed that men would be culturally compelled to force women to have sex with them in order to prove their masculinity.
>
> (2011, p. 9)

These findings indicate there exists a spectrum of transactional sexual behavior and that the roots of these activities may stem from changing gender conceptualizations. Wayomi and her colleagues argue that men in Tanzania have become aware of changes in power relations between men and women and associate women's power with their demands for money and goods. Thus, in the past, a man could just force a woman to have sex with him as his right without negotiating consent. These days, as women have gained power in sexual relationships, they expect to be given something in return. However, even in this study, the power that men and young women perceived was short term. Ultimately, the men decided the value of the exchange, condom use, and when to engage in sexual activities. In patriarchal situations where young women are negotiating sex with older men, exploitation still remains at the core of the transaction. This becomes apparent in Wayomi et al.'s discussion of sexual and reproductive health risks. Despite an awareness of the danger of contracting HIV or other sexually transmitted diseases, most young women were unable to negotiate safe sex with the men. Interestingly, many of the parents in Wayomi and colleagues' study saw the expansion of transactional sex as another aspect of the emergence of a cash economy in that region. Wayomi and her colleagues hypothesize that as the economic situation in sub-Saharan Africa has worsened, women have been forced into a continued economically dependent relationship with men. Sexuality becomes a commodity to be bartered and sold without the stigma that this transaction has in many Western contexts.

Sexual Exploitation in Refugee Situations

The exploitative aspects of transactional sex become most apparent in refugee situations. Ferris (2007) describes that it is not unusual for UN case workers to take advantage of this type of exchange relationship and that parents often force their daughters into these transactions. The most frequently exploited girls tend to be between the ages of 13 and 18, living in single-parent households, and girls who are street traders. What becomes apparent in all of these examples is the economic vulnerability of the young women and the fact that they are primarily exploited by older men. As Lalor (2008) points out, merely labeling these behaviors as "prostitution" does not convey the true circumstances surrounding this phenomenon. It is more accurate, instead, to see these transactions and behaviors as a form of child sexual abuse.

The disturbingly high incidences of sexual exploitation described above point to the low social status of girls and women in many places and the cultural patterns and beliefs that allow for the growth of this phenomenon. But it is also important to note that sexual exploitation has strong linkages to poverty, globalization, and exploitative economic conditions. For instance, structural adjustment programs and neoliberal economic policies have led to serious socio-economic dislocations in many low-income countries. As women in particular have lost jobs, they and their families have been put at risk and many have fallen into dire poverty. In order to survive, women have sought various solutions. At times they have ended up engaging in risky survival strategies such as exchanging sexual services for basic needs. At other times, young girls and women have been forced into prostitution due to their circumstances, as in the case of refugees, or due to a lack of knowledge. It is this linkage between economic policies, increases in poverty, and the greater potential for sexual exploitation that needs to be brought out into the open and dealt with.

How are Girls and Women Entrapped into Prostitution?

The growth of the sexual services industry is fueled by demand and by the large supply of girls and women who are available to participate in this sector of the economy. This leads us to explore the questions of why there is a greater availability of girls and women, and how they are at times coerced and at other times persuaded to participate in their own sexual exploitation.

We have already seen that a combination of factors entice and force girls and women into the sexual services industry. However, globalization has facilitated the growth of sexual exploitation of girls and women in other specific ways. For instance, large transnational networks facilitate the flow of women over national boundaries, and often have complex, highly organized mechanisms to enslave the women. In fact, most instances of sexual trafficking are not as benign as Penttinen's (2008) initial ethnographic descriptions would suggest. For instance, many girls and women are often recruited into the contemporary sex industry by organizations that seem legitimate on the surface. Many of these organizations lure girls and women to join through the promise of attaining domestic jobs, careers in modeling, or finding a marriage partner. They often promise to assist girls and women make a better life for themselves in a high-income country. Hughes (2000) cites that Interpol-Ukraine estimates that about 75 percent of recruited girls and women are not aware that when they sign up to go abroad, they will actually be forced into prostitution. They are duped in part because the interview processes to attain the promised employment tend to be lengthy and complex, adding an aura of legitimacy to these enterprises.

In a relatively new trend, trafficked women (also known as "the second wave") are used as recruiters, offering up hope and their own "positive" experiences to the potential applicants. Women often work as recruiters in their native countries as it may be their only means of escaping the situation that they have ultimately found themselves in (Hughes, 2000). Commonly, most recruited women do not realize the fate that awaits them until they have already left their home communities.

As part of this process, once the women reach their destination countries they are told that their jobs as nannies, domestics, or dancers are non-existent. Especially in cases of international trafficking, women's options now become extremely limited. They find themselves in a new environment, without their families and social support networks. Oftentimes they do not speak the language of the host country and are unfamiliar with its laws and practices. This social isolation rapidly makes the women dependent on their traffickers for their survival. Traffickers commonly confiscate the women's travel documents or give them false documents, making them even more vulnerable and subject to deportation should they be discovered. They usually also pay the costs associated with the transportation of the women to the new locale. The girls and women then incur this as a debt that needs to be repaid in order to regain their freedom. Even women who are aware that they will be engaging in the sexual services industry are usually not aware of the degree of deception and violence that they will be subjected to in this process.[6] The traffickers, in turn, use a variety of tactics to make the women more reliant on them, such as engaging them in fraudulent activities in order to pre-empt them from seeking out legal authorities to regain their freedom. Other common strategies used by traffickers are the use of extreme violence, rape, and threats. As one young girl who was trafficked from Laos to Thailand stated, "After eight days of torture, I thought I will accept the job to save my life" (quoted in Zimmerman et al., 2003, p. 46).

Compounding these problems is that trafficked girls and women receive little sympathy in their home and host societies. Many times they are blamed for the crimes that have been committed against them. They are labeled as prostitutes and often shunned by their families and communities, even in cases where they unknowingly entered into their exploitative situations. Trafficked girls and women have trouble receiving adequate health care both at home and abroad, and are excluded from health care initiatives that stress prevention and safe sex. Instead, they are harassed and ostracized by local officials, and forced to fend for themselves. A study of South Asian prostitutes found that these women not only suffer from a high risk of sexually transmitted infections but are also much more likely to have a wide range of health issues related to forced, early sex such as pelvic infections and chronic pelvic pain. Because they often live in highly polluted environments with poor air circulation and heavy tobacco smoke, many girls also suffer from conditions such as asthma and bronchitis (Joffres et al., 2008). Thus, once a young girl or woman enters into the cycle of prostitution, her life chances are severely curtailed. Exacerbating this problem is that legal officials may accept, and even support, the traffickers. A number of studies indicate that government officials may themselves be collaborating with the traffickers, and at times even be buyers of prostitution (Hughes, 2000).

Globalization has not only facilitated the conditions that allow for an increased exploitation of women and children but it has also contributed to the creation of new and different forms of sexual exploitation. Through the pervasiveness of the Internet, traffickers can conduct their negotiations in private spaces with little chance of being discovered (IOM, 2000). The Internet also allows for new types of participation and sexual exploitation. For example, traffickers are now able to set up sites where sexual fetishes and violence can occur in "real" time allowing for voyeurism from different parts of the world. Encryption technology that hides public access to these practices allows this type of exploitation to proliferate in places where law enforcement can be bribed or where prostitution is legal or at least accepted. These practices can then be transmitted to clients all over the globe. While some of the most notorious sites have been shut down in recent years due to public outrage around the world, many more continue to operate and flourish.[7]

Macroexplanations for the Rise in Sexual Exploitation

This discussion raises the question of why sexual trafficking and exploitation is on the increase despite large-scale efforts by transnational organizations such as the United Nations, UNESCO, the International Labor Organization (ILO), the International Organization for Migration (IOM), and many other human rights groups concerned with women's issues. Some anthropologists in particular argue that despite these large-scale efforts, sexual trafficking continues to remain hidden from the public eye. They hypothesize that because the sexual exchange of girls and women has always been an integral aspect of so many cultures and societies, it remains embedded in the norms and values of family and kinship systems. From this perspective, the sexuality of women is perceived as something to be bartered and exchanged (Mauss, 1990; Long, 2004). Historically, societies and groups traded women to achieve peace and as a form of "gift." The exogamous marriage rules that are the basis of most cultural systems require specifically that it be women who are exchanged between groups. Thus, there exists in many places a cultural template that deems transactions and negotiations involving women and their sexuality as commonplace. In other words, from that perspective the sexual bartering of girls and women is not exploitation but a cultural norm embedded in a variety of societal beliefs. This viewpoint may explain, in part, why sexual trafficking remains outside of mainstream discussion despite its proliferation, and why its perpetrators are not always punished in the same manner as for other types of crimes.

Other explanations for the increase in sexual trafficking and exploitation also point to the public representation and commodification of women in Western societies. Young women are portrayed and marketed as an object to be acquired. Western images of girls and women focus on their sexuality and beauty in advertisements, music, and a wide variety of media outlets. Sexual servitude, thus, does not always provoke the same outrage as older forms of slavery. The fact that there is no real consensus as to what constitutes sexual servitude exacerbates the problem. Many Westerners, for example, feel that women have the "right" to participate in the sexual services industry if they so choose. However, this perspective hides the fact that poverty and domestic abuse are often the real culprits, and force young women to make choices that are ultimately destructive to their physical and psychological health. This perspective also obscures the issue that there are vast differences between those who "choose" to enter the sex industry versus those women who are coerced or tricked into participating. Moreover, women's rights organizations that advocate that all forms of prostitution are a form of violence against women, ignore the complex social and economic conditions that force women to choose to enter the sexual services industry in the first place. Blanket statements that are based on the experiences of middle-class Western women do not adequately convey or take into account the multitude of conditions that define the lives of vulnerable girls and women and that may encourage them to seek options that would be unfathomable to more well-to-do women.

Synopsis

As we have seen, sexual trafficking and exploitation is an extremely complicated phenomenon because it is a hidden and a highly contested and controversial topic. The victims are usually vulnerable individuals without financial or social resources, and the perpetrators use a combination of coercion and violence to perpetuate their agendas. This issue is compounded by the fact that in many jurisdictions legal sanctions against sexual traffickers are minimal when contrasted with the types of penalties that are applied to drug traffickers. Hughes (2000) also points out that in certain places, such as the countries of the former Soviet Union, the line between organized crime and government is increasingly blurred. Transnational networks of organized crime are gaining in influence and are proving to be instrumental in preventing the passing of any type of legislation that would stem the tide of sexual trafficking. Under those circumstances it becomes extremely difficult to break the cycle of corruption, networking, and profit-making that is endemic of this industry. For example, Kateryna Levchenko from La Strada-Ukrain made the following statement when asked to comment on the proliferation of criminality and the trafficking of women:

> the main part of income from this criminal business is obtained by foreign criminal organizations that are the ones interested in preservation of the current situation. They do not want any improvements in the status of Ukrainian women or in Ukrainian economy as a whole. The scale of this illegal business, huge monthly and annual turnovers, merging with certain power structures (first of all, the police) in the countries of Central and Eastern Europe, make it a real national security issue.
>
> (quoted in Hughes, 2000)

In a world where poor young girls and women have become more vulnerable, factors such as poverty, the lack of sustainable, safe jobs, and the corruption of some authority figures conjoin to create a hostile environment. In Chapter 8 we will examine policies and initiatives that can bring about change and decrease the susceptibility to sexual exploitation of girls and women who are at risk. I would like to point out, however, that in order to address this issue in a systematic manner, both macro- and microstrategies are needed. The first step in accomplishing any form of transformation is raising awareness of these issues. We need to understand the conditions that force girls and women into situations where they can be susceptible to being sexually exploited. Moreover, we need to identify and prevent the various parties that are involved in the proliferation of sexually exploitative practices from continuing with their quest. In part this can only be accomplished by making engaging in this industry less lucrative for them. Thus, the focus needs to be on those perpetrators who create, legitimize, and support these trafficking networks and industries. We also need to ensure that issues of poverty, inequity, and gender discrimination are addressed by global and local initiatives. Next we turn to migration, aspects of which are, in the eyes of some, closely related to sexual exploitation and trafficking.

Notes

1 This scenario is a composite of the various ethnographic descriptions that Penttinen provides (2008).
2 While men are also facing increased risks in the globalized economy, with respect to sexual exploitation women are the predominant victims.
3 The AIDS epidemic is also on the rise due to the prevalence of using prostituted boys for sex. This is a complex topic to research, however, because of the stigma associated with homosexual sex in so many non-Western societies. In areas of sub-Saharan Africa and South Asia, governments are reluctant to acknowledge that this is a situation that exists in their countries. For example, in India sexual relations between men is treated as a criminal act under the law. As a consequence, many men hide their homosexual relations.
4 See Lalor (2008) for an extensive discussion about the complexities of gathering data on HIV/AIDS among children in sub-Saharan Africa. For ethical and legal reasons, most studies do not include questions on abuse in studies of children.
5 There are fundamental differences between transactional sex and bride price or bride wealth. Bride wealth is an exchange between parents while transactional sex occurs between the young woman and the man. Thus, despite reports of forced sex and coercion, young women may feel a certain sense of power through the transaction.
6 See Hughes (2000) for disturbing examples of how these women are threatened and coerced.
7 There are horrific depictions on the Internet of the types of services and fetishes that individuals can indulge in, many of them involving the sexual slavery and extreme abuse of young women. These raise serious questions about "free speech" and the rights of individuals to exercise their wishes over others with virtually no limitations.

6

NEW DIRECTIONS
Migration, Women, and Transnational Motherhood

Consider the following scenario.

Yolanda, a young undocumented domestic worker from Mexico, becomes extremely agitated when a nurse in the emergency room asks her if she has children. She explains that she has four daughters, but only one is here in the United States with her. Teary eyed, she explains that she left her native village due to extreme poverty and the lack of opportunities. She only brought her youngest, a 22 months old, on the arduous, dangerous border crossing into New Mexico. One day, when she has papers and some money, she hopes to send for her other children who are being cared for by her mother and an aunt. Worried, she debates if she will ever achieve her dreams of finding a steady job with decent pay, and if her daughters will recognize her by the time she is reunited with them.[1]

Now contrast this case with the following situation.

Fatima, a young Pakistani woman living in the Netherlands, stares at the people from social services with disbelief. They have just informed her that she may lose custody of all of her children because she left them with an acquaintance while she spent ten days in Pakistan dealing with the aftermath of her father's death. They are claiming that she is an "irresponsible mother" who does not put the best interests of her children first. Fatima explains to the social service officials that according to her culture because she is the oldest child, she is responsible for getting the families' affairs in order when a parent dies. The social service workers are not swayed by her argument and instead proclaim that now that she lives in the Netherlands, she needs to adhere to the laws and cultural beliefs of her host society. Fatima is confused as she feels that she was being very responsive and responsible as she came back to the Netherlands immediately after taking care of the funeral arrangements for her father. Her children were properly taken care of and from her point of view not neglected in any form. What is the problem she demands? And why would social services take her children when she has a consistent record of taking excellent care of them?[2]

Yolanda and Fatima symbolize one of the most controversial phenomena of our contemporary globalizing world: women who migrate to high-income countries due to work incentives, while simultaneously being mothers. To many in the general public in their home and host countries, they embody contentious issues about economics, movement, citizenship, and what constitutes being a good parent, and a good mother in particular. It is easy to get caught up in the complex debates about neoliberalism, economic downsizing, Structural Adjustment Policies, and the like. However, it is the human factor that is often forgotten in these debates, and it is this aspect that rises to prominence in an examination of the gendered nature of contemporary migrations.

Transnational Migration and Transnational Families

Transnational migration is in and of itself not a new phenomenon. Throughout the nineteenth and twentieth centuries many individuals, first from Europe and then other parts of the world, migrated most commonly to the United States, Canada, and Australia, and sent their remittances back home to their families (Glick Schiller, 1999). They stayed in touch through letter writing and hoped for an eventual reunification through return migration. In proportion to the global population, there are actually fewer migrants today than one hundred years ago. The IOM estimates that there are currently about 214 million migrants, which is about 3.1 percent of the world population (2012).

Today there are significant differences between the transnational families of those earlier times and contemporary ones. For contemporary transnational families, communication and transportation technologies make it much easier to stay in touch and to maintain ties. The Internet allows families to share in each other's lives on an instantaneous basis, and the relative ease of travel permits more consistent visits. However, the conditions for poor transnational families have also become more complex. Changes in manufacturing and a sharp increase in temporary and subcontracted work have made upward mobility more challenging for those individuals who migrate to high-income countries. Further, declines in global economic conditions have put the most vulnerable members of low-income and high-income countries at even greater risk. This problem is coupled with a peculiar, new and unique aspect of globalization: money and capital move more freely between countries and regions, however, the movement of individuals has become more restricted (Mitropoulos, 2001). In response to an increased labor migration combined with security concerns, nation-states have closed borders and tightened immigration laws in an effort to keep people out and to discourage them from staying on in their countries. Those who do manage to enter illegally, stay in their host countries at great risk, and are likely to face harsh restrictions and the constant fear of being caught in their daily lives.

Despite these obstacles, both legal and illegal migration is on the rise. This phenomenon can be primarily understood from an economic perspective. As global conditions worsen for the poor, an increasing number of individuals are seeking better prospects. Due to their economic susceptibility, they or their families may feel extremely vulnerable in their home communities. This leads individuals to be willing to risk everything, including at times their lives, in order to create new opportunities for themselves and their families. Some persons also migrate because of the lack of opportunities for skilled professionals in their home societies. This is often referred to as the "brain drain." Nurses, doctors, teachers, computer specialists, and the like seek new lives in high-income countries where they will be able to further their careers and earn considerably higher salaries. For these highly skilled professionals, remaining in their home countries is an unappealing option since they are underpaid and there is often no chance for advancement. Other factors such as wars, famines, and the collapse of governments, as in the countries of the former Soviet Union and the Eastern bloc, also contribute to the growing movement of people from one area of the world to another.

Impacting the flow of people is also the increased access to information that individuals have these days. Television, movies, and the Internet allow images about different lifestyles and consumer goods to proliferate and reach far corners of the earth. Today people are exposed to new ways of living that they may never even have imagined. This fuels their desire to get out of oppressive situations and to seek a better life. Thus, the technological aspects of globalization are closely linked to the economic and social ones.

The Feminization of Transnational Migration

An integral aspect of the new wave of migration is its increasingly feminized nature. This feminization of migration is closely linked to a global labor flow that has encouraged and at times forced women to seek work in higher-income regions and countries. By 2010, 49 percent of all individuals who migrated internationally were women (IOM, 2012). There is some variation by region of the world, with Eastern Europe at the top of the list at 57 percent and Western Asia at 39 percent, but generally speaking most countries that sent migrants averaged close to 50 percent (Bose, 2011).

The increase in women's migration is closely related to the changes brought on through globalization. As manufacturing jobs have moved to export processing zones and service sector jobs have increased in urban areas and in high-income countries, a new demand for female workers has arisen. An increasing number of women are migrating often first from rural to urban areas. Then due to economic disruptions, they may locate to other countries as "contract workers." Contract workers travel to other countries for a specific period of time in order to work in certain industries such as child or elder care, domestic work, manufacturing in global export processing zones, or in food, services, or entertainment. It is noteworthy that migrating women take up different employment niches than their male counterparts. Male migrants are more likely to work in construction and information and communication industries, while women as noted primarily end up in the manufacturing and service arenas (Raghuram, 2008). Even highly skilled women who migrate often do not end up working in their areas of expertise in destination countries. In other words, they become "deskilled" (Allan & Larsen, 2003).[3] Migration also affects men and women in other gender-specific ways. Women tend to have a heavier responsibility vis-à-vis their families and thus, when they migrate, they need to balance their work and family obligations in a different manner than men who have traditionally relied on the wives that they left behind.

Female migrants have become a key aspect of the global economy. Both sending and receiving societies rely on them because they provide a new form of low-cost labor and they send home remittances. These remittances are an important source of income for their families and, increasingly, their communities' and countries' economies. In a number of low-income countries, remittances sent home by migrants now make up a substantial aspect of the GDP and may even equal or exceed the amount of money brought in through exports (Orozco, 2002). In the Philippines, for example, somewhere between 34 to 53 percent of the population depend in their daily lives on migrant remittances (Parrenas, 2010). According to IOM estimates, about $440 billion in remittances were sent home by migrants in 2010. Despite the current global economic downturn, this is an exponential increase in comparison to 2000, when approximately $132 billion was sent home by migrants. The IOM also notes that the actual numbers for remittances are probably much higher since the unrecorded flows through formal and informal channels are unknown. At $48.3 billion, the United States is by far the largest source of the outflow of remittances. The top recipient countries for remittances are India, China, Mexico, the Philippines, and France (IOM, 2012).

Despite a strong interest in the economic role of remittances by a number of international lending institutions such as the World Bank, we actually know very little about the gendered nature of these transmittals. We do not know specifically who in the recipients' households profits from remittances, how the money is actually saved (that is, what is it not being spent on), and how gender comes into play with respect to decision-making around the distribution of the money. Moreover, while there is a growing dialogue on the role of remittances as an important economic contribution of migrating individuals, less attention has been paid to the neoliberal principles that underlie this global trend. As a growing number of states abdicate their responsibility to provide jobs and social welfare nets to their citizens, these policy and programmatic changes are legitimized by an entrepreneurial ideology that encourages individuals to take care of themselves. However, due to a series of interrelated factors, in many low-income areas of the world opportunities have actually worsened with respect to economic prospects. This situation, combined with a need for specifically female labor in urban areas and high-income countries, has led to the current rise in female migration. Paradoxically, in both sending and receiving countries, female migrants tend to be criticized, socially excluded, and ostracized. This is particularly the case for women who migrate abroad if they have children. In this chapter we examine this phenomenon in greater depth.

Transnational Motherhood—Creating New Conceptions of the "Good Mother"

A contemporary aspect of the new feminized migration is the phenomenon often referred to as transnational motherhood: women who leave their children behind with husbands and relatives while they seek employment abroad. Several countries have recently emerged as primary sending countries with respect to transnational mothers including Sri Lanka, Mexico, Poland, and the Philippines. It is estimated that in the Philippines alone, about 9 million children are being raised without at least one parent and that this represents about 27 percent of the youth population. Parrenas (2012) points out while the gender breakdown of transnational parents is not available, one can assume that a majority of these children are growing up with a mother who is working somewhere else. She cites the fact that from 2000 to 2006, over 70 percent of newly hired migrants were women and they were working in over 130 countries in Asia, Europe, and the Americas (Parrenas, 2010). The total number of transnational mothers around the world is, however, unknown.

While transnational mothering is becoming increasingly common in certain places, it is a highly controversial topic. In many cultures, traditional gender roles continue to persevere and to advocate that women are the spouse who is best suited to taking care of the home and to nurturing and raising children. As Glenn (1994, p. 3) suggested, "Mothering—more than any aspect of gender—has been subject to essentialist interpretation: seen as natural, universal, and unchanging." Simultaneously, according to this perspective, the main role for men is to be the economic providers. While this is an overt cultural and religious value in places like the Islamic Middle East and parts of Southeast Asia, it is also a pervasive notion in many other areas of the world including many of the high-income countries of the West. In the United States, this phenomenon is often referred to as a universal model of exclusive mothering. This perspective advocates that the best caretaker for a child is its biological mother and that, conversely, this is a woman's primary role in life. As Nancy Chodorow (1978) stated, this is "a socially and historically specific mother–child relationship of a particular intensity and exclusivity and a particular infantile development that this relationship produces" (p. 76).

This particular version of motherhood is rooted in beliefs stemming from nineteenth-century psychology and sociology, and has actually, according to some perspectives, grown in importance in the late twentieth and early twenty-first century. As an increasing number of women have entered the formal labor force in the United States, an intensive mothering model has simultaneously taken hold. Research on work–family life indicates, for instance, that working mothers today spend as much time with their children as stay at home mothers did in the 1960s (Bianchi, Robinson, & Milkie, 2007). Mothers are expected to participate in organized activities with their children, provide extra stimulation for their physical and social development, and be involved in every aspect of their lives from infancy through college. Simultaneously, in contemporary U.S. society there is less emphasis these days on the household labor of middle-class women. Studies indicate that women spend less time on housework and cooking than in any previous generation. Many women are relying extensively on convenience or fast food and outsourcing household responsibilities, often to other paid women. For women who have children, it is increasingly their role as mothers that is central to their identities, much more so than their role as homemakers. As women's roles have changed, the demand on men to be actively and emotionally involved with their children has also expanded. A model of involved fathering advocates that being engaged in the raising of children is not only beneficial to men but also contributes to children's psychological development (Palkovitz, 2002). From a mainstream, societal perspective, men continue to be expected to be the primary breadwinners in their families but with the added dimension of involved fathering.[4] In fact, recent studies indicate that for young American men, work–family stress is now greater than it is for women. Despite these enormous societal changes, mothers continue to be upheld as the primary influence in a child's life, and are vilified if something goes wrong with their children. Popular opinion advocates that women who have children need to prioritize their physical and psychological proximity to their children. This view on motherhood is also prevalent in many other societies around the world.

Female migration and transnational mothering displace and alter these traditional gender role concepts in complex ways. Female migration is associated with a rearrangement of household roles and a redistribution of domestic labor. When the mother leaves, someone still has to cook, clean, raise and nurture the children, and take care of all the other basic tasks that keep a family running. In Western middle-class households, a reorganization of domestic responsibilities is now commonly associated with the distribution of some of this care work to either husbands and/or paid domestic workers. However, the situation for low-income women in Western and non-Western contexts is quite different. For instance, Gamburd (2000) documents in her study of Sri Lankan female migrants that in many non-Western contexts it is not men but other female kin who take care of the domestic chores and care work in the absence of a mother. In fact, men may become resentful and try to emphasize their role as the "man" of the house by purposefully not helping out or, even at times, by becoming abusive. Ethnographic evidence also indicates that among some cultural groups individuals believe that men cannot help out in the home because they may be "naturally" averse to child care (Parrenas, 2010).

The dominant societal view of transnational mothers in many of their home societies is that they are abdicating their natural female role by "abandoning" their children in the process of migration. They are subjected to similar views in receiving societies where the fact that they have left their children behind makes them objects of scorn and derision. Migrating women are often caught in complex paradoxical situations where they are represented as "irresponsible mothers, immoral wives, and selfish consumers," while they argue that they are forced to seek opportunities abroad due to the economic conditions of their home societies (Keough, 2006). This perception is coupled with a popular perspective in many places that by leaving their children motherless, so to speak, they make these children more vulnerable to abuse. For instance, a Romanian economist quoted in the *New York Times* called the "outmigration of women a 'national tragedy,' one that has triggered social upheaval in Romania."[5] These types of critiques raise the question of why migrating mothers cause such a societal furor when, as was noted at the beginning of this chapter, migration is not a new phenomenon. Men have been migrating throughout recorded history and sending remittances home.[6] The historical record abounds with stories of fathers who were away for years at a time involved in military maneuvers, at sea, or taking on various types of employment. Thus, if this is not a new phenomenon, then why do women who migrate make headlines and are blamed for the downfall of their countries? For instance, Parrenas (2010) describes a recent speech by the president of the Philippines that called for strategies to encourage mothers not to migrate. She writes:

> As President Ramos stated, "we are not against overseas employment of Filipino women. We are against overseas employment at the cost of family solidarity ..." By calling for the return

migration of mothers, President Ramos did not altogether disregard the increasing economic dependence of the Philippines on the foreign remittances of its mostly female migrant workers. However, he did make clear that only single and childless women are those who are morally permitted to pursue labor migration.

(p. 1836)

This outraged response that seems to characterize virtually every sending society, including the Philippines, Poland, Romania, and Lithuania to name just a few, can best be understood by examining the gender ideology that emphasizes that women's most "natural" role is that of being a mother. That belief must be contrasted with the actual sentiments of many migrating women with children. Many of these women feel that they are actually selflessly sacrificing for their children and are better mothers than the ones who cannot provide economically for their children. Yet, as Suurmond (2010) suggests, it is particularly the term "good mother" that carries strong symbolic value. This concept is subject to variation depending on cultural context and interpretation as her depiction of the case of Fatima, the Pakistani woman, illustrated.

Deconstructing Motherhood

It is through the work on transnational mothering that the concept of motherhood and its strong ideological underpinnings is being analyzed, reflected on, and transformed. Until recently, scholarship on motherhood stressed that this was an activity mainly associated with the care and raising of children. Motherhood was contrasted to fatherhood, which was primarily conceptualized as providing children with economic support and educational opportunities. The phenomenon of transnational motherhood has led to a renewed interest in how the roles of mothers are perceived and practiced in different contexts. In turn, this is leading to a new focus on men and masculinity in cross-cultural contexts.

Case Study: Mexican Migrating Mothers Need to Retain their "Traditional" Functions

Dreby (2006), who researched migrating mothers and fathers from Mexico, describes how mothering there, similar to many other places, is associated with the daily care for children, and fathering is related to providing economic security for the family. But she points out that Mexican mothers' caregiving role is also associated and celebrated as being self-sacrificing and martyr like. For instance, mothers are

131

likened to the selfless qualities of the Virgin of Guadalupe. This version of motherhood is termed *marianismo,* and accordingly women should be self-negating and give up their wishes and desires for their children. An integral aspect of this construction of femininity is that women are morally and spiritually superior to men. Men, conversely, are to be honorable and represent and protect their families. The question arises what happens to these gender constructs in transnational contexts. Do these concepts become transformed? Strengthened? Do they influence concepts of motherhood and fatherhood in home and host societies?

Dreby's (2006) study only begins to answer some of these questions. Interestingly, she found that in the Mexican case, women and men who migrated to the United States maintained similar relationships with the children they had left behind in Mexico: they communicated regularly with them and sent them financial remittances and gifts. Thus, a form of gender convergence was at work here with men and women exhibiting similar behaviors while abroad. However, similarities between mothers and fathers were only present with respect to their actions. When it came to the traditional beliefs about motherhood and fatherhood, Dreby found that those beliefs were not altered. While other studies have shown that migration may transform gender expectations within marriages, Dreby found that with respect to parenting, traditional beliefs about mothering and fathering persevered, even in a transnational context. Working in the Philippines, Parrenas documents similar findings (2010). When women migrated, despite the fact that they were sending home remittances, men did not take on new roles or re-define fathering. In the Mexican case, the relationships that fathers built with their children continued to be directly related to their ability to fulfill the economic provider role. If they were economically successful, they maintained regular contact with their children. Mothers were judged through a different lens. The Mexican mothers' primary goal with respect to their children was to demonstrate to them that even from a distance they were able to stay emotionally intimate with them.

Changes in Conceptions of Motherhood and Fatherhood Among Migrants

While Dreby's (2006) study points to a certain stasis in beliefs about parenting roles, Mummert (2005), also studying the parenting roles of Mexican migrants in the United States, arrived at a different conclusion. She found that while it is true that Mexican fathers needed to maintain their economic provider status role, increasingly "a certain physical presence and closeness have become requirements of fatherhood" (2005, p. 7). Mummert's analysis speaks to the fact that gender roles are not necessarily static. Instead, they are influenced by context, external factors, and ideologies. Transnational parents are not immune from the trends they are exposed to in their host societies. They may migrate with certain beliefs but it is almost impossible for those beliefs not be become altered during the course of their migration. Transformations in the values and beliefs of migrants remain a fruitful area for the exploration of the dynamism inherent in globalizing processes. They suggest that the spread and changes in values and beliefs are not just based on images transmitted through popular media and the Internet but are also reliant on interpersonal relationships and communications. We are only at the beginning of understanding these underlying processes and how they alter marital and parental relationships in subtle ways.

The Relationship Between Breadwinning and Motherhood

Parrenas (2010) suggests that transnational motherhood expands the notion of mothering by emphasizing breadwinning as one of its key elements. However, other studies on transnational parenting dispute this analysis— while in some contexts concepts of fatherhood may be changing and expanding on the breadwinning role, transnational motherhood has not integrated breadwinning into mothering in the same manner. Many women who migrate and leave their children behind do so due to financial reasons. However, breadwinning has not uniformly replaced caretaking as the core concept of motherhood. Hondagneu-Sotelo and Avila (1997, p. 562) suggest:

> Rather than replacing caregiving with breadwinning definitions of motherhood, they appear to be expanding their definitions of motherhood to encompass breadwinning that may require long-term physical separations. For these women, a core belief is that they can best fulfill traditional caregiving responsibilities through income earning in the United States while their children remain "back home."

The construct of transnational mothering brings to the forefront that which a number of scholars have been advocating for several years now: that the ideal of exclusive motherhood that has been considered normative for middle-class women is not something that poor women or women of color have been able to adhere to either in the past or today. Instead, economic circumstances almost always drive people's choices and actions, and do not necessarily conform to the norms that may be prevalent in a society. For instance, in order to meet their child-care responsibilities, many women of color in the United States have traditionally shared this obligation with extended kin and fictive kin.[7] Transnational mothers represent a contemporary version of the same dilemma—but for them the situation is even more complicated. They have to engage in a particularly difficult form of joint mothering that is characterized by significant geographical distances, arduous journeys, and, oftentimes, loneliness. Transnational motherhood points to the fact that ultimately it is not necessarily race, ethnicity, or culture that drives individual actions. Instead, economic need plays a pivotal role even in those decisions that are thought of by many as "inherent" or "traditional," as is the case with motherhood. Women's desire to protect and enhance their children's lives are not just defined by physical presence or caretaking, but take on other forms. The decision to migrate indicates that some women also feel that by being able to provide financially they are taking care of their children in the best way they are able to, according to their specific set of circumstances. A mother's absence, while understood as being challenging and complicated, is not necessarily perceived as interrupting a child's upbringing or its sense of being nurtured (Nicholson, 2006). From a Western normative perspective, this is very difficult for many people to understand.

By deconstructing transnational motherhood, we broaden our view of what a "good mother" is and her role in society. The analysis of transnational motherhood also assists us in moving away from dichotomies such as public and private, and work and household. For instance, Denise Segura in her work on Mexican immigrants found that "Mexicanas, raised in a world where economic and household work often merged, do not dichotomize social life into public and private spheres, but appear to view employment as one workable domain of motherhood" (1994, p. 212).

As an increasing number of women around the globe take on paid employment, a broader perspective on the various responsibilities of motherhood will probably take hold. Increasingly, in many middle-class contexts, women's paid work outside of the home is an integral aspect of their identities and of the family economy. Among middle-class families in Western and non-Western contexts, the dichotomy associated with a traditional family breadwinner–homemaker model is slowly dissipating as an increasing number of individuals telecommute, run their own businesses out of the home, and create a myriad of other arrangements. This suggests that we are moving to a reconceptualization of motherhood that will increasingly feature work as one of its central tenets. In other words, breadwinning is becoming an integral aspect of motherhood for more skilled individuals—even if it is not formally acknowledged as such, and not necessarily popular as a social ideal. Moreover, as Nicholson (2006) suggests, the migration of women for work and economic reasons has significant implications not just for the present context. Migrating mothers do not just provide financially for their children. Through their experiences, these women create a new vision of what is *possible* in the future. In other words, these women introduce the elements of hope, opportunity, and change to their children. Through the new resources and ideas they provide, the children of migrating mothers learn that it is possible to effect change in one's life. Thus, the children benefit materially as well as ideologically. Since many of these families live in conditions of great poverty with few opportunities, the migration of women introduces new, often unimagined elements into the children's and communities' lives. On the one hand, migrating women are sacrificing physical time with their children, but, on the other, they feel they are actually giving their children something even more valuable—a better future than they may be able to achieve for themselves. Ultimately, this is a universal motivator—the desire on parent's parts to improve the conditions of their children's lives. Transnational mothering needs to be understood from this perspective. However, complicating this discussion is the role that current national and international policies play with respect to migration. We turn to this issue next.

The Growing Role of Nation-States in Restricting Migration

While transnational migration is on the rise, the international response of receiving nation-states has been to intensify efforts to restrict the flow of people across borders and to limit their lengths of stay. In the United States, the popularity of current restrictive immigration legalization policies can be attributed to public sentiment that assumes that the U.S. labor market is overrun with Mexican and Central American laborers. Public opinion polls and policy-makers stress that instead of opening borders the government should be sending people home "where they belong." This perspective is accompanied by the view that the state should also institute policies that will prevent migrants from taking the "rightful" jobs of American citizens. This pejorative view of migrants has gained further traction with the downturn of the global economy. Thus, in order to halt undocumented immigration and to limit legal immigration, a variety of measures have been put into place including the erection of physical barriers between the United States and Mexico, and the creation of a human fence of Border Patrol agents in El Paso, Texas. In the same vein, California voters recently approved a referendum that prevents undocumented citizens from receiving publicly financed social services.

In Europe, similar negative sentiments about undocumented and documented immigrants are also on the rise. Spain recently passed stringent family reunification laws and other countries are following suit. Moreover, in a variety of European countries, including France, the Netherlands, Italy, Hungary, and Sweden, right-leaning political groups are gaining seats in their country's parliaments based on stringent anti-immigrant platforms.

In a recent survey of the Italian public, 70 percent of those questioned responded that immigration had a bad impact on their country (Pew Research, 2010). In response to these views, European countries have also tightened their residency and citizenship requirements. For instance, many countries now require a strict language and cultural test, in addition to other lengthy formalities as part of the citizenship process. As the case study of Fatima at the beginning of this chapter described, strict adherence to what are perceived as the norms of the host society are increasingly being applied to all foreigners. Another example comes from France where a recent reform to the immigration laws now includes behavior guarantees by parents for their children.

Despite these negative sentiments, documented and undocumented workers continue to stream into the United States and other high-income countries. This migration is fueled by the perception that there *is* work available in these places and that migrants can be more successful in areas with thriving economies than in their home societies. Much of this information is conveyed through transnational networks of individuals who are forming new twenty-first-century versions of chain migrations. Rodriguez (2006) refers to this phenomenon also as autonomous migration—a movement of individuals independent of state agreements whether it be legal or illegal. He states, "It is important to understand that autonomous migration means more than unauthorized ('illegal') border crossings: it means a community strategy implemented, developed, and sustained with the support of institutions, including formal ones, at the migrants' points of origin and ... points of destination" (p. 23).

Rodriguez goes on to point out that because so many core institutions such as local governments and employers support this strategy, many undocumented migrants do not perceive this method of entering other countries as a criminal activity. Instead, illegal migration is a mechanism for them to maintain and further their personal and familial interests.

Perceptions about Immigration are Context Dependent

It is important to note that legal and illegal immigration has somewhat different causes and effects in the United States and Canada, in contrast to Europe. The United States and Canada are historically immigration destination countries. Thus, while the current sentiment about migrants, especially in the United States is relatively negative, the fact remains that most of the population has immigrant roots. This is not the case in Europe. Most Europeans pride themselves on the supposed homogeneity of their societies and the unique culture, language, and traditions that marks the distinctiveness of each country. However, today most European countries are faced with a paradoxical choice: many of their birth rates are so low that they are virtually completely dependent on immigrant labor.

This situation persists despite many citizens' negative sentiments about foreign migrants. For instance, Germany reached a milestone in 2009: for the first year on record there were more elderly over the age of 65 than youths 25 and under. Moreover, approximately 45 percent of children under the age of six were the children of immigrants. Countries such as Germany thus need migrants to help sustain the labor force. Despite these realities, restrictive immigration laws and policies are taking hold across the United States and Europe. These measures are firmly supported by the majority of the citizenry, and further limiting the rights of legal and illegal migrants is encouraged.

Restrictive Immigration Policies and Family Life

The impact of restrictive immigration policies is particularly detrimental to the family lives of migrating workers. As countries work to limit family reunifications and make even return visitations to their home areas more difficult for documented workers, parents with children are often faced with lengthy separations. This situation is the most problematic for women who are undocumented and mothers. They are often compelled to prolong their absence from their families and have to draw on a complex web of family members and friends in order to ensure that their children are taken care of. Moreover, they do not have the luxury of visiting their families on a regular basis or having their children come to them. As Yolanda's example in the beginning of this chapter illustrated, these women have to worry when and under what conditions they will see their children again. The most efficient strategy for most undocumented migrants is to stay as long as possible in their host country in order to maximize their earnings. These mothers have no options but to conduct their mothering and kin work from afar. Thus, an important distinction among transnational mothers is their legal status: if they are documented workers or in a country illegally matters with respect to visitations and their abilities to move across borders. Their legal status plays an important role in the types of work they are able to access, their relationship to their host society, and the connections they are able to maintain with the families that they have left behind. Undocumented migrant women are excluded from most jobs and their status makes them vulnerable to exploitation and abuse. They remain at the margins of their host society, and are often unable to access even the most basic services. Being undocumented affects their everyday lives and forces them to maintain clandestine relationships with their families back home. As states continue to tighten borders, even legal migrants have to deal with the consequences. It has become increasingly complicated for non-citizens to renew visas and to re-enter societies they may have left for a visit home. All of these restrictions stand in stark contrast to the increasing number of individuals who want to leave their home societies in search for better lives.

The Consequences of Migration: Creating New Transnational Connections and Meanings

An outcome of transnational female migration is the development of new networks among women. In migration studies, networks have always been a key aspect to understanding migratory patterns of migration, settlement issues, and employment links. The process of establishing networks creates and reinforces relationships and at times links migrants with members of their host societies. These relationships provide critical information. They influence decisions about who migrates, they provide information about jobs and social programs, and they supply knowledge about the living conditions in host countries. However, current research indicates that at least at this juncture, new emerging female networks are often not embedded in the more established transnational networks. These networks tend to be dominated by men, NGOs, and business partnerships (Dannecker, 2005). This is a noteworthy phenomenon because from a historical perspective men's success was dependent on these relationships. In order to succeed, men needed the information and support that transnational relationship networks provided. Chain migration was based on this concept: men would assist each other before and after the migration. However, in the contemporary migration pattern, men's and women's migratory networks do not overlap or support one another. Thus, women do not benefit from the resources that men from the same society may have access to.

Women's Networks

Despite the often loose and informal structure of women's networks in contrast to those of men, ethnographic evidence indicates that women still gain from these associations. One problem with understanding women's networks stems from the class divisions between women themselves. For example, Ehrenreich and Hochschild (2003) have illustrated that women from low-income countries form global care chains, which can be described as "a series of personal links between people across the globe based on the paid or unpaid work of caring" (Hochschild, 2001, p. 131). These types of networks are composed of socially disadvantaged female migrants that originate in low-income countries but are joined through their sharing of similar types of work and migration experiences. This illustrates that even women with few resources often utilize a variety of strategies to form associations. For instance, they may pool money amongst themselves as in the case of evolving credit systems, or they may assist female migrants in forging new identities in their host societies. These networks also provide women with information about work and residency alternatives, or with emotional support. Transnational networks also permit women in remote areas to gain access to information about migration possibilities and alternative sources of employment.

The role that transnational networks play in the lives of migrants is also very dependent on the presence of local networks. Whether in the home or host societies, local networks assist women with the practical aspects of migration and relocation. Empirical evidence indicates that when local networks are available, women rely less on transnational networks for information and support (Ryan, 2007). Local networks assist women with community formation, permanent settlement, and practical assistance. Women may also change their associations and networks over time. For instance, they may access different networks if after a migration they experience social and geographical mobility in the receiving society.

The Growth of Transnational and Local Networks

Varied types of transnational and local female networks are emerging as migrants themselves become more heterogeneous. For instance, there has been an increase in skilled professional migrant women who migrate independently and become integrated into new types of transnational associations. Women who are nurses, doctors, technology experts, and teachers are increasingly migrating to high-income countries where they can earn a significantly more lucrative salary than in their home societies. Through their access to communication technologies they are able to forge new connections and build both physical and virtual communities with each other. This group of migrants is often ignored in policy and scholarly debates about female migration (Raghuram, 2008). However, more and more female migration encompasses both highly skilled individuals and those workers who are employed in the service sectors of high-income countries. It is important to remember that these different groups may have very diverse experiences in their host societies. An exclusive focus on the service sector misrepresents the totality of the migrant experience and the varied contributions that migrants make to receiving countries. It also obscures the role that skills, education, age, and immigration status have on the formation of female transnational and local networks. We also need to keep in mind that networks are dynamic and change over space and time.

New Roles for Migrating Women through Network Associations

Besides providing social support, networks also facilitate the creation of new roles for migrating women. For instance, they may participate in their new communities by organizing group activities or by becoming community leaders. This can provide even low-status women the opportunity to be socially active and to regain some self-esteem or prestige in their migrant community (Raijman, Schammah-Gesser, & Kemp, 2003). At times women also join religious organizations in order to find support and make connections. In many countries, migrant churches are now primarily female, indicating the importance of this form of institutional support for some women. For instance, studying Latina immigrants in Israel, Raijman et al. (2003) found that churches provide a form of a "surrogate family" for migrating women. The church was perceived as a new place to feel a sense of belonging. The women's close relationship to a church stood in stark contrast to many of the women's feelings of uprootedness and displacement in the areas where they lived and worked. Churches were a protected space where women were safe, no matter what their legal or economic status happened to be. Socially, churches also allowed women to regain the status that they felt they were missing in their host countries.

The creation of uniquely female physical and virtual networks marks an adaptation of migrating women to their circumstances. Despite often feeling alienated from their host societies and, at times, being forced to the bottom of the social ladder in their new environments, migrating women are creating innovative social spaces for themselves. They are redefining the migratory experience in a different manner from men, and forging new identities for themselves.

The Transformation of Gender Relations

One consequence of growing female migration is a transformation in gender relations between men and women in sending societies. While most recent scholarship has centered on the experiences of migrating mothers, a number of scholars are beginning to compare the experiences of both migrating women and men, and the impact of their experiences on family life. Migrating women and men gain the knowledge of living in two different societies with different values and practices. Women may also for the first time in their lives gain a measure of independence through earning an income and living independently.[8] Despite some similarities in their migration experiences, however, men's and women's actual encounters are quite varied. Usually mothers and fathers live in different types of transnational families, and they have different emotional bonds with their children. As we have seen, men usually continue to prioritize their roles as economic providers while women emphasize emotional intimacy with their children—even if emotion work is conducted over a distance.

There are other changes that occur as well. For instance, when women migrate and earn an income abroad, they may experience a certain personal autonomy and independence. Men, in the mean time, lose ground as the authority figures in their households (Mahler & Pessar, 2006). This is particularly the case when women's earnings are relatively high in comparison to the males in the household. But we need to be very cautious about drawing any conclusions that suggest that women's employment improves the balance of power vis-à-vis men in highly patriarchal contexts. A number of ethnographic accounts indicate the appearance of a cross-culturally widespread phenomenon: as men are displaced as the main breadwinner, they may compensate by attempting to increase their control over their wives and daughters. Thus, under certain conditions, female earnings actually raise women's risk of psychological and physical abuse. Ferree aptly coined this phenomenon as "employment without liberation" (1979). We know very little about how changes in women's status as a result of migration affects male self-esteem and how these factors are tied into issues of race, class, religion, and cultural values. However, there is some evidence that the response of some migrating women to their husband's negative attitudes has been to prolong their time abroad (Pessar, 1986). Women who return to abusive situations often also decide to migrate again. Time abroad has taught them that there are alternative options to the life they were leading in their families and home communities. Upon returning home, female migrants often reject local practices that subordinate female civic and economic empowerment. In other words, migration leads to personal and social transformations, many of which have not yet been explored in a more systematic scholarly manner.

What Can We Learn from Female Transnational Migration Experiences?

The bulk of scholarship on work and family issues is primarily based on middle-class experiences in the United States, and to a lesser extent in Europe. A recent shift in scholarship has broadened the discussion to include some of the experiences of low-income and single-parent families. Those studies emphasize the structural difficulties involved in surviving on a meager income, with inadequate child-care options, and a lack of social mobility. The data on transnational families further expands the work–family discussion. It forces researchers to examine new domains besides the traditional ones such as work–family role strain and work–family balance. These are topics that have dominated the discourse over the last 20 years but in reality only apply to one sector of Western high-income populations. By incorporating work-based migration, and especially transnational mothers into the mix, issues such as geography and region, cultural diffusion, and immigration policy become critical aspects of understanding work–family dynamics.

While transnational mothering is perceived in the scholarly and policy communities as a "new" phenomenon, ethnographic evidence indicates that it is really a contemporary adaptation to economic circumstances. Migrating mothers are building on a model historically enacted by women of color in the United States. To be separated from their children and entrust their care to others is a necessary response to extremely limited economic choices. These women are reworking a familiar family form—one in which women work in order to assist their families financially. However, in the case of migrating mothers, geographical distance plays a new, critical role. Women who migrate cannot easily see their children or other loved ones, and they often do not know when they will be reunified as a family. Moreover, transnational motherhood is usually a phase in the life of these families—it is not a permanent situation. Scholarship on transnational motherhood indicates that most women who migrate fully expect to be reunified with their families (Parrenas, 2010). These women see their separation from their families as temporary. However, in most cases, family reunification cannot happen based on the desires of the migrants. They need to abide by the laws of their host states and the wishes and regulations of their employers. Migrants are thus very much at the mercy of other parties with respect to the length of their absence from home.

Many contemporary migrants wish to bring their children with them, as we saw in the case of Yolanda at the beginning of this chapter. But the chances of this actually happening have become virtually impossible, unless migrants do this in an undocumented fashion. Restrictive policies in high-income states encourage and force migrating women to return to their native societies. As nations tighten their borders, many migrants are given no choice but to return home when their contracts are completed. They are seen as temporary, cheap labor and in many countries stringent laws are in place that make it virtually impossible for temporary migrants to become permanent residents or citizens.

We need to be cognizant of the fact that transnational families are a direct result of unequal global economics and the changes brought on through globalization. While the women who make the choice to migrate are often scapegoated in the process as "bad mothers," we need to understand that they are individuals who often have few options. Their choices need to be framed as part of what Sassen (2002) has referred to as "survival circuits." Women are migrating in order to provide for their families and to help them overcome the lack of economic opportunities in their home societies. Migration for both skilled and unskilled workers is a response to global inequalities that privilege the members of certain societies over those from others.

It is also important to note that transnational migration does not occur in isolation. Women who decide to migrate do so in consultation with their spouses and/or extended families and friends who then take over their domestic responsibilities. We need to be cautious and not apply an ethnocentric lens to perceiving these women's choices as autonomous, and as a form of self-actualization. Currently not much is known about the internal negotiations in families that lead to female migration and the subsequent care arrangements. Some studies such as Parrenas (2010) indicate that while many men understand the economic motivation behind their wives' migrations, they do not necessarily change their caretaking behaviors in response. But besides the division of household labor and child care, we still do not know much about how gender relations within marriage change across distances. For instance, what occurs upon the return of a migrating mother? Does she now have more status in her household, vis-à-vis her husband? In societies where distinct gender socialization remains in place, do the new impressions and experiences a mother may bring back change family values? How do parenting practices change when a mother becomes re-incorporated into a household from which she has been absent for several years? Do women who return from working abroad become more entrepreneurial and set up their own businesses? These are just some of the topics that could expand our understanding of work–family–gender issues and their interrelatedness with economic and cultural contexts.

Synopsis

Much of the Western work–family literature conceives of work as a "choice" that women make which they then balance with the other demands in their lives. As we have seen, this is usually not the case for most transnational mothers. As a general rule, contemporary migrating mothers who choose to work abroad do so in order to improve the life possibilities of their children and to provide for their extended families back home. Many studies indicate that when mothers migrate they entrust the care of their children to a solid extended family network that is in place in their home country. It is precisely this emotional security and family bond that allows them to make this choice. While this is not a model that is familiar to Western middle-class women, it is one that reflects the social reality of African American and immigrant women historically in U.S. society. As they are relatively sure that their children will be well taken care of, they can refocus their energy on breadwinning—an activity that is increasingly reframed by women as a new form of caretaking. Migrating women still perceive themselves as good mothers who are fulfilling their traditional roles—but this role has been re-conceptualized to include economic provision.

From a Western middle-class perspective, breadwinning and caretaking are two distinct activities. However, when looked at through a cross-cultural lens, breadwinning and caretaking are not necessarily dichotomous activities. For instance, in Latin America and West Africa, women

have consistently contributed to the economic welfare of their households in any number of ways. They have sold goods in markets, worked
as traders, cared for other people's children and have run home store-
fronts. These women have participated in economic activities while still
taking care of their children and their homes, and they have blurred the
public–private dichotomy that is an integral aspect of the work–family
debate in the West. Thus, transnational mothers' financial contributions
to their families are not in and of itself a new or major redefinition of
motherhood or caretaking. However, what makes their situation novel
and complicated in ways not previously seen is the distance and often
danger associated with their choices. This is especially true for those
migrants who participate in dangerous border crossings and work illegally in host societies. It is also important to note that many migrants
suffer from extreme social isolation, often not speaking the language and
having little contact with the surrounding culture. They often participate
in the lowest levels of economic activity with little knowledge of their
rights and no recourse to the law should they suffer from abuse or exploitation. Moreover, their separation from their families and communities is
absolute until they return back home. Most migrants are not able to
afford return visits and, thus, must focus their energy on making and
saving as much money as possible. They may form relationships with
other migrants but otherwise are usually not well integrated into their
host societies.

A myriad of complex factors point to the determination of migrating
women to be "good mothers." They endure loneliness and separation in
order to give their children something that they believe would not be possible otherwise—a new and better future. Thus, in this context, caretaking
becomes redefined as a future-oriented activity and not just one that takes
place in the here and now. Transnational motherhood needs to be understood through this lens and not just through a normative model that only
stresses the traumatic aspect of a mother's separation from her children.
When men migrate, they are still perceived as fulfilling their role as
economic providers. In fact, migration may bolster a man's status as it
supports his dominant role as breadwinner. When women migrate, the
cultural ideals and gender scripts that dictate that mothers belong in the home
rise to the forefront. However, in reality the decision to migrate is an economic
one for both men and women. And as ethnographic evidence indicates,
women remain emotionally closely involved with their children despite
their physical absence. They work hard at parenting from afar and attempt
to mitigate any possible consequences of their absence for their children.

The consequences of migration are more traumatic for women than for
men. Men may suffer on an individual level, but women are often also vilified and ostracized on a societal one. As Nicholson (2006) eloquently states,
"A greater awareness of the realities of these women's lives is, I believe, an

indispensable first step toward altering the economic and political patterns that have created the necessity of mothering across national borders" (p. 30). Instead of criticizing and excluding transnational mothers, we need to work on policies that will improve the social and economic conditions that cause them to leave in the first place, while simultaneously refashioning our own immigration laws to allow for family reunification and visitations. High-income societies benefit immensely from the cheap labor that is provided by migrants while delegating them to the lowest rungs of society. It is only by incorporating a stronger social justice perspective into our laws and policies that we can start to improve the conditions of their lives instead of creating even greater obstacles for those who are destitute and seeking new opportunities for themselves and their families.

Notes

1 This example is summarized from Sternberg's introductory work (2010). Dreby (2006) also provides a variety of examples that illustrate the complexity that Mexican families in particular deal with through legal and illegal border crossings.
2 For an extensive discussion of this real case, see Suurmond (2010).
3 A new scholarship is beginning to examine the effects of skilled migrants leaving their home countries. For instance, South Africa is experiencing an epidemic with respect to HIV/AIDS while simultaneously losing its doctors and nurses to other countries. See, Allan and Larsen (2003).
4 This traditional perspective perseveres.
5 Parrenas (2010) has an extensive discussion of this newspaper article and its implications.
6 Even classical literature like the *Odyssey* by Homer depicts the long-term travels of men away from their families and home societies.
7 Fictive kin refers to those associations and friendships that take on a familial aspect.
8 As will be discussed further on, there is a great deal of variation with respect to what women gain in terms of finances and autonomy.

7

THE GLOBALIZATION OF CARING LABOR

The Re-Arrangement of Social Relationships In and Outside of Families

Consider the following scenario.

Laura is a young 32-year-old middle-class teacher in a private school in the Philadelphia suburbs. She is pregnant with her third child and contemplating the next several years of child-care responsibilities. Currently, Laura is legally paying her American college-graduated nanny about two-thirds of her paycheck every month. However, once the third child arrives, she would have to increase her nanny's salary. As she does the math, she realizes that she will be working full-time, however, after she pays the nanny, taxes, social security, and the paycheck company that she uses, she will have $50 left over at the end of the month. Her best friend Suzanne employs a young Dominican mother who has been in the United States for less than a year. Suzanne pays her nanny under the table, thus avoiding paying for the various taxes and the paycheck company. She also pays her a fraction of what Laura pays her "legal" nanny. Suzanne claims that her Dominican nanny is "fabulous" because she has lots of experience with children, being a mom of four herself. However, the children are back in the Dominican Republic and do not "interfere" with the woman's domestic responsibilities here in the States. Now Laura is torn, should she quit the job that she loves and is an important part of her identity? Should she take over all the child care herself and leave the breadwinning to her husband? Or should she join what her friend Suzanne calls the informal economy, and find a cheaper migrant woman to assist her with her home responsibilities? As she debates her options, Laura, who has always been a law abiding individual, also wonders how she really feels about employing someone "under the table" so to speak, and a woman who may also have children but in another country?

The global movement of women entering the paid formal workforce has been coupled with a complex crisis of care. In most societies until relatively recently, care was provided within familial and household settings. This resulted in the private costs of caring labor being hidden from societal view. However, as middle-class women in high-income countries have joined the paid labor force, they have had to rearrange their care responsibilities at home. In some cases, they have negotiated their obligations with their spouses. More commonly, working women have sought out other women and paid them to take over at least some of their household responsibilities including care work. This trend has helped fuel the outmigration of women from low-income countries. In some cases, as we saw in the previous chapter, poor women are leaving their societies in search of new opportunities. However, the trend of transnational migration is not just limited to women with few skills. Increasingly, highly skilled, trained professionals such as nurses and teachers are leaving ill-equipped hospitals and schools in their native countries and taking on jobs in the better paying countries of the world, often leaving behind their own dependents.

Caretaking is Becoming a Global Phenomenon

Labor migration brings together individuals from many different backgrounds, areas of the world, ethnicities, and ages. Hochschild (2001) has termed this phenomenon "global care chains," which she defines as "a series of personal links between people across the globe based on the paid or unpaid work of caring" (p. 131). These global care chains have created new types of relationships and transformed existing ones. This has occurred because caring labor entails emotion work. As Pyle (2006) quotes from a chapter in the United Nations Development Program's (UNDP) *Human Development Report 1999*:

> Studies of globalization and its impact on people focus on incomes, employment, education and other opportunities. Less visible, and often neglected, is the impact on care and caring labour—the task of providing for dependents, for children, the sick, the elderly and (do not forget) all the rest of us exhausted from the demands of daily life. Human development is nourished not only by expanding incomes, schooling, health, empowerment and a clean environment but also by care. And the essence of care is in the human bonds that it creates and supplies. Care, sometimes referred to as social reproduction, is also essential for economic sustainability.
>
> (UNDP, 1999, p. 77 in Pyle, 2006)

Women's entry into the paid labor force has decreased their ability to devote themselves to unpaid care, but this trend has taken place alongside many other changes as well. Demographic trends in the industrialized world have resulted in low fertility rates and high life expectancy in many places. While in some European countries governments have responded by increasing the provision of day care and work–family leave for parents with young children, other care responsibilities such as care for the sick, the elderly, and the disabled have not always garnered quite as much attention. In other parts of the world, other complex care issues have also emerged. For instance, the burden of care for families in sub-Saharan Africa has increased due to the HIV/AIDS pandemic which has killed so many adults. In China, rural–urban migration is leading to whole villages being devoid of healthy adult men and women to farm the land and take care of young children. Some estimates suggest that about one-third of all rural Chinese children are now living with a single mother or their grand-parents, for at least part of the time (Razavi, 2011). However, in low-income countries, the primary cause for the crisis in care stems from the response of governments to a free market, neoliberal economic ideology that focuses on export production and the implementation of Structural Adjustment Policies. As the pressure to reshape their economies has intensified, many governments have reduced state support for social service programs. This move has resulted in many women losing their jobs and simultaneously having reduced access for themselves and their families to much needed social programs.

The Growing Demand for Care Workers

As the number of professional women in high-income countries has grown, a new demand for domestic workers has arisen. Women in poorer countries have seized on this employment opportunity and have responded by migrating to find work in the rapidly expanding service economy. While traditionally the home was the realm of family caring labor, conducted out of emotional bonds and feelings of obligation, increasingly care has become a commodity, bought and sold on the open market. Increasingly in high-income contexts, women are outsourcing their traditional care responsibilities to other women who are typically strangers to them. They are dependent on these women to provide both physical and emotional care to those individuals they may be closest to: their babies, young children, elderly parents, relatives, and the disabled and ill. This relationship between work and emotion makes care labor a somewhat unique market commodity. As Nancy Folbre (2008) states:

> Whether provided to children or adults, care involves personal connection and emotional attachment. Care services are often "co-produced" by care providers and care recipients. Parents and teachers must elicit cooperation from children; similarly,

nurses and home care providers must elicit cooperation from patients. Care is often person- and context-specific. As a result, its quality is heterogeneous and difficult to monitor or measure. The intrinsic motivation of the care provider often affects the quantity and quality of the services provided. Indeed, the sense of "being cared for" is an important by-product of inherent value.

(p. 375)

Despite the importance of caring work on an individual level, employment in care labor is routinely poorly paid and often temporary in nature. Non-familial caregivers have few legal rights, especially if they are migrants or undocumented or both. This results in a form of employment that is at the bottom of the social hierarchy with respect to benefits, pay, and working conditions. The devaluation of care labor is routinely associated with its feminized nature. In other words, because women perform this work it is seen as not as important or as valued in society.

While the "crisis of care," as it is often termed, has drawn a great deal of scrutiny in high-income countries, care arrangements in developing countries have not received the same level of attention. As women in the developing world have entered the paid labor force, they also have had to face the same dilemma as women in high-income countries: who will now care for their dependents. Women who work locally as well as women who migrate continue to be responsible for their domestic tasks. Of primary concern is that they need to work out care obligations. For women who work outside of the home, this may entail finding someone who takes over their responsibilities throughout the time that they are away from their families. For women who migrate, the situation is even more complex. These women need to arrange their home lives in such a way that their care and domestic responsibilities are met on a longer-term, consistent basis (Rodriguez, 2006; Parrenas, 2012). Some women in developing countries who take on paid employment rely on spouses. However, employment reports indicate that more frequently these women rely on their daughters, mothers, or other female kin for assistance. In fact, men may become resentful at the expectation that their roles are to change due to their wives' employment status (Connell, 2005).

Complicating the caring labor dilemma is that we are witnessing a global increase in households with young children that are maintained by single parents, primarily women. For instance, according to the 1960 U.S. Census, 9 percent of children at the time were living in a single-parent household. By 2010, that number had increased to 27 percent. And worldwide, about 16 percent of children live in single-parent households, of which about 80 percent are headed by women (Rampell, 2010). These single mothers have to balance the complexity of formal paid labor and family caregiving often with few social supports. Many programs and policies do not take the situation of the single caregiver into account. In fact, even feminist scholarship often emphasizes unequal relationships between heterosexual couples, with little or no regard for the fact that many women in both high- and low-income contexts do not have a male spouse or partner to rely on for economic or household assistance. Chant (2010) calls this the "feminization of responsibility and/or obligation."

Issues around care have begun to elicit scholarly attention with a special focus on Asia, the United States, and Europe. These are the regions of the world that are the primary recipients of migrating care workers and where public sentiment about these workers is often quite negative. In the public mind in high-income countries, the physical presence of migrants is often associated with illegality (even if they are documented), increased crime, depletion of state funds, and the exploitation of federal programs. There is little public discourse about the needs that are being filled by these migrants and the conditions under which they perform this work. Moreover, Pyle (2006) points out that despite the extensive interest in migration and the increased flow of transnational caring labor to high-income countries, very little notice has been paid to what she calls the "care deficit." Here, Pyle refers to the care that the dependents of migrants need, as well as the often difficult conditions under which these individuals work in host societies.

Scholarship on caring labor has drawn attention to the mechanisms through which households and families are embedded in globalization processes. They illustrate that the reproductive work of the home is now an integral aspect of the global economy, and that non-material resources such as emotion work are also an aspect of globalization. The changing nature of global migration patterns particularly points to the mechanisms through which women and households have become integral parts of global markets. By examining the growing phenomenon of paid caring labor, we can more clearly identify the interaction of micro- and macro-level factors. Caring labor has moved out of the private domain of the home and become a commodity, to be bought and sold in the public marketplace. Thus, the private–public dichotomy that has been a characteristic of family–workplace relations in industrialized societies is rapidly disintegrating. The needs of the household have become something that is negotiated in a more open forum and that has become in many places a service, the price of which is dependent on the marketplace. In addition, the linkages between those individuals that need to purchase caring labor and those who sell this labor, highlight new types of relationships. Increasingly, these are associations between women from very different backgrounds, and from varied cultural and regional parts of the world. These new global care chains point to interdependent relationships that cross multiple boundaries (Hochschild, 2001). Global care chains shed light on the feminized nature of current migratory patterns and serve to illustrate the ever-increasing closer linkages between individuals, house-holds, markets, and states.

Much scholarship on caring labor is primarily focused on the transna-tional flows of domestic workers, the employment niches they fill, and what are seen as the plusses and minuses of migration. As was mentioned previously, little attention has been paid to the care needs of women and families in low-income contexts. This deficiency complicates a compre-hensive discussion of caring labor. However, the scholarship on care that does exist, points to five clear trends: 1) both paid and unpaid care is mainly performed by women; 2) care work is increasingly commodified; 3) state support for care labor is declining; 4) care labor creates new social relationships that span geographical distances; and 5) care work creates and increases status distinctions between women with respect to class, education, race, and ethnicity. We examine these trends more closely in this chapter.

Care Labor as "Women's Work"

In virtually every part of the world, caring labor is very much a part of "women's work." In particular, women's unpaid caring labor has drawn the attention of feminist scholars who point out that women's involve-ment with care in general contributes to their lower wages (England & Folbre, 1999). In order to be clear about what is meant by the term "care," we will use the Daly and Lewis (2000) definition as the activities and relations involved in meeting the physical and emotional needs of dependent adults and children. The term "care" also implies the social and economic context and the associated values and behaviors that are integral aspects of these frameworks.

Despite the fact that an increasing number of women with young chil-dren have entered the paid labor force, research indicates that there has not been any significant gender changes with respect to child-care respon-sibilities. That said, some analysts have recently become critical of the almost exclusive focus on women in global care chains. They point out that a disproportionate focus on women has ignored the involvement of an increasing number of men in domestic labor (Kilkey, 2010). But even these critics acknowledge that, specifically when it comes to care labor, this remains a female responsibility, and has also evolved into a primarily female-dominated profession. These days in the industrialized and devel-oping world, men may find employment in households; however, they will usually be hired as domestics in order to clean, garden, or cook. Men are very rarely employed as carers unless it is in a caring facility such as at a hospital or old age residence. Caring for others, be they children, the elderly, the sick, or the disabled, remains virtually completely within the female domain. This is true in the realms of caring based on individual desires and feelings of obligations, as well as with respect to caring as a profession.

In the contemporary situation, even if they work full time, women remain responsible for the unpaid work of taking care of young children, the disabled, the ill, and the elderly. Despite the complexities of the current social environment, Folbre (2008) points out that surveys conducted on this topic in the United States consistently indicate that regardless of gender, most men and women disapprove of women who do not fulfill their care responsibilities themselves. However, increasingly, women in both Western and non-Western contexts are being forced to negotiate their care obligations with paid employment. In response, women employ a wide variety of strategies to meet the challenges of their daily lives. Some women rely on daughters, other female relatives, and close friends to assist them. Mothers and sisters are particularly important sources of support, specifically with child care. Well-to-do women often respond to their care obligations by turning to the marketplace.[1] Nowadays working professional women often pay low-wage female service workers to assist them with care responsibilities in their homes. If they have children, they increasingly place their children in day-care centers that are virtually 100 percent female run. Women who do not have many economic resources often work out barter arrangements with relatives and friends (Ryan, 2007).[2] They exchange services in kind in order to assist one another with their work and domestic responsibilities. This continuation of a gendered division of caring labor is called by some analysts "relations between women" (Rollins, 1985). Even though gender role beliefs, particularly in the United States and Europe, have moved toward a gender convergence model, caring labor remains primarily a female issue. Middle-class men in Western societies increasingly support an ideology of gender equality and are now more likely to help with household chores and child care. However, virtually every study and survey indicates that women remain the primary caregivers for infants, the ill, the elderly, and the disabled. Thus, caring labor consistently remains in the female realm to be negotiated within the home, and increasingly in the marketplace.

The Commodification of Care Work

The increased commodification of caring labor provides insight into the changing roles of families, markets, and the role of governments. While the care of vulnerable individuals was once a service that was primarily performed privately and without pay, this work is quickly moving into the marketplace. As care labor becomes a commodity to be bought and sold, it is also directly influenced by state policies. Governments play a role with respect to care because they establish work policies and provide resources that can assist families with their care responsibilities. As an increasing number of women from low-income countries migrate to high-income countries to take up employment in care-related occupations, states determine their citizenship status, residency requirements, and legal rights with respect to employment. Caretaking, a formerly private activity, has thus moved into the public sphere. However, caretaking tends not to be part of the formal market economy. Instead, the need for care workers has assisted, in part, the tremendous growth of the informal economy.

The emergence of the informal economy is very much a critical aspect of globalization. As markets have become deregulated and companies have shifted their work to low-income countries, the conditions for workers have changed. Large portions of the labor force in low-income countries are now employed in informal activities that include self-employment and subcontracted work conducted out of the home. This type of employment is characterized by unstable working conditions, lack of formal regulations, and often no legal protections. One consequence is that the relative bargaining power of individuals with a lack of skills has lessened (Beneria, 2007a). In high-income countries, the informal sector has grown as well. A need for low-wage workers has fueled the increase in informalized jobs, especially in the domestic arena. Women, in particular, have been affected by these changes in the marketplace. In low-income countries they are often part of the informal economy, conducting their work out of their homes and balancing their care-taking responsibilities with market work. In the case of out migration to high-income countries, women are increasingly the workers who are subject to state regulations but with little bargaining power vis-à-vis their employers. An often overlooked point is that middle-class women in high- and low-income contexts are also a part of the informal economy as they are the ones who hire domestics and carers, set the working and payment conditions, and negotiate the spectrum of care responsibilities.

Caring labor and the individuals who provide these services are an integral part of today's informal economy. Women engaged in caring labor usually do not have formal employment contracts, nor do they have unions they can turn to in cases of abuse.[3] Women who migrate transnationally and take up work as live-in domestics or nannies often face the hardship of being isolated within households. Their living and working conditions are hidden from view and they may not know who to turn to in cases of abuse. For instance, Chin (1997) reports that many Filipina and Indonesian domestic workers are considered "girl-slaves" in Malaysia. At times, despite being caregivers, they may have to perform dangerous tasks such as washing windows in high-rise apartment buildings, or being exposed to other health and safety risks.[4] Cultural norms also differ with respect to the treatment of domestic workers. Due to their isolation, these workers may be subjected to verbal and physical abuse and may experience humiliating treatment from those they care for (Pyle, 2006). In some cases, they may not be given adequate food, enough time to sleep, or much personal privacy.

Despite the intimate nature of this form of employment and the high level of responsibility that it entails, in most places migrating women cannot set their own price—the price for their labor is determined by market conditions, which include the availability of other laborers and the needs of that particular community. The informal economy thrives on these unregulated transactions. Through the lack of regulations and oversight, employers can establish their own conditions without regard for the rights and feelings of their employees. Ethnographic evidence indicates that employers tend to place many limitations on domestic workers, and have very high expectations of them (Ehrenreich & Hochschild, 2003). Even in societies such as Singapore, which is often upheld as an exemplary modern society, domestic workers have few rights and many obligations (Yeoh, Huang, & Willis, 2000).

Domestic workers who migrate are often unable to change their jobs due to legalities with respect to visa restrictions. However, their actual experiences in households are often outside of the purview of the legal system. In many countries, that which happens within a household is understood to be outside of the jurisdiction of the state and is perceived as a private matter. This situation points to the interesting paradox where caring labor is a commodified aspect of the marketplace but understood to be outside of the realm of the government. However, this is actually not the case. The state plays an important role with respect to caring labor, especially in helping determine work–family balance, and in regulating the supply of migrants who can enter a country to fill that particular employment niche.

Differential State Support for Care Labor

The issue of care is restructuring the overall relationship between families, markets, and the state. It also encompasses a potential change in gender norms. Under the male breadwinner–female homemaker family model, women were obligated to be full-time caregivers and received compensation for their work through their husbands' economic provision of them. In many countries around the world, states supported this model based on the belief that the family is the best provider of care. Benefit policies also upheld this family model, and states provided little in the way of social services to assist with caring responsibilities. Changes in gender ideologies and in employment opportunities, however, have negated this model.

From a global perspective, governments have responded in a variety of ways to the work–family dilemma that has been brought on through women's increased formal employment. In high-income countries such as the United States, backing for programs that assist families with care work have not garnered much political or social support. In contrast to, for example, European high-income countries, the programs that do exist in the United States are means tested and available only to those people who live in poverty. Despite this fact, family support programs have experienced dramatic reductions over the last decade. And virtually no new programs have been created that would assist families with their care labor. The United States is not alone in this movement. Many high-income countries in the 1980s and 1990s witnessed some form of decline with respect to the services provided by welfare states. Social service programs were eliminated, federal responsibility has been transferred to the state and local levels, and faith-based and community organizations are taking over the provision of basic social welfare services (Mattingly, 2001; Trask, 2010).

In the European context, a concern with rapidly declining fertility levels has recently led to some renewed legislative efforts to assist families in reconciling work–family responsibilities. For instance, in the Scandinavian countries, a move to allow women to enter the labor force was subsequently supported by the development of quality child care and other social policies designed to help families reconcile work and family life. These changes were instituted as early as the 1970s. Other European countries have followed suit, but depending in great part on the state of their fertility rates. As women in European countries have entered the paid labor force, if they were faced with inadequate care options, their response was to remain childless (Esping-Andersen, 2000). This is a particularly striking phenomenon in countries such as Italy and Spain that have very strong culturally sanctioned familial orientations. In other words, popular rhetoric espouses the importance of families and of having children in particular.

Despite a stated emphasis on families and the importance of raising fertility levels, there has been a wide range of responses to instituting family-friendly policies throughout Europe. For instance, in order to stem declining fertility levels, Spain has introduced laws that mandate paid and unpaid leaves for care work. In France and Finland, governments have instituted high-quality day-care programs and flexible working hours which has helped facilitate the negotiation of families' employment and domestic responsibilities. It is interesting to note, however, that in France the *écoles maternelles* or preschools, which admit children from the age of three and which virtually all children between the ages of three and six attend, were formed for educational purposes and to create loyal citizens— not necessarily to assist families in reconciling work–family issues (Morel, 2007). While there is a great deal of variation throughout high-income countries with respect to subsidies and support for carework, an increasing number of European countries are increasing their child-care provisions and taking into account family caregiving for the elderly. We will examine some of those policies in greater detail in Chapter 9.

The Problem of Care in the Developing World

The situation with respect to care in low-income countries, as well as India and China, is quite different. A byproduct of globalization has been a decrease in state support for those activities that strengthen and assist families. This move has been closely tied to the economic shift of many low-income countries to export production. The policies of transnational institutions such as the International Monetary Fund (IMF) have facilitated this transition as they have encouraged the removal of price controls, declines in state subsidies and employment, and the weakening of social programs. In many of these areas, there is a rising prevalence of households with young children maintained by mothers who are negotiating paid employment with caregiving with virtually no assistance from men or government services (Shahra, 2011).

In many countries today, in addition to cuts in programming and services, benefits are increasingly tied to strict citizenship requirements. What we find is that while legal residents, particularly in high-income countries, have witnessed the reduction of social services, non-citizens have experienced the growing denial of benefits to them. Throughout Europe and the United States political hostility toward migrants has focused on their use of social programs, leading to the further elimination of benefits, and creating an environment where immigrants feel unwelcome and at times frightened to access services.

Citizens and non-citizens are not just separated by legal status but by economics as well. In order for an economic niche for service workers to exist, they need to earn quite a bit less money than their employers. Women will not pay for dependent care if the income they make is equivalent to what they are paying an outsider to take care of this responsibility for them. As we saw in introductory case study of Laura the middle-class American teacher, there is little incentive for a woman to continue to work if most of her income needs to be used to pay someone else to take care of her domestic obligations. Thus, in one sense citizens in high-income countries are benefiting from the global economic restructuring that is encouraging and forcing workers to take on low-wage jobs in other places. Through the maintenance of a pool of low-wage workers, citizens in high-income countries can continue to pursue their interests and occupations. This creates an environment where relatively high-earning women now have affiliations with low-income women from geographically disparate places. A complex aspect of this relationship is the often forgotten domestic situation of these low-income women. As was mentioned previously, they too have to negotiate work–family obligations, but with considerably fewer resources.

Care Labor Creates New Relationships that Span Geographic and Social Distances

The move of care labor out of the home and into the marketplace highlights the increasing number of relationships between migrating women and their female employers. As Mattingly (2001, p. 373) states, "Since one group employs the other, the two groups of women are tied together through transactions of caring labor." Both groups of women face the same challenge of having to negotiate care for vulnerable dependents. However, this is where their commonalities end. Women who have economic resources also have a certain amount of power, within their households and over their employees. They can dictate the conditions under which their employees work, and how much care their dependents receive. For instance, it is not uncommon for well-to-do mothers in cities such as New York and Los Angeles to employ multiple nannies, so that they have 24/7 child care, even if they themselves do not work. Low-income women do not have the same options. Instead, they must negotiate their dependent care with the resources they have access to. At times, low-income women may use monetary resources but more commonly they exchange favors, gifts, or dependent care.

In the absence of state support for working mothers, women in low- and high-income contexts have constructed complex networks amongst themselves to fulfill the needs for caring labor. Many of these relationships occur outside of the purview of the formal economy and at times may even be in violation of government rules. As the need for employees in households has expanded, that niche is increasingly filled by undocumented workers. Employers tend not to ask for residency papers when hiring someone to clean their houses, take care of their dependents, or do other home-related chores. And in those few cases when they do ask for those papers, they are unable to identify legal documents from forged ones. Thus, household caring labor has become a domain where illegal transactions can occur, but not necessarily with intent by the employers. Most domestic workers never report their income, do not pay taxes, and are otherwise not visible in the formal economy. The black market nature of domestic work makes paid caring labor an extremely difficult occupation to track and support. Paradoxically, many of the same individuals who hire undocumented workers to work in their homes support tightening the rules around immigration and are not supportive of providing benefits to non-citizens (Mattingly, 2001).

Due to the needs created through women's employment outside of the home, care labor is now a vital part of the market economy. Around the world, dual-earner households or working single parents increasingly rely on low-wage service workers to assist them in fulfilling their home obligations. As has been noted, this niche is rapidly being filled by migrant women. However, unlike in export-processing zones or call centers, caring work cannot be removed and conducted in a geographically isolated region. Instead, an individual's physical presence is necessary to conduct this work. Thus, a necessary condition of the growing service sector is the presence of the individuals who serve as domestics and carers. Migrants need to set up their own households and live in the areas where their services are needed. We thus have a paradoxical situation in many high-income countries: migrants are often unwelcome and face hostile social climates. Laws and policies constrict their movements and they are often a socially invisible part of host societies. However, the relatively affluent citizenry is dependent on the relatively cheap labor of these non-citizens. Migrant service workers inhabit a new transnational zone where, with respect to political rights, they do not belong to their host societies, but their labor is a crucial aspect of the economic functioning of those respective markets.

Complicating this discussion are also the elaborate networks of care labor that characterize so many relationships *between* women in low-income contexts. However, what is unclear in these discussions is the extent to which women benefit or are constrained by these relationships. For instance, Hondagneu-Sotelo (1994) argues that despite a certain cost women primarily benefit from their involvements in care networks with other women. Mattingly (2001) disputes this analysis and points out that there are real costs and constraints embedded in exchanges that occur within family networks. In other words, certain obligations are set up when family members exchange caring labor. This exchange is not purely altruistic and comes with either a social or economic expectation, or both. When a migrating woman enters into a caring labor exchange relationship with another woman, even if she is a relative, she becomes embedded in a transaction of mutual responsibility. In other words, in exchange for care, she becomes obligated to repay the caregiver for her time and services. As the French sociologist Marcel Mauss explains in *The Gift* (1923/1990), exchanges between individuals are built on self-interest *and* concern for others. We enter into exchange relationships due to our desire to help out, but also to profit from the relationship. Nowhere are those principles more evident than in exchanges that involve caring labor. Women who draw on family members to assist them with their caring labor often take on a longer-term financial responsibility for these relatives. For instance, a portion of the money migrants send back home may be delegated to a mother or aunt who is taking care of the children or other dependents who have been left behind. That obligatory exchange relationship does not necessarily end with the return of the migrant. It may extend far into the future depending on the relationship and the cultural context within which the negotiation took place.

At times migrating women delegate the care of vulnerable dependents to their oldest daughters. In order to negotiate work–family obligations, many women in low-income contexts employ this same strategy. The consequences for young girls in participating in domestic caring labor are very serious. By taking on increased domestic responsibilities, girls may not be able to continue their education, take on new training opportunities, or pursue work that may be more lucrative. In this system of stratified hierarchical female labor, a differential value is put on women's work. Within this hierarchy, young girl's labor is the least valued. Girls are forced to support their mothers by working with little or even without pay and may lose out on future educational and job opportunities for themselves. The cost of participating in caring labor decreases the market value of the girls even though their mothers may benefit financially from this situation. We, thus, have a paradoxical situation where women in the same family are differentially affected through participation in the market economy. This situation can have equally negative consequences for girls if the mother works outside of the home or if she migrates.

Care Work Creates and Increases Status Distinctions Between Women with Respect to Class, Education, Race, and Ethnicity

Women who are engaged in care work in other countries face a situation of double jeopardy: they are female and migrants, and often also belong to a group that is a minority in the society in which they are working. Socially, they are often even separated from men from their home countries. Due to the female stereotypes associated with caring labor, men for the most part are unable to enter this profession. The few men that are employed in jobs such as nurses are stigmatized for taking on an occupation that is perceived as "women's work." Both in high-income and low-income contexts, generally employers do not want to hire men to take care of their children or elderly dependents. The employment of women in caretaking jobs is based on gender-stereotyped assumptions that suppose that women are more nurturing and docile, and will be more willing to take orders from other women. It is also assumed that they will accept low wages based on the belief that they are secondary earners in their households (Yeoh, Huang, & Willis, 2000).

The pronounced preference for female caretakers creates divisions between men and women who stem from the same home societies. This situation also creates an even greater distance between migrants and their host societies. The migrants do not have many supports to draw on—not even other citizens of their respective countries, further isolating them. Moreover, in high-income countries, the increasingly commodified version of caretaking is now an entity that is more and more associated with, and delivered by, women who belong to minority groups in their host societies. These racial and gender stereotypes and prejudices further feminize and marginalize care labor, even as this responsibility moves from the household into the marketplace.

Women who migrate transnationally to provide caring labor often face various types of discrimination. A number of ethnographic studies indicate that the religion, ethnicity, and race of women come into play with respect to the types of jobs they can access and how they are treated if they work in a household. For instance, Indonesian women in Taiwan are often placed in more labor-intensive jobs (such as caring for the aged or very sick) while Filipina women are channeled into easier domestic employment situations (Loveband, 2004). In Singapore, Filipina domestic workers may receive one or two days off per month, while women from Sri Lanka receive one or none, and Indonesian migrants may receive no days off. Other types of discrimination come into play as well; for instance, whether women belong to the racial majority versus the racial minority. Studies of migrant nurses indicate that those belonging to the racial minority in a certain society may receive more difficult shifts and have less access to training and promotion opportunities. Immigrant nurses working in the United States and in Saudi Arabia reported that they are looked down upon by colleagues and patients despite possessing good English skills (Pyle, 2006). Women who work in families and households are often the most vulnerable to abuse and exploitation. They are at the mercy of their employers with respect to the number of hours they work, the conditions under which they work, and even how much they are paid. Studies have documented that household employees often do not receive adequate food or time off. They are also susceptible to physical and sexual abuse. While workers are aware of the prejudice and discrimination they face, they are also aware of the vulnerability of their situations. This makes them reluctant to report illegalities to the authorities.

Transnational care workers commonly find themselves in situations where others have power and control over them, leaving them with limited means to negotiate their employment and living conditions. Depending on their legal status, they may also suffer from the psychological pressure that accompanies having to worry about deportation if they are undocumented residents. As Pyle (2006) points out, "The level of care they experience in their own lives is often seriously deficient" (p. 300). Due to the low status of caretakers and particularly migrant carers, few programs or policies address their living or working conditions. They are viewed as outsiders and often as infringing and exploiting their host societies. It is not uncommon to hear politicians highlighting the supposed abuses of the social system that are perpetuated in particular by undocumented migrants. It is much less popular to emphasize the contributions of migrants to the social and economic functioning of their host societies.

Care Work is Increasingly Within the Domain of Lower-Income Women

As this discussion has indicated, in the contemporary context of market exchanges of caring labor, racial, ethnic, and economic inequalities between women are highlighted. Differences in region, race, ethnicity, education, and class manifest themselves in the relationships that are constructed between different groups of women. As care labor and other previously unpaid household responsibilities shift out of the domain of middle-class women in high- and low-income societies, they have become the paid responsibility of lower-class women. While Western feminists of the last several decades predicted that the growing economic power of women would lead to a rearrangement of roles between men and women, this has not necessarily happened. Especially with respect to caring labor, those responsibilities have remained female centered and, at most, are negotiated between different groups of women. However, the women who have taken over a paid version of caring labor have even less social support than the middle-class women who used to perform this work. As Nancy Folbre (2008) suggests, these aspects of caregiving point to the growing divisions between women. Instead of uniting women in a shared enterprise, the new networks of female caregiving emphasize the inequalities between them.

The uneven levels of state and social support for caring labor, force women around the globe to create their own solutions for balancing work–family obligations. Depending on the local environment and the economic resources at their disposal, women work out very different solutions to caring for their vulnerable dependents. In the European context, where there is public support for the importance of care labor especially for families with young children, women have the option of placing their children in high-quality child-care programs. They also receive support in terms of family leave for taking care of the ill and the elderly. In the United States and many countries in the developing world, families have to rely on the informal economy for their caring solutions. Women have, thus, created female-centered exchange networks in order to cope with these obligations. However, in each of these scenarios, be they state supported or purely financial transactions in the market economy, migrant women are playing an increasingly important role in the delivery of care labor. In order to understand the complex dynamics underlying the delivery of care, the marginalization of caregiving and its primarily feminine nature need to be kept at front and center of any analysis.

Case Study: The Omission of Male Domestic Workers

While, as has been discussed extensively, care work is almost exclusively in the female domain, a small but growing number of analysts are pointing out that the domestic arena more broadly defined is not always exclusively dominated by women. For instance, Kilkey (2010) highlights the fact that approximately 10 percent of individuals employed in households across the European Union are male, and that the rate is higher when looked at from a country by country basis. For instance, she points out that between 2004 and 2007 approximately 39 percent of individuals working in individuals' homes in the UK were men. A study about India (Qayum & Ray, 2010) in the 1990s revealed that one-third of the domestic workers in Bengal were male, and there is an even higher percentage in select countries in Africa, such as Zambia (Bartolomei, 2010). Kilkey also reminds us that having male domestics is considered "status enhancing" in certain contexts (2010, p. 131). Moreover, we know little about the types of work that male domestics do these days as virtually all scholarly attention is focused on females.

The few studies that exist in the area of male carers reveal that male domestic workers must negotiate the tensions that result from participating in what is generally regarded as "women's work." Men attempt to resolve this issue by re-conceptualizing their work as "bread-winning activities," thereby adding masculine overtones to their activities (Qayum & Ray, 2010). They may also refuse to participate in some of the most intimate aspects of domestic work (such as hand washing underwear) in an attempt to distance themselves from the feminine aspects of domestic work (Chopra, 2006). Kilkey (2010) also points out that employers have to cope with stereotypes inherent with employing males to work as carers and domestics. Many employers do so by hiring migrant men. The fact that these men are foreign allows employers to portray them as an "other" in a manner that would not be socially acceptable should they hire a native citizen to perform the same duties.

These days, most employers in Western high-income contexts are more comfortable hiring men to garden, maintain the exterior of houses and yards, and for home repair. For instance, currently, in popular culture in the United Kingdom, the "Polish Plumber" has become a common stereotype. However, as Kilkey (2010) highlights there are currently very limited scholarly efforts to situate "men within global care chains" (p. 138). Thus, while there is a burgeoning literature on the *feminization* of care, there are much sparser efforts when it comes to *gendering* care and domestic work in general. Moreover, because much of the type of work that is often performed by men is not conceptualized as domestic labor, their contributions to social reproduction, more broadly defined, are ignored and/or marginalized. As Kilkey (2010) astutely points out, however, exploring the kinds of work that men perform for pay in the domestic sphere would give us greater insight into how class, gender, and race intersect and how meaning is created around work, boundary formation, and concepts of masculinity and femininity.

Potential Models for Ensuring Gender Equity in Families

As the male breadwinner model in which heterosexual couples divided work and care labor along gender lines loses its relevance, particularly in the contemporary Western context, new family arrangements are taking its place. This has led to debates as to which societal models should replace this long-term normative prototype. For instance, Fraser (1994) explicates a "universal breadwinner model" where either men or women are wage earners and care is shifted out of the home to the market and the state. As an alternative, she also suggests a "caregiver parity model" in which women who have significant care responsibilities are able to support themselves and their families through a system of caregiver allowances. In other words, women would be compensated for their caregiving work and would also be able to enter the formal labor force on a part-time basis. In this model, care would remain in the home and not be outsourced to the market or the state. However, Claassen (2011) disagrees that these types of models ensure gender equity. She points out that the universal breadwinner model rewards the male norm of paid work and that caregiving becomes relegated as an activity that has little economic and, thus, social worth. The universal breadwinner model also creates a second shift for women since even though they are working they still need to make care arrangements. The caregiver parity model is also not recognized by her as a satisfactory solution. She explains that the labor market becomes divided into those individuals who are full-time caregivers and the ones who are on a part-time work path, the "mommy track." When this happens, caring remains associated with being female, and being the main breadwinner remains a masculine activity (Fraser, 1994).

Fraser suggests a new, utopian option in which work and care would be associated with masculinity and femininity equally. She delineates a model in which all jobs would presume that workers also have caregiving responsibilities. In order to meet their care responsibilities, workers would be able to work a shorter week and have more flexible schedules. The state would support care work through a network of government-funded institutions and quality child-care providers. Her model even includes a societal transformation wherein some care work would be taken over by friends and associates on an informal basis. In other words, care work would move out of the hetero normative nuclear family. Claassen (2011) refers to this idea as the universal caregiver model since it shifts caring to a central role in the lives and activities of individuals, on a par with wage labor. From this perspective, neither work nor care would predominate. Both would share an equally important role in individuals' lives.

Claassen also suggests another possible societal option: a modification of the caregiver parity model. A complex compensation schema would reward caregivers either through direct payment for their care labor or would allow them to be compensated for buying care services. By employing this strategy, no specific model of care compensation would dominate and individuals could work out solutions to their unique situations. The underlying principle of a modified caregiver parity model would be that each family has its own distinctive set of circumstances and that different situations require varied alternatives and solutions. This option recognizes that individuals need to have agency and choice when negotiating their domestic circumstances. By being able to draw from different types of compensation schemas, carers could decide on the optimal arrangements for their dependents. Or conversely, for instance, in the case of an elderly adult who needed care, that individual could decide for his or herself if they would prefer to be taken care of by a family member or if they would prefer market-based care services. This model allows the care recipient a certain element of freedom of choice and could free up adult children from a personalized obligation that they may not be able to fulfill.

These various possibilities raise the question as to which scenario is the one most likely to be instituted in high- and low-income countries in the near future. As the above discussion has illustrated, since states are reducing expenditures across the board, new policies that shorten working weeks and institute government-run quality care facilities are unlikely options in many places. Instead, it is the universal breadwinner option that seems to be most promising in high- and low-income contexts. As women around the globe assume an equivalent breadwinner role as men, they increasingly find themselves in situations where they need to purchase or negotiate care arrangements. And despite a general growing move away from the normative heterosexual breadwinner–homemaker family, caregiving remains a highly gendered activity.

Given current global trends, it is likely that even more women are going to join the paid labor force. This suggests that balancing work and family obligations will continue to be a growing issue. Shahra (2011), however, points out that there are certain new developments that have been omitted in discussions of care. For instance, outside of sub-Saharan Africa, fertility levels have declined in many parts of the developing world. Declining fertility levels translate into lesser care responsibilities for women. Also, many places now have clean water, electricity, and better domestic technologies that reduce the amount of housework women have to do. Even though this is happening in an uneven manner around the world, there is also a concurrent rise in the availability of pre-primary education and child care. As a whole, this means that at least for some groups of women there are fewer domestic obligations and that some traditional care responsibilities have shifted out of the home to other institutions.

Shahra (2011) points out that it is not clear from the current evidence that the overall need for the provision of unpaid care has increased everywhere. We do know, however, that in some places and for certain groups of women, there is most definitely a crisis of care underway (Folbre, 2006). Moreover, given the aging of the global population, including in the developing world, the issue of care for the elderly is sure to rise in importance.[5] There is a tendency in the care literature just to focus on women with young children. However, the care of the elderly, the ill, and the disabled is an equally important matter, and often even more difficult to reconcile with work obligations. In many places care of the elderly, the ill, and the disabled is naturally assumed to be a family responsibility and there are no formal venues to turn to for families that do not have those capacities. As an increasing number of women work outside of the home and also migrate for work, this issue is certain to create even more problems than are associated with care today. Thus, while Shahra (2011) may be correct in her assessment that there are improvements on some fronts with respect to care issues, it is likely that new care complexities will emerge in the global arena. It is thus instructive to consider the potential of varying care models, even if they seem utopian in nature in the current context.

Since we know that issues of care, especially care of the elderly are bound to increase, given current demographics and improvements in helping keep elderly individuals alive, we need to be working toward advising policy-makers as to possible scenarios and solutions. The complexities of care are an issue that has universal implications. Virtually everyone has someone in their realm of close acquaintanceship that will at some point require care. Even for those individuals who have no children or elderly parents and relatives, it is not inconceivable that one of their close friends or work colleagues will at some time require some form of caregiving. While an increasing number of individuals in metropolitan areas are choosing to live alone, they are still enmeshed in relationship circles.[6] Issue of care will arise in those situations and we will need societal solutions.

Synopsis

As this discussion has indicated, when women become involved in care networks they also pay a cost—be it in monetary terms or social obligations to others. Those who are able to buy caring labor services become an important part of the informal economy. They help determine the price of the labor and working conditions of other women. However, we know little about the emotional side of the equation. When women hire other women to take care of their caring labor, they are also passing on some of the emotion work that comes along with the relationship to the young, the sick, the elderly, and the disabled. Having someone take care of your aging mother or your six-month-old infant is not the same type of responsibility as having someone wash your clothes or clean your house. Despite a prolific literature on caring labor, many of these analytic distinctions have not yet been subjected to close scrutiny. Oftentimes, every type of domestic labor is placed under the same umbrella, and domestic workers are spoken of as a unified group. But caring labor is distinct from other domestic services and the individuals who perform this work are not a homogeneous group. Citizenship, race, ethnicity, regionality, education, and class create sharp dividing lines between women, despite the fact that increasingly they are joined by similar needs in complex economic and emotion work transactions.

Economic inequalities have been exacerbated as globalization has facilitated the growth of markets and the decrease in social policy spending. These inequalities are present in every aspect of social life and affect the lives of individuals in high- and low-income contexts. Both women who need to purchase care and those who provide care are enmeshed in complex relationships where they are increasingly dependent on the care labor of other women. Women are now inextricably tied to other women in a global environment where much of their labor is under paid and undervalued. In order to effect change and assist individuals balance their work–family responsibilities, we need to enact policies that acknowledge care labor and the global connections that are now such an integral aspect of this process. Also, we cannot limit the discussion to child-care and fertility concerns.[7] Care labor involves every age group and has as its central elements both physical and emotional requirements. Issues of care highlight the economics of domestic responsibilities, the role of the state in the private lives of families, and the emotional work that is an intrinsic aspect of caregiving. Moreover, as many feminist philosophers point out, quality care is an ethical obligation in a socially and morally just society. Every individual regardless of their age, gender, race, ethnicity, or sexuality deserves adequate care. Conversely, family and external caregivers require support, respite, and adequate compensation. We cannot treat care purely as a commodity that can be bought and sold at its lowest cost. Care is part of the human condition and must be recognized as such.

Notes

1 Folbre (2008) cites a finding from Catalyst that about 33 percent of working professional women in the United States who have not yet reached leadership positions do not want to have children. She also cites the statistic that 49 percent of women who make more than $100,000 are childless.
2 See the ethnographic account *All our Kin* by Carol Stack (1974) for one of the first in-depth descriptions about how poor families assist one another to survive. Many of her early observations about obligations between fictive kin still hold true today.
3 There is currently a movement underway to organize domestics across transnational spaces to ensure that they gain more rights vis-à-vis their employers. This is an excellent example of globalization potentially working to the benefit of individuals.
4 Pyle (2006) reports that in Singapore approximately 100 maids die every year in falls from high rises.
5 The statistics with respect to aging in the developing world are staggering. For instance, according to United Nations estimates, individuals over the age of 85 are expected to make up 24 percent of the population by 2030. By 2050, China is predicted to have 99 million individuals over the age of 80 and India, 48 million.
6 See for instance, the article "One's A Crowd," February 5, 2011, *New York Times*, http://www.nytimes.com/2012/02/05/opinion/sunday/living-alone-means-being-social.html?src=me&ref=general.
7 There are extensive analyses that document the fact that more conciliatory work–family policies and higher-quality child care in Europe can be attributed to the concern around falling fertility rates. See in particular Esping-Andersen (2000).

Part III

POLICY RESPONSES IN DEVELOPING AND INDUSTRIALIZED COUNTRIES

8

INVESTING IN GIRLS AND WOMEN IN THE DEVELOPING WORLD

Ensuring an Equal Start

Consider the following statistics:

- When women attend school for seven or more years in Africa, Asia and Latin America, they have on average two to three fewer children than those women who have less than three years of schooling (Plan UK, 2009).
- In many countries in the developing world, the mortality rate of children under the age of five is highest among mothers who have not attended school. The mortality rate goes down if a mother has several years of elementary school, and it goes down even further if a woman has some secondary schooling (Plan UK, 2009).
- According to a study by the World Bank, when a country experiences a 1 percent increase in the number of women who attend secondary school, its annual per capita income grows by 0.3 percent (Dollar & Gatti, 1999).
- A study conducted among rural Ugandan girls indicated that those who had attained a secondary school education where three times less likely to be HIV positive than girls who had not attended school (De Walque, 2007).

As has been argued throughout this book, many girls and women, particularly those who live with little access to material and educational resources, continue to be disadvantaged in today's globalizing world. This is the case in both developing and industrialized societies. Moreover, as multiple feminist scholars have pointed out, globalization itself is a highly gendered phenomenon. The dominant public arena of globalization prioritizes the world of global finance and stresses individualism and entrepreneurship. This approach to social life is associated with a Western capitalist emphasis that highlights the masculine nature of economics and rational decision-making. The other less obvious aspects of globalization are characterized by gendered and racial subordination in various arenas, and a dependence on a low paid, unskilled labor force. This secondary facet of globalization is increasingly associated with women: in ever-growing numbers they provide the cheap labor that is either low-paid or unpaid, and allows for economic globalizing processes to flourish. Thus, the masculine realm of global political and financial activity is in actuality closely related to the feminized realm of low-paid and unpaid women's work (Kolarova, 2006).

Globalization has had very different consequences for the day-to-day lives of women and men (Freeman, 2001; Oza, 2001). Many women continue to lack access to economic, social, educational, and employment opportunities. However, especially from a Western perspective, their experiences are hidden from view. These women tend to be part of the poorest and marginalized sectors of their populations and their experiences are of little interest within contexts that are characterized by multiple complex social and economic problems. This troubling set of circumstances exists despite the spread of ideals and opportunities that have given many women chances that far exceed those that were available to their mothers and grandmothers.

For the average middle-class Western woman, it is virtually inconceivable to imagine that she would not be able to attend high school or university, that she not choose her field of study, or that she not enter a profession of her choosing. Contemporary Western middle-class women are socialized to believe that they have the equivalent rights as men to fashion their life course with respect to educational opportunities and careers. While they are aware that they may still face salary discrimination at their jobs or a "glass ceiling" at the highest level of a career ladder, in particular younger women are convinced that their lives will mirror those of men with respect to access to opportunities. Yet despite the global spread of increased egalitarian ideas about the roles of women and men, and the rapidly increasing number of women in every country's workforce, many women are extremely disadvantaged in a globalizing environment. For instance, Ruth Pearson writes:

> However, it would be more sensible to re-conceptualise women's work in most areas of the developing world as being by definition unregulated and unprotected regardless of whether it takes place in large-scale workplaces, small or family-based workshops or within women's own houses or compounds. Women provide "cheap" labour, which is part of the so-called "informal" economy. The informal economy is not the exception in most developing countries—it is the norm, and by all statistical accounts it is growing both because the formal sector is becoming informalised,

and because the range of market-oriented informal economic activities is expanding to meet the needs of poor households for cash. Women are playing a bigger and bigger role in this economy, and policies and demands which might improve their position should be based on this reality.

(2004, p. 118)

Globalization is predominantly linked to specific gender differentials. For instance, globalization has brought about an environment where a greater openness to trade is accompanied by a need and demand for skilled labor that is paid at higher wages than low-skilled labor (Baliamoune-Lutz, 2006). In much of the developing world, women fill the ranks of the unskilled or low-skilled workforce that is paid at this lesser level. They are thus the principal group affected by the wage gap that comes about though the integration of their economies with global markets. Standing (1999) has pointed out that trade liberalization did not automatically improve gender wage inequality or the conditions under which so many women work. And Seguino (2005) explains the widely noted gender differential in earnings by pointing to the fact that poor women in the developing world tend to have fewer skills and have no choice but to take on what are often highly exploitative jobs.

Globalization is also often associated with deteriorating working conditions for women that often include longer hours, compulsory overtime, lack of safety standards, restrictions on trade union organization, and unstable employment. In certain industries and in various locales around the world, women tend to be concentrated in jobs with no benefits and no recourse for voicing their complaints, and where they are likely to be employed in low-paid services to others (Denis, 2003).

The deteriorating working conditions for women, particularly in the developing world, are compounded by the fact that governments, policymakers, and other significant organizations usually focus on issues such as economic development and international relationship-building over the social concerns and restrictions that so often mark their societies. The concerns of marginalized groups such as poor girls and women often do not rise to the forefront of national agendas.

Social Policies in the Developing World

Social policies and programs emerge as the consequence of a specific socio-historical context. Currently two opposing perspectives dominate the social landscape with respect to development agendas: the neoliberal approach and the human development perspective. Different institutions and governments have adapted and instituted these agendas with varying success. The World Bank and International Monetary Fund have primarily promoted the neoliberal perspective by enforcing Structural Adjustment Policies and encouraging developing societies to engage in free trade and join the global marketplace. In contrast, the United Nations has increasingly turned to the human development program advocated by Amartya Sen (1999). Initiatives are evaluated by how well policies and programs are working at expanding the capabilities of individuals. By utilizing this perspective, economic growth becomes *one* aspect of success—but is not the final determinant. Instead, the focus of policy goals becomes the well-being of individuals with an emphasis on social justice, equity, and political participation.

A problematic aspect of discussions in general on social policies is defining what a policy is. Definitions tend to be broad and encompass the range of guidelines, principles, legislation, and activities that affect the conditions under which people live. Policies can be explicit, meaning that they are designed to achieve specific objectives, or they may be implicit, which means they were designed with one goal in mind, but in actuality have important consequences for another group or segment of society (Kamerman, 2010).

Curiously, in much of the developing world there has been little emphasis on social policies that link the lives of women who are increasingly involved in export-oriented industries with broader societal concerns. Even feminists who are concerned with this topic have tended to concentrate on wage and gender-based wage gaps, agency in households, communities, and factories, or they have explored the working conditions of women in the so-called global factories. Razavi and Pearson (2004) suggest that there are three possible factors contributing to this omission: 1) that the wages generated through employment in export-oriented industries are very low; 2) that women entered these industries just as states have reduced services to their citizens; and 3) that the capital that has financed many of these industries has enjoyed "special" privileges which absolves it in the minds of many of having to take into account workers' welfare. However, from a social justice perspective, this argument is not credible. Why would states and industries be released from protecting workers' rights because they are curtailing services or because these workers earn very low wages? Is it not this very vulnerability that deserves protection? In fact, Razavi and Pearson go on to point out that from a historical perspective welfare states in Europe arose directly in response to the economic vulnerabilities of workers. It was precisely the need for greater social protection and cohesion that influenced the creation and maintenance of supports for individuals and families (Gough, 2000). Esping-Andersen, a leading supporter of the European welfare state, has argued that despite fears about the relationship between globalization and welfare policies, most advanced industrialized countries have continued to maintain their social agendas and have actually become even more successful (1996). From this perspective, welfare regimes can coexist and flourish alongside open trading markets. This then begs the question as to what is currently happening with respect to social policy concerns in developing countries.

Any discussion on these issues, however, needs to begin with the understanding that developing countries are not homogeneous—there are marked differences between nations in terms of political economies and the types of investments that are nurtured and used to create the export bases that fuel contemporary foreign trade. For instance, in many locales national capital has provided the stimulus for growing export-oriented production and not necessarily foreign direct investment. In some countries, development has also been part of a larger national project that *did* emphasize a form of welfare state and social protection. In these places, the low wages earned by employees were supplemented by a range of other benefits that included cheaper housing, land reforms, and income re-distribution. As the world economy has worsened, social policy debates have sprung up in many of these societies, emphasizing the dichotomy between workers and national interests. What has been missing from these debates is an emphasis, for instance, on the gendered constellation of labor in export-processing zones and how women need to be compensated in a broader social and economic sense for exercising efforts that help uphold their economies.

There are multiple explanations and underlying motives for understanding the omission of women's well-being with respect to supportive social policies in developing countries. One problem is that a great deal of financial capital and strong state administrative capacities are needed in order for social policies to make a significant difference in the lives of citizens (Razavi & Pearson, 2004). This poses a significant challenge for developing nations that are struggling with state reforms and restructuring imposed by international entities in order to pay off their debts. But there are other underlying causes as well. As Barton (2004) points out, rules, policies, and laws that stress the centrality of the market in relation to individuals, families, communities, and nations enforce an agenda that does not highlight the structural and social barriers to women's equality and rights. On a most basic level, many of these very rules and laws are in opposition to the aspirations of gender transformations. In fact, they do not deal with the fundamental reality that women and men need to have equivalent access and control over resources, to decision-making, and to the benefits of their work. It is only in those contexts that gender equality becomes a reality.

The discrimination and lack of opportunities faced by girls and women, especially at the poorer levels of societies, are not just "women's" issues. These are ethical and human concerns that require a serious reassessment of our national and transnational policies and structures. The same forces that are bringing new economic relationships and social concepts to the farthest corners of the globe could and need to be used to also realign policies and programs to improve the lives of millions of individuals, making them more productive, and physically and psychologically healthier individuals. There are multiple examples from around the world where thoughtful social policies and new initiatives are lifting girls and women out of great poverty. They range from simple programs instituted by local NGOs to complex policies and strategies formed through collaborations between states, transnational entities, and local communities.

In those places where governments, NGOs, or other entities have begun investing in girls and women, the results have been nothing short of astonishing. Not only have individual lives improved, but communities and whole societies have benefited in unexpected ways. There is extensive documentation that educating girls and women and giving them the tools to ensure that they have a strong economic and social foundation has strong societal implications: it leads to lower fertility levels, delayed age of marriage, better health for young women and their children, increased societal and political participation, and greater societal productivity. As the upcoming examples in this chapter will illustrate, investments in girls' and women's education, nutrition, and health not only improves their individual well-being and economic status but also has long-term positive implications for their families and communities (Bouis et al., 1998). Moreover, the successes witnessed at the individual, familial, and community levels allow us to understand that girls and women are not victims of their circumstances. Instead, even the most rudimentary tools and opportunities allow women to achieve great successes. In particular, educational and empowerment initiatives allow women to flourish. For instance, Ganguly-Scrase (2003) describes:

> However, during fieldwork, my preconceived ideas were challenged. Against the overwhelming evidence of the negative impact of economic liberalization, I found that women do not perceive themselves to be the victims of neoliberal policies. Instead they emphasize their own senses of self-worth and advancement of women's everyday lives. Such responses may be understood in the context of changing gender relations, as a result of both women's own changing perceptions as well as the postcolonial state's structural interventions in education and employment.
>
> (p. 547)

When women are perceived as empowered actors in their own scripts and they are given even the most rudimentary chances, many are able to turn their lives around. Globalizing processes may contribute to new social problems—but globalization also provides the tools for potential solutions.

This chapter focuses on some successful initiatives in developing countries and highlights the fact that there is no one solution that fits every group of women, every locale, or every situation. Instead, the most successful initiatives are the ones that take into account local circumstances and that evolve over time as a response to feedback and evaluation from the participants. The wide range of successes with respect to educational attainment, better health-care provision, and employment opportunities for girls and women indicates that gender equality is an achievable goal. While globalization creates challenges for contemporary women and men, it also provides us with mechanisms that ultimately may lead to greater social justice and a better quality of life for all individuals.

The Impact of Local, National, and Transnational Collaborations

Some of the most successful human development initiatives in developing societies have arisen through the collaboration of local, national, and transnational organizations. For instance, Denis (2003) describes how in Barbados various women's groups worked with individuals in government and international organizations to organize lectures and public get-togethers that raised awareness about women's poor social conditions. Women's organizing led to new independent programs and initiatives aimed specifically for women and families who needed welfare supports. Denis points out, however, that as admirable as such initiatives seem, they also encourage governmental disengagement and back a neoliberal agenda that privatizes social efforts instead of making them the responsibility of the state. Doyal (2002) takes a different stance and points to the achievements of the UN conferences in Cairo and Beijing as examples of local and global mobilizing. Doyal suggests that by drawing on a framework of human rights that has been emerging since the 1950s, diverse participants were able to come together to advocate for the sexual and reproductive rights for women. The Platforms for Action that resulted from the two conferences have become the foundation for policy-making in a wide spectrum of countries.[1] Specifically, effective and safe reproductive health care has moved to the forefront of many societies local agendas, as has the concept that women have the basic right of access to social and economic resources.

In Asia, the collaboration of local and national women's groups have expanded the concept of the workplace to include informal sector and home-based work. This has facilitated the coming together of women with very different backgrounds and concerns. Some of these initiatives have led to the identification of health hazards at the workplace and to broader environmental concerns (Kaplan, 2001). In addition, global networks of sex workers and migrant women across national boundaries have allowed women to organize in new ways to protect their interests and to promote their right to safer living and working conditions. Many of these campaigns are now partnering with women in the industrialized world who share in the common goal of protecting and promoting women's rights.

Addressing Female Health Concerns with an Emphasis on HIV/AIDS

Some of the most significant successes with respect to collective organizing have come about in the health-care domain. While both men and women face challenges to their health on an everyday basis, women have specific issues that need to be recognized in the global arena. The most important aspect concerns women's biology: a woman's reproductive potential makes her vulnerable if she does not have the power to control her fertility and to carry out a pregnancy and child-birth safely. As (Doyal, 2002) points out, this is an example of the uniqueness of women's situations from men: women's biological needs must be recognized and met if women's health is to be prioritized on a social agenda.[2] The fact that so many women are poor also directly plays into health concerns. Not only do women often have less access to health care but also their physical and psychological exhaustion as they try to help their families survive often makes them more vulnerable to a range of health problems that can be cumulative over time. Especially during their reproductive years, women may have very stringent demands put on them while their access to nutritious food may be low. This situation can lead to iron-deficiency anemia and increases a woman's susceptibility to a range of illnesses and pregnancy-related ailments. Maternal deaths stand at around 600,000 annually, and more than 15 million women per year sustain injuries and disabilities related to childbirth and pregnancy worldwide (Doyal, 2002).

The gendered relationship between health, poverty, and global restructuring is particularly evident when viewed through the lens of the HIV/AIDS epidemic. While HIV/AIDS is thought to be a disease that mainly affects gay men in the industrialized world, it is a serious threat to many poor women, specifically in developing countries. According to the World Health Organization, in sub-Saharan Africa, women constitute 60 percent of individuals living with HIV. Among the most vulnerable individuals in sub-Saharan Africa are younger aged girls (between   15 and 24). Many of these girls have not begun having children yet, and are for the most part inexperienced in managing their social and economic lives. Many of the most vulnerable girls do not live with their families, do not attend school, and do not have permanent places to live. Most typically, they have migrated from rural settlements to urban areas in search of work and better opportunities. In the 12 countries most ravaged by the

HIV epidemic, currently an average of 33 percent of urban girls between the ages of 10 and 14 are living with neither parent and 28 percent live with one parent (Bruce et al., 2011).

Until recently there was little knowledge about the lives of adolescent girls in low-income and slum areas of urban centers, such as in sub-Saharan Africa. However, new ethnographic evidence about the conditions of their lives reveals a dismal picture. For example, in the Nairobi slums of Kenya, 58 percent of girls aged 15–17 are not living with their parents in comparison with 41 percent of boys. Often, these girls are working as domestic servants and/or living with extended family members. Most of these girls (83 percent) are not attending school and are barely surviving by doing menial labor. The circumstances under which these girls live makes them particularly susceptible to health related concerns, and specifically HIV infections.[3] The vulnerability of young girls is exacerbated because they do not have the protective realm of the family or the trusted relationships that come with community connections. Their lack of connectedness allows them to enter unwittingly into abusive relationships, become involved in sex and money exchanges, or to engage in other temporary exploitative relationships. Poor homeless girls tend not to be recruited into youth-development and school-based family-life education programs, making them an invisible and unheard element of their respective societies.

Many girls who occupy the bottom rungs of their societies are very vulnerable to contracting HIV infections because HIV transmission is often the direct outcome of rigid gender roles. In every society, cultural and societal gender norms directly influence the number and types of sexual partners women and men expect and say they have, the circumstances surrounding sex, the negotiation around when to have sex, contraceptive usage, and the role that the threat and role of violence in forcing and keeping women in sexual relationships plays (Bruce et al., 2011). In places where restrictive patriarchal gender rules are in place, young girls often do not have a say over when to have sex, nor do they have the power to refuse men who want to have sex with them.

Women are affected by the link between gender roles and HIV infections in other insidious ways as well. For instance, women are responsible for a disproportionate share in caring for those who become ill through HIV, they have less access to resources and property when a partner dies, and they suffer from a whole spectrum of social, health, and economic costs. In situations where women have few economic options for supporting themselves and their children, women are often also compelled to stay with men, even if this means that they are putting their health at risk. If they refuse to partake in unsafe sex, men may withdraw their material support, leaving these women with no viable means to live. And for some women their only option is to participate in paid sex work, which especially puts adolescent girls at risk (Hallman, 2005). Women's greater susceptibility to serious health issues is, thus, not just based on biology but also on social factors and a lack of alternative means of subsistence. Moreover, the acceleration of global restructuring has also diminished the protective familial and social support networks that previously existed even in very poor communities.

While a variety of local and global programs have attempted to target some of these issues, most youth programs aim to reach a broad age spectrum that ranges over 15 years, and usually focuses on both boys and girls. Because they cast such a wide net, most health-based international programs are relatively ineffective at stemming the tide of HIV infections, in particular because they do not take into account the social circumstances of boys and girls in various cross-cultural settings. The end effect is that boys tend to dominate the activities in these programs and young girls are often marginalized and excluded (Hallman, 2005). Moreover, there are intrinsic problems within the delivery systems: peer educators tend to direct information about HIV toward boys, while girls are educated about contraception and pregnancy. This is a highly problematic situation because in sub-Saharan Africa the HIV infection rates of adolescent girls are three times as high as those of boys (UNAIDS, 2004a, 2004b). Many of these programs ignore the power differentials in sexual relationships among these young people as well as the role of poverty. Instead, these initiatives usually focus on abstinence and on the mechanisms of how HIV is transmitted. Programmatic messages about sexuality are based on the concept that sex is consensual (a Western concept), and that adolescent girls have control in sexual situations (which they often do not even in Western contexts). Moreover, until very recently most health-related initiatives have not included any insight or guidance on the types of activities that could guide young people to more productive futures. In other words, these programs have not concerned themselves with the circumstances that force young women to live in hazardous environments and to become susceptible to dangerous health-related behaviors.

Lately, the recognition of these complex linkages between health, poverty, social circumstances, and global processes has led to research and programming that does not focus solely on the sexual behavior of men or women in isolation. Instead, many of the newest initiatives target male–female relationships in families and communities (Hallman & Roca, 2007). A primary focus of these pioneering programs now are issues such as power and inequality differentials between women and men, as well as conceptualizations of masculinity that encompass the acceptance of violence to control women. Most of these new, inventive programs focus on HIV/AIDS and are located in sub-Saharan Africa. Many of them are being implemented by free-standing NGOs, or by partnerships between local, national, and transnational NGOs. The main funding for these enterprises stems from the U.S. government, including USAID and NIH and private donors.[4]

Successful programs take a variety of approaches. Most do not just target females in isolation, but also focus on the men in their lives. For instance, in certain contexts the greatest benefit to adolescent girls comes from programming aimed at their fathers in order to discourage them from marrying off their daughters at a very young age. Other programs focus on coercion and the often socially legitimized sexual preying of older men on young girls. Men are taught that these are unacceptable behaviors that have long-term health implications for women and their communities.

A contemporary example from Kenya illustrates ones of these new inventive initiatives. This particular program addressing HIV/AIDS has been highly successful through its emphasis on mass media and community education, female mentoring, counseling, and testing. The curriculum is aimed specifically at married young women, and those who are in the process of getting married, by introducing them to the dangers of HIV/AIDS, family planning, safe motherhood, and other related topics. There is also programming aimed at men. Amidst various strategies, the program uses an activity known as Magnet Theater to teach local drama troupes about health concerns that come with early marriage, HIV, and issues around reproduction. Female mentors bring girls together on a weekly basis to discuss these topics and to encourage them to pursue counseling and testing. Since its inception, approximately 20,500 males and 17,300 females have been contacted, and nearly 100,000 individuals have been reached through the mixture of mentors, religious leaders, radio spots, and the theater pieces (Ochieng & Erulkar, 2008). In particular, the theater pieces have influenced audiences through the demystification of how HIV/AIDS is spread and contracted, as well as through creating affinities between community members and the audiences. Many participants have reported changing their sexual behaviors after attending one of these plays (Ochieng & Erulkar, 2008).

A recent survey by the Population Council indicates that the most successful health-related initiatives maintain programmatic flexibility and respond to feedback. By consistently tweaking aspects of established programs, these projects tend to function more efficiently and effectively. For instance, a report by Bruce et al. (2011) offers a variety of suggestions for best practices with respect to instituting programming that truly benefits girls and women. Some of the steps they recommend include:

- Targeting females based on specific criteria that make them vulnerable to abuse or sexual coercion.
- Focusing on geographic areas where there are concentrations of vulnerable young women (for instance, districts where many girls who perform domestic service live).

- Including women in the creation and planning processes of programming by having them identify the most influential men in their lives (partners, fathers, brothers, peers, friends).
- Producing programming that separates men and women into same sex and age working groups.

The Population Council report also highlights another complex issue that was mentioned previously: that in many developing countries, youth policies focus on individuals aged 15–35. The most vulnerable group, young girls who are going through puberty, are omitted from these initiatives. For instance, a number of development reports indicate that in Zambia, Liberia, and Haiti, girls who are 15 and younger are often the most frequent targets of rape. Many of the current youth-oriented programs focus on an age range of girls and women after the worst experiences have already been inflicted on them.

An important conclusion of the Population Council report (Bruce et al., 2011) is its observation that in order for targeted programs to be effective, they need to include an understanding of relationship patterns in specific cultures. In many areas of the world, girls report that their initial sexual experiences were unwanted or forced (Hallman, 2005). Later on, girls are often involved sexually with older men for economic reasons. The report also highlights the fact that while many contemporary initiatives *state* that they focus on gender relationships, frequently their curricula only target men and boys, and exclude girls. Girls and women are perceived as dependents of men and more difficult to reach in many non-Western community settings. Thus, most preventative programs *do not* assist women and girls in learning to protect themselves in sexual relationships. Ultimately the Population Council report stresses that the key to preventative programs being truly effective is to identify the most vulnerable populations. Thus, targeted programming focused on differentiated age groups of both women and men is extremely important. The report points out that programs that are directed at females need to be focused on efforts that *protect* girls and women, while a focus on men needs to prioritize appropriate male behavior. These need to be distinct, separate efforts and priority needs to be given to the most vulnerable groups.

The Population Council report (Bruce et al., 2011) also stresses the importance of rigorous formal evaluations of programs that include other measures besides self-reports. It is, in general, difficult to assess accurately attitude and behavioral changes. These are moving targets and need to be gauged through multiple measures. Ongoing process and outcome evaluations are thus a necessary, and often missing aspect, of implementing effective programming. These types of evaluations are only now becoming more commonplace in international contexts, and are slowly being incorporated into new initiatives.

Efforts to Limit Sexual Trafficking and Exploitation

Closely related to women's health issues is the sexual trafficking of girls and women. This issue has drawn closer scrutiny in the last several years due to its connections with human rights violations and because the sex industry impacts the spread of HIV/AIDS. As was discussed in Chapter 5, sexual trafficking and exploitation continues to grow exponentially despite the efforts of transnational and feminist organizations to stem this phenomenon. Yet, as Joffres et al. (2008) state:

> Women and children have a right to be protected from any forms of trafficking and to be treated with dignity. This requires a comprehensive anti-human trafficking strategy embedded in a human rights approach since violations of human rights are both the cause and consequence of human trafficking. Such an approach requires the systematic development and implementation of policies and programs that address the socio-economic, political, environmental, and cultural factors that increase vulnerability to trafficking at the local, regional, state national, and international levels.
>
> (p. 9)

From a global perspective, there is increased recognition that a human rights approach to trafficked children and women needs to be implemented. Instead of blaming those individuals who have been forced into prostitution (a common previous tactic), there is more appreciation today for the fact that sexually trafficked individuals deserve the same rights to health care and safe surroundings as their other fellow citizens. Human rights advocates are working to raise awareness that health-care workers and officials in positions of authority need to be more sensitive to the conditions that force women into prostitution, and they have turned attention to the fact that it is often powerful officials who assist in perpetrating these crimes. These campaigns have led to various successful initiatives to assist vulnerable girls and women who are caught up in the sex industry.

A review of the literature indicates that in order to stop sexual trafficking a multi-pronged approach is the only solution to this difficult problem. Successful policy and programmatic initiatives incorporate educational, economic, and legal dimensions and combine them with advocacy. Due to its complex nature, sexual trafficking can only be stopped by intercepting the process at various points, including in the home society, in transit, and in the receiving countries.

Some of the most successful initiatives that combat sexual trafficking are based in Nepal. For instance, the ABC/Nepal NGO has been running the Better Life Program for Adolescent Girls since 1995. This training skills initiative introduces girls to family life education and focuses on empowerment, the formation and support of women's cooperatives, and raising public awareness. It also provides limited financial resources to very poor families so that their daughters can take part in their programs. Maiti Nepal, another highly influential NGO that has received international attention, has a different approach. It has prevented the trafficking of 6,000 girls and women by intercepting trafficking efforts at the border and by providing shelters for those who are rescued. They also provide programs to assist girls and women who have been rescued to recover their self-esteem and make it possible for them to return to their families. Maiti Nepal also hosts educational programs about migration and awareness in order to educate high-risk girls and women, and sponsors lectures for police personnel to assist them in identifying traffickers (Kaufman & Crawford, 2011).

Strikingly, most successful efforts have been initiated by NGOs working in conjunction with local communities. However, larger-scale efforts are also needed to keep this phenomenon from spreading. For instance, the SAARC (South Asia Association for Regional Cooperation) has brought together representatives from Nepal, India, Pakistan, Bangladesh, Bhutan, Sri Lanka, and the Maldives to draw up a Convention for Preventing and Combating the Trafficking in Women and Children for Prostitution. This convention promotes:

> co-operation amongst member States to effectively deal with various aspects of prevention, interdiction and suppression of trafficking in women and children; repatriation and rehabilitation of victims of trafficking, and preventing the use of women and children in international prostitution networks, particularly where the SAARC member countries are the countries of origin, transit and destination.
>
> (Kaufman & Crawford, 2011, p. 658)

This convention is based on the idea that through collaboration, regional states will be more effective in both the prevention and intervention of sexual trafficking.

From a specific policy perspective, strict laws that focus on the traffickers and the clients would do much to deter the current situation. For example, an interesting and potentially promising legislative response comes from Sweden. Under Swedish law, prostitution is considered to be a type of male violence that is perpetrated against women and children. In a twist from that which is more typical in other parts of the world, this prohibition allows the men who purchase sexual services to be prosecuted instead of the women. Concurrently, women involved in prostitution are provided with programming and educational provisions that allow them to leave the sexual services industry. Research indicates that since the inception of this law prostitution and trafficking have remained stable or even declined. The Swedish case stands in stark contrast with neighboring countries such as Finland and Denmark where the sex industry has grown exponentially since the 1990s (Ekberg, 2004).

Policy-makers and researchers also point to the Swedish example in an effort to stem the tide of growing sex tourism, and the exploitation of vulnerable women and children by aid workers and United Nations peace-keepers. For example, Hynes (2004) and Ferris (2007) describe in detail how UN aid workers often trade critical emergency supplies and food in exchange for sex with young girls. A more universal implementation of laws such as the Swedish one would cut down on these types of abuses and provide a form of protection for susceptible young people.

It is crucial to note that despite the many efforts on the part of govern-ments, NGOs, and local communities, sexual trafficking is a growing prob-lem. This is an illegal, clandestine activity that is difficult to track and to monitor. Moreover, accessing the girls and women who become involved in the sex trade is at times virtually impossible. Different factors force and sometimes even encourage girls and women to become involved in sexual trafficking. As was noted in Chapter 5, a laxity in laws and the corruption of highly placed officials further contribute to the growth of this concealed activity. Moreover, the fact that there is a "market" for these activities pro-vides incentives for those involved to be vigilantly adapting their processes and movement of individuals in order to evade detection and discovery. Communication technologies have eased the secretive nature of the process, and governments with their stricter laws pertaining to migration have inad-vertently made it more difficult for women to escape from their traffickers.

In order to stem the tide of sexual trafficking and exploitation that has become so endemic, attention needs to be turned to the factors that create the conditions that encourage this type of abuse in the first place. Addressing the underlying poverty conditions that make women and children vulner-able is a key factor in any prevention initiatives. This can be accomplished through advancing the implementation of vocational skills training programs and economic incentives. These types of services need to be combined with educational initiatives that promote gender equality within the family and community. Moreover, raising awareness about this issue empowers girls and women and, simultaneously, makes their communities more responsible for their safety.

Educational Initiatives as Key

From a global and historical perspective, the single greatest recent differ-ence in the lives of girls and women in the developing world is associated with greater access to education (WHO, 2013). Increased involvement of international organizations with gender education policy-making and the recognition of the importance of educating a broader segment of their populations have led states in the developing world to focus on providing greater educational access in general. This strategy has been further encouraged by the year 2000 publication of the United Nations Millennium Development Goals (MDGs) that highlighted the need to improve global development by decreasing poverty. As part of the MDGs, gender equality in relation to education has become one of the yardsticks with which nations can evaluate their development progress. Global gender targets allow states to identify the scale and effectiveness of their programs and to measure the variety of factors that are associated with gender inequality. While gender equality is now increasingly understood as a fundamental human right, it still comes with its own problematic: gender equality is often perceived in non-Western contexts as part of the neoliberal economic package that moves countries toward Western-style models of contemporary life.

The complexity of attaining gender equality goals has been highlighted by the *Global Monitoring Reports,* published by UNESCO (2003/4) that reported that two-thirds of the world's illiterate individuals are female and that about a quarter of the world's countries are not able to achieve gender parity with respect to access and enrolment for primary school (Fennell & Arnot, 2008). These reports raised awareness that the failure to achieve gender parity with respect to schooling was based on multiple factors and that governments needed to reshape their educational provision and policy approaches. For instance, gender equality reform movements are often locally based and operate unevenly, even within the same society. These initiatives are often also patched together by ideologically diverse groups composed of NGOs and government policies that have been created in response to international pressures. The UNESCO reports have highlighted the severe challenges to educational development with respect to gender in poor communities such as limited curricular resources, inadequately trained female teachers, no focus on gender-sensitive teacher training and skills, and limited awareness of the conditions needed to promote gender equality. Feminist scholars have also called for more insightful indicators beyond access to education—such as the extent to which girls are empowered and encouraged to use their individual and collective agency. From this perspective, education is directly associated with attaining social capital and access to social networks.

Strong Schools as a Proven Successful Strategy

An important aspect in attracting and retaining all children in school is determined by the quality of the schooling that is available. Quality is linked to gender because, as we have seen, in many parts of the world girls from poor families are more likely to be kept out of school by their parents than boys. However, parents and communities view education differently when a number of factors are in place: these include conveniently located schools with flexible schedules, motivated teachers, access to books, and skills-based learning that is perceived as being financially lucrative in the future. Under certain conditions, the refashioning of the services provided by schools ends up translating into positive community effects. For example, in some areas of the world with large minority or indigenous populations, such as New Zealand or Canada, providing bilingual education in schools has served to better integrate the communities into the local surroundings. When local children do not speak the language that is used in the school, as for example the Roma in Eastern Europe, parents are much more reluctant to enroll their children. But through the availability of language classes, children and parents begin to become part of the larger social environment.

Another means of strengthening schools is to address the specific local concerns of the parents of the community. For instance, in some areas parents do not want their daughters walking to school due to safety concerns. In Pakistan, locating schools in village centers has dramatically increased the attendance of girls. In heavily Muslim areas, girls are often not allowed to travel beyond village limits after they reach puberty due to cultural fears surrounding their sexuality. By locating schools near to their homes, this barrier is ameliorated (Sathar, & Lloyd, 1993). In addition, incorporating female teachers and creating single-sex classrooms allows for families to feel more comfortable with sending their daughters to school. Further, there is increasing evidence that poor families prefer to send their daughters to school if the curriculum focuses on "hard" subjects such as science and math. Thus, it is imperative that in low-income regions girls be given greater access to math and science education, and that they be depicted in the broader media as scientists, doctors, and other such professionals.

Supporting outreach programs to parents, bringing parents into the classroom, giving cash incentives to parents who are reliant on their children's labor, and providing food at school can all work to motivate parents to allow particularly their daughters to continue their education. Educational initiatives also need to focus on socially marginalized families and groups: there is very little research in this arena, and there are very few policy recommendations that concern themselves with the experiences of minority populations in developing countries. In general, the focus of most policy and programming initiatives is on mainstream children and their educational experiences. But especially in places that are characterized by significant minority populations, efforts that look at additional services for integration are pivotal to ensuring the success of children. Providing programs such as summer classes that assist children in catching up to "mainstream" children can benefit marginalized families. Moreover, research and evaluation of the needs of excluded groups would strengthen the types of services that could be provided to vulnerable children. Traditional incentives are often not the appropriate way to reach these groups, and at this point we know very little about which successful interventions will specifically keep girls from marginalized populations attending school.

Case Study: Bangladesh as an Example of Directed Policies and NGO–State Collaborations

Bangladesh provides an interesting example of a place where directed policy decision-making has led to a significant rise in girls' education and an overall increase in the adult literacy rate from 34.6 percent in 1990 to 54 percent in 2007 (UNICEF, 2010). During this time, a number of new primary schools were opened around the country and primary school attendance doubled. Gender parity was achieved during this period and girls began to outperform boys. In order to understand these trends, we need to look backwards at the policy steps that led to this impressive outcome.

In 1990, the Bangladeshi government made a significant policy decision by determining that it was imperative to provide free and compulsory education for all members of the society in order to move the country forwards. Backed by the financial support of the World Bank, the Asian Development Bank, and a number of international donors, the government restored old schools, built new ones, developed innovative curricula, and provided textbooks to students. Currently, there are about 18 million children enrolled in approximately 38,000 primary schools in Bangladesh making this one of the largest primary education systems in the world (Chisamya et al. 2011).

The efforts to revitalize the primary school system did not occur purely through the efforts of the state. Instead, these initiatives were supported by a number of local NGOs. Historically, NGOs have played an important role in educational reforms in this part of the world. For instance, even before the government restructured its educational policies, NGOs had already created an extensive number of primary schools around the country. These schools were supported by government-paid salaries to teachers and through the donations of textbooks. However, the revitalization efforts to the education system were provided through NGOs. For instance, the Bangladesh Rural Advancement Committee (BRAC) initiated a rural educational program in 1984 that spread to 35,000 primary schools by 2008 (Plan UK, 2009). BRAC schools are distinguished by their inventive teaching practices and the implementation of creative approaches such as flexible hours, convenient locations, parent involvement, and the teaching of practical skills. These innovations assisted in encouraging parents that live in remote rural areas to allow their daughters to attend school.

The Bangladeshi government built on the BRAC initiatives by introducing some other unique policies. For instance, in order to encourage secondary school attendance among the poorest populations, the government supplied cash stipends to rural girls and their families. Other measures included making food available in schools, screening texts and curricula for gender biases, and enforcing the hiring of female teachers. This last measure resulted in a doubling of female teachers in schools, an important aspect for parents who preferred having their daughters interact with women rather than men due to modesty concerns (Plan UK, 2009).

The most successful measure attributed to changing school attendance was the provision of monetary stipends to poor parents in rural areas. In particular, secondary school stipends have influenced many parents' decisions to allow their daughters to continue their schooling. Instead of having their daughters work, monetary stipends accomplish the goals of both education and financial remuneration. Small stipends are provided to girls in grades 6–10, as long as they remain unmarried, attend school up to 75 percent of the time and achieve a minimum score of 45 percent on annual examinations. Promoting female secondary school attendance has had another positive social outcome: it delays marriage and childbearing for young girls (Plan UK, 2009).

In order to effect a cultural and behavioral transformation among rural parents, the government has employed a variety of communication strategies to spread the message about the importance of educating girls. For instance, the Female Education Awareness program, which is supported financially by the World Bank, has allowed the government to implement a number of measures including advertising on television and using radio ads, print materials, and face-to-face communication. The goal of this outreach is specifically to encourage fathers and older men to allow their daughters to continue their schooling. Another goal of the program is to foster interest in the school stipend program and to inspire teachers and school officials to foster gender parity (Schuler, 2007). In Bangladesh, instituting flexible school times and instituting child and sibling care has also been a measure that has had significant success in attracting and retaining female students. Girls are able to fulfill their house responsibilities without having to give up on their desire for an education

(Sathar, & Lloyd, 1993). Other successful programs include promoting adult education and higher wages for women, which also increases the likelihood that mothers will send their daughters to school for an education (Herz & Khandker, 1991).

Another highly effective strategy has been a cartoon campaign by the Meena Communication Initiative to raise awareness of gender disparities. This initiative that is funded primarily through UNICEF depicts a female character who is the victim of various gender inequities that are characteristic of the lives of Bangladeshi girls and boys. For example, in one scene a grandmother defends the fact that she gives the best food at each meal to the boy in the family rather than the girl, with the explanation that he has "more difficult" work to do. Consequently, in this cartoon, the girl and boy trade places. The girl takes on her brother's chores and is now wandering through the fields with the family's cattle while the hungry boy, with great difficulty, has to perform all the household labor. In another scenario, the daughter turns out to be the only member of her family who can read the instructions on a package of seeds, and, thus, is able to help her family to grow new food (Schuler, 2007). These forms of communication have been disseminated widely throughout Bangladesh and have proven to be unexpectedly effective.

While there have been no formal specific evaluations of any of these strategies, the gender parity that has been achieved in the Bangladeshi school system indicates the success of the totality of these initiatives (Plan UK, 2009). The ethnographic data of Schuler (2007) reveals that there is a widespread perception that gender norms with respect to women are changing. Women are now recognized as being more educated and informed about the world, as having necessary and valuable skills in a changing economy, and that they are more resourceful than they used to be. In particular, women's contemporary ability to contribute to the family income was highlighted by virtually every individual who Schuler (2007) interviewed. These findings are extremely encouraging because even just ten years ago only men represented their families in the public sphere. At that point, modesty and submissiveness were considered to be the most important aspects of a woman's personality, and violence against "disobedient" women was deemed appropriate. While obviously many families have retained traditional gender norms, the successes with respect to schooling and gender parity indicate that behavioral and social change can be effected through relatively simple initiatives (Plan UK, 2009). Schuler (2007) provides an interesting example of an illiterate rickshaw puller who was arrested on false charges. Subsequently, his illiterate wife was cheated by all those around her. This experience taught the man the value of insisting of an education for both boys and girls "so that no one could outwit them again" (p. 189). In the same study, Schuler found that for girls being educated is increasingly equated with making a better marriage and being treated well in their marital homes (Mahmud & Amin, 2006). Moreover, parents cite the ability of girls to take care of themselves should something go wrong in their lives as an important reason to encourage female education. Schuler quotes the following from a young Bangladeshi girl, "Nowadays illiterate girls who have not gone to school have no value. When they visit a girl's house to see the [prospective] bride, the bridegroom's side first asks her parents about her educational level. If a girl is not educated, even an illiterate man would not want to marry her" (p. 190). Other girls pointed out that families do not ask about the size of dowries in the same manner as before, since the abilities and marketable skills of the girls are now considered the dowry.

Schuler's (2007) qualitative data indicates that increased education and earning an income do indeed bring about positive changes in women's lives. Especially in poor families, men at times desert their wives and children, leaving them destitute with no means of support. Having a formal education allows women to support themselves—and sometimes encourages husbands to return to their families. Earning an income has also raised the self-worth of women, in their own eyes and by others (Plan UK, 2009). Simultaneously, as women learn to network, they are empowered to take care of themselves and their families.

Girls' and Women's Empowerment Programs

Besides traditional educational initiatives, local empowerment and skills-based programs have been proven to make some of the greatest improvements in women's and girls' lives. Alongside their stated educational goals, many of these programs have larger aims such as delaying marriage and increasing the ability of girls and women to choose their own husbands. One example comes from Burkina Faso, which is listed in the United Nations Human Development Report as one of the poorest countries in the world.[5] In Burkina Faso, the Mille Jeunes Filles (MJF) program (translated the Thousand Girls program) is often cited as a creative initiative that illustrates the power of collaboration. Mille Jeune Filles is a governmental effort that was begun in 1994, initially to teach girls agricultural skills. This initiative involved a collaboration of the Ministry of Family and Social Welfare, the Ministry of Health, UNFPA, and the Population Council, and was geared to girls between the ages of 14 and 18. The initial goal of the program was to strengthen the country's agricultural sector by utilizing a neglected part of the labor force, young women. This residential program enrolls 1000 girls and in addition to learning crop cultivation, each participant is educated in reproductive health, reading, dressmaking, and financial management. Upon completion, each girl is given some money with which she can return to her village and make an initial investment in business supplies. The success of the program can be attributed in part to its empowerment features: girls return to their villages with new skills and encourage other females to participate. Families and communities have benefited from the programs due to the increased economic advantages that their daughters now bring with them. Thus, despite initial resistance, parents now vie to enroll their daughters to participate in Mille Jeunes Filles (Brady, Salouco, & Chong, 2007).

Another noteworthy collaborative initiative is based in India and is entitled Mahila Samakhya. This is a government-initiated development program that began in 1988 and now covers 21,000 villages over 83 districts in nine states. Mahila Samakhya is a rural women's empowerment program that seeks to increase the capacity of girls and women through skills training and by educating them about their rights and entitlements. Based on a collaboration of non-governmental agencies, female activists, and officials from the Department of Education, a unique feature of Mahila Samakhya is that rural women are part of the development and implementation of the program. Women describe the success of this initiative because it has "let them come out of their houses" (Gupta & Sharma, 2006). A pivotal aspect of Mahila Samakhya is the concept of self-empowerment. Women are taught how to create a positive self-image, develop self-confidence, and learn to think critically.[6]

Economic Empowerment: Microcredit, Microfinance, and Conditional Cash Transfers

Besides education, economic empowerment through microcredit, microfinance, and cash transfer initiatives, constitute the other most popular programs that are currently thought to empower women in developing countries. All of these economic projects are widely encouraged by international donor agencies as mechanisms specifically to lift women out of poverty. In particular, microcredit refers to the extension of very small loans to impoverished borrowers who usually lack steady employment and collateral. Microcredit is a part of microfinance which refers to the provision of a range of services (particularly savings accounts) to the poor. The programs are designed to support entrepreneurship, alleviate poverty, empower women, and uplift their families and communities. Since its inception, microcredit and microfinance initiatives have spread widely to other parts of South Asia, Africa, and Latin America. However, over the last decade microcredit in particular has become a controversial development tool.

Microcredit revolves around a lending principle: members save small amounts of money in a group fund every month. They may then borrow from this group fund for a variety of needs including school fees or a household emergency. As borrowing groups establish a repayment history and prove that they can manage their funds, they become eligible to take out larger bank loans to fund more significant entrepreneurial activities. Foundational to the concept of microcredit is a loan fee that is charged to borrowers. The loan fee was introduced based on the idea that while the borrowers may not have any resources, they should not be thought of as charity cases (Eisenstein, 2005).

Microcredit is a highly gendered activity. It is currently estimated that about 84.2 percent of the poorest microfinance clients around the world are women. Most of the women who are targeted to participate in microcredit programs range in age from their mid-twenties to late forties, the goal being to reach women who are primarily finished with childbearing and can focus on improving their economic status.[7] Microfinance is a popular development strategy as it specifically targets girls and women and provides them with a "pathway" out of poverty. In contrast to other development initiatives, microcredit has had fewer problems focusing on women because in many places women take on the financial responsibility for managing the household. In general, loans are relatively small and borrowing remains within groups, negating the need for collateral, which women in the developing world often do not have.

Proponents argue that microfinance is a mechanism for incorporating women into the mainstream economy. While microcredit is associated with a host of gender-specific problems, including men forcing their wives to gain access to loans, loans being perceived as a type of dowry, and increased violent behavior of men toward their wives, ethnographic reports indicate that most women want to continue to participate in microcredit initiatives. Some studies indicate that women engaged in microfinance programs had an improved standard of living and increased self-empowerment with respect to decision-making, other studies have illustrated that some women became entangled in a spiral of debts or they became part of too many microfinance programs and could not keep up their payments. Concurrently, multiple donor institutions have begun to question the continuation of these programs. Still, many women feel that by participating in microcredit endeavors they are able to step out of the private sphere, they become less dependent on their in-laws, and that they receive greater social acknowledgment from their communities

(Hofmann & Marius-Gnanou, 2007). Women also perceive microcredit as a way of increasing their contributions to the household and improving the lives of their children. In order to better understand the role of microcredit or microfinance, as it is also referred to, it is useful to give a brief overview of the history of this strategy.

The concept behind microcredit came about as a response to U.S. development policies which were critiqued as early as the 1970s for "ignoring" the plight of women in poor countries. USAID responded by creating an Office of Women and Development, and by restructuring the Foreign Assistance Act to include women as part of foreign aid policy (Poster & Salime, 2002). USAID then adopted the idea of microcredit lending to poor rural women as one of its primary strategies.

Microcredit is primarily the brainchild of Muhammad Yunus, an economist who in 1977 initially tried out this concept in the village of Grameen in Bangladesh.[8] His experiment began in the following manner: he observed that rural village women tended to borrow money from middlemen in order to make bamboo stools and mats, and then sold these products back to the middlemen at the end of the work day. Thus, he initiated a process whereby he took a small loan from a Bangladeshi bank and lent out $27 to 42 women in one village. Muhammad Yunus discovered that this small amount of money allowed these women not only to survive but also to develop entrepreneurial skills. Each of them managed to start a small business that eventually pulled them out of poverty (Grameen Bank, n.d.). The success of this initial enterprise led Yunus to develop what is now referred to as the "Grameen model." The Grameen model proposes bringing together six unrelated individuals from similar socioeconomic circumstances into a group and then providing them with individual loans. These groups are expected to meet weekly and to make regular payments. If everyone repays their loans in a timely fashion, then the group is allowed to borrow a larger sum of money. This initial trial led to Yunus founding the Yunus Bank in 1983, which was then renamed the Grameen Bank, and has since its early start grown at an exponential rate. By the late 2000s, the total borrowers of the bank numbered 7.34 million, with 97 percent being women. Approximately 80,257 villages are currently covered under the auspices of the bank. The bank also claims a loan recovery rate of 98.35 percent (Grameen Bank, n.d.). The success of Grameen's strategy led to the first international Microcredit Summit held in New York City in 1997, with the stated goal being to reach 100 million of the world's poorest families.

The success of microfinance can, in part, be understood against the backdrop of the growth of the global informal sector, which was originally perceived by economists as a form of transitory employment. The informal sector, however, has been growing exponentially not just in the developing world but even in high-income countries. In response to the negative effects caused by Structural Adjustment Policies, the World Bank established Social Funds as a form of a social safety net. These funds contribute to microenterprises by giving out microloans through non-governmental organizations and monitoring the collection of interest payments. Some analysts argue that this popularization of microcredit symbolizes the importance of the informal sector and the dissolution of "true" economic development (Elyachar, 2002). In those countries hardest hit by Structural Adjustment Policies, it has been particularly women who have had to take on the complex set of problems caused through lost jobs and benefits. Critics of microcredit point out that these types of endeavors are part of a larger trend that shifts familial financial burdens onto women and their families. Observers of these developments have become increasingly ambivalent to what were initially thought to be a panacea to poor women's financial woes. These more recent perspectives suggest that microcredit is in reality a "feminization" of debt and may in the long run portend unfortunate consequences for women's lives (Khondkar, 2002; Yunus, 2002).

In part, microcredit is also financed through remittances sent home by migrating women who work in other parts of the world and send their incomes back to their husbands, children, and extended families. For example, in 2007, global remittances amounted to approximately $318 billion with the Philippines alone receiving approximately $17 billion (http://migration.ucdavis.edu/mn/more.php?id=3408_0_5_0). Significantly, the worldwide flow of remittances is larger than the combined total aid and credit from both public and private sources that is given to poor countries. In a chain reaction, the influx of this money into the local banking systems allows poor rural women to take loans in the form of microcredit and to become microentrepreneurs. This money circuit, born primarily by women, then continues to support the policies put into place by high-income countries and their elites and which, according to some analysts, are associated with the increased poverty of populations in less developed countries.

One of the principal challenges of microcredit is the process of providing small loans at relatively affordable prices. Interest rates tend to be very high due to the transaction cost relative to loan size. Advocates for microcredit argue that high interest rates are unavoidable and that the opportunities provided by the loans outweigh their disadvantages. However, only limited progress has been made to solve this problem. The result is that microcredit has limited effectiveness for fighting poverty. Moreover, critics of microcredit argue that by focusing exclusively on microcredit initiatives, governments have abdicated their responsibilities for poverty reduction and that poor households end up in debt traps. From this perspective, money from the loans is used for household consumption and does not help foster entrepreneurial activity, alleviate poverty, or improve access to health care and education. Critics also point out that microcredit does not reach the very poorest segments of society. In order to participate in a microcredit fund, members need some kind of capital to invest—even if it is a very small amount. Despite these criticisms, microcredit and microfinance programs are flourishing. Moreover, new types of initiatives that take into consideration some of the critiques of the older models are emerging.

Case Study: TRY—Targeting Vulnerable Adolescent Girls in Nairobi

In 1998, the Population Council and the development arm of a bank designed specifically to assist low-income individuals (K-Rep Bank) combined forces to offer new economic and social opportunities to the adolescent girls in the slums of Nairobi.[9] The overall goal of the project was to reduce adolescent girls' vulnerabilities to detrimental social and health outcomes, and, specifically, HIV infections by improving their economic opportunities (Erulkar et al., 2006).

The program which is referred to as TRY (Tap and Reposition Youth) was a pilot initiative that adapted elements of the group lending model to the needs of poor adolescent girls. The program goals recognized that the traditional microfinance model would not work for most of the targeted adolescent since entrepreneurship and repeated borrowing were not their primary concerns. Instead, what they needed was to accumulate social capital. The girls needed social support groups, friendships, mentoring relationships, physical safety, and the chance to save their money in a safe accessible place away from their male partners, husbands, and personal temptations. Once these foundations had been laid, credit opportunities and entrepreneurship were thought to follow.

In 1999, K-Rep, after recruiting 130 girls who formed themselves into five groups, undertook weekly sessions to educate girls about credit policies and procedures. They participated in a six-day training that focused on entrepreneurial skills, life skill, gender roles, and business management. Participants learned how to develop a simple business plan and savings and credit procedures were covered.

As part of this model (known as the juhudi model), girls had to demonstrate that they had the ability to save money before receiving any sort of a loan. Members showed financial discipline through making small weekly payments to the savings account. These funds were then reserved in case a member fell behind in repaying her loan. At the girls' request, the amount they saved increased rapidly. Approximately 70 percent of the girls had previously saved their money at home but stated that it was difficult to hide their money from their boyfriends and husbands, and they were thus thankful to have a place to leave their money. These savings groups then functioned like a merry-go-round with 15 girls making contributions in each group, and receiving a lump sum every 15 weeks. Group meetings took on a social character and became a place for sharing personal stories and tribulations:

> For my part, I enjoy the boosting we give each other, be it in terms of solving social problems, business issues, or helping each other out with family or marital problems. Since I joined the group, I have acquired a number of friends with whom I share problems or with whom I just have fun. I don't feel lonely. (Focus-group participant, age 22, divorced, eight years of education; Erulkar et al., 2006, p. 22)

Several months after the groups began saving, the first loans were given out. The groups decided themselves who should get the first loans and the girls negotiated the choice of recipients. They considered how the members saw the girls, the type of business plan they had developed, and the likelihood that they would be able to repay the loan. By December 2000, the end of the first phase of TRY, 132 loans had been granted, 26 of which were second loans.

The girls who had the greatest difficulty repaying the loans were younger, less educated, and poorer. Thus, K-Rep and the Population Council initiated the Young Savers Clubs in order to reach the youngest and most vulnerable populations. These clubs stressed social support, mentoring, and saving—even though the girls were not required to save on a weekly basis. TRY represents a fascinating experiment in adapting economic livelihood models for the most vulnerable adolescents. From this model we can learn about the importance of mentorship, staged interventions, and the importance of savings for young girls as they move from adolescence to adulthood. While traditional micro-finance models may work well for older women, they are not always appropriate for the most vulnerable adolescents. Group lending does not improve these girls' lives nor does reduced collateral and lower interest rates make a difference. Instead, group mobilization and support using individualized credit plans may have a greater chance of success.

The TRY initiative illustrates a fundamental problem that parallels the stories of other girls in the many developing countries: adolescent girls are often extremely vulnerable, specifically to HIV infections, and risky sexual relations are often not something they are able to exercise control over (Erulkar et al., 2006). Moreover, although borrowing was a central concern to the TRY participants, many of the girls also wanted to establish saving accounts, create friendship networks, and learn skills in order to attain some form of employment. This requires programs that have multiple foci and dedicated trainers and mentors who function as enforcers of credit policies but are also able to assist the girls in accomplishing their goals. This multifaceted approach stands in contrast to many Western economic models that focus purely on the market nature of the business transactions.

Despite their growth, microcredit and microfinance programs have elicited wide criticism from various constituents but remain popular among the individuals who actually participate in them. Proponents of microcredit argue that this strategy encourages women to get out of the confines of their homes and families, and to interact in the public sphere. Moreover, even women from very "traditional" backgrounds are now forced to work with mostly male program officials helping disestablish some of the traditional gender norms that have preserved separate gender roles and hierarchies (Schuler, 2007). There is ethnographic evidence that even in those cases when the loans had to be handed over to the husbands in the family, there is some familial and societal recognition that this cash is only available due to the presence and actions of the woman. Thus, even if just in a very subtle manner, microcredit slowly begins to empower women in their families, communities, and societies.

In part, microfinance and microcredit are controversial because they are seen by some as an abdication of state responsibilities to the poor and by others as a form of feminization of debt. As this cursory overview indicates, microcredit and microfinance approaches are not necessarily static uniform approaches to alleviating poverty and gender injustices. In spite of the problems associated with these initiatives, ethnographic evidence indicates that girls and women profit from participating in these programs and, thus, we cannot just summarily dismiss them as not functioning. While they may not alleviate extreme poverty, microcredit and microfinance serve other social functions. Some feminists have suggested that in order to overcome some of the challenges associated with microcredit and microfinance, what needs to happen is that critical linkages to other venues of social change need to be established. For instance, associating women's networks and women's lobbying groups with microfinance initiatives would add a protective element to these programs and would promote human rights with a focus on women (Guerin & Palier, 2007).

Incentivizing Gender Equality through Conditional Cash Transfers

Over the last several years, the provision of cash benefits has become another key social protection strategy in developing countries. Increasingly, the provision of cash benefits is linked to specific individual and familial behaviors such as regular visitations to health clinics, and enrollment and attendance in secondary school. Conditional Cash Transfers (CCTs) were initiated in Latin America, but have also become popular in parts of Asia, Africa, and the Central and Eastern European countries.

An overview of recent CCT initiatives indicates that in order for CCT programs to be effective, certain conditions need to be in place. These include that the benefit be an adequate amount of money, that the appropriate populations be targeted, and that there are reasonable conditions associated with the cash transfer. For instance, if there are conditions attached to the CCT, then an adequate social infrastructure is a critical precondition to guarantee the effectiveness of the program.[10] Thus, if the targeted population is required to visit health-care facilities in order to receive the cash benefit, then an adequate number of health-care facilities need to actually be available. Kamerman (2010) suggests that some other factors need to be taken into consideration as well. For instance, she points out that vulnerability needs to be defined apart from low income, that the mothers in families need to be made the beneficiaries in order to guarantee gender equity, and that "carers" (grandparents, relatives) need to be eligible to receive the benefits in those cases when there are no parents in the home. This latter provision supports families that have been devastated by HIV/AIDS and child-headed households. CCTs have been proven to be effective in reducing child labor and have prevented the most vulnerable individuals in developing societies fall into abject poverty. They are, thus, rapidly gaining in popularity as a form of social protection.

Synopsis

Throughout the developing world, girls' and women's lives are changing. Most striking is the increased public visibility of women and their participation in the paid labor force. Despite the many negative conditions under which so many women work, there is also evidence that there are simultaneously positive shifts under way. Ethnographic evidence indicates that women perceive themselves as benefiting from educational and employment opportunities. Simultaneously, men are recognizing that improvements in the lives of women advantage them as well. As women attain more access to education, employment, and political participation, they become a source of pride for the men in their lives. In an ethnographic study of lower middle-class Bengali's, Ganguly-Scrase (2003, p. 554) found that "for men, it is a recognition of improvement and a sense of pride that 'my' wife goes out to work or 'my' daughter is doing well in her studies and the hope that she will be well placed in a good job." In fact in a fascinating turn of events, a corollary has appeared: when women do not participate in the workforce or are not in school, this is increasingly perceived as a type of "backwardness." In part, some of these changes are coming about as the result of global advertising. Men's views are subtly linked to ideologies of consumerism and "rising up in the world." To be "modern" now means that one needs to acquire certain consumer goods that are promoted by the media—and increased resources are needed to make this happen.

Young women increasingly also have greater aspirations than their mothers. Whereas in the past unskilled labor and microcredit were the only options open to many vulnerable women, education is increasingly the pathway to a more secure and lucrative future. Education allows young women to market themselves in new ways to potential marriage partners and has increased their value and influence in their families.

Despite the promise of some of these successful initiatives, it is important not to generalize to "all" girls or adolescents when creating programming that may give them a head start in life. Instead, it is critical to target subsets of young people differentiated by age, culture, marital and social status, economic class, living arrangements, and urban-rural differences (Brady, Salouco, & Chong, 2007). Another important step is to take a strength-based approach to investigate what kind of programming is already in place in various areas. Many communities and organizations around the globe are currently attempting to address young people's needs—however, much of the programming focuses on school attendance, targets urban populations, and favors the participation of older boys. Girls living in rural areas and young married females are often excluded or neglected in programs and policies. Awareness of cultural values and examining specifically the needs of girls can go a long way to assisting girls and women create brighter economic and social futures for themselves.

The shift in gender roles portends another important trend: as women's lives improve, their families and communities benefit simultaneously. And for women, increased training and the ability to earn an income brings confidence and a sense of autonomy (Ganguly-Scrase, 2003). Self-empowerment leads to collective action, and this ultimately is what truly can affect social change.

There has been a shift around the globe in terms of thinking about market forces. For example, some of the individuals most closely associated with the World Bank, such as Joseph Stiglitz (2002), have come to realize that just letting the market reign supreme without any regulations does not necessarily benefit the poorest individuals in low-income countries, and may in fact have hurt them. Moreover, increasingly the failure of the neoliberal model is understood to lie not just in economic factors but also in cultural explanations. The neoliberal model remains grounded in a

Western, individualistic perception of human nature. By forcing poor individuals and families in rural areas and low-income countries to become more "entrepreneurial" and to take on the responsibilities of paying for health and educational services completely negates centuries of collectivized action and thought (Tikly, 2004). This shift in thinking has forced the World Bank to acknowledge that in certain cases the levels of poverty in low-income countries have increased under its structural adjustment programs (Gore, 2000). This realization has led to a new interest in "social capital" as a critical corollary to "human capital." In particular, there is increasing concern in building social solidarity instead of individual self-interest as a necessary aspect of creating prosperity and growth (Tikly, 2004).[11]

The extreme shift in thinking is based in part on the work of Robert Putnam who defined social capital as "trust, norms and networks, that can improve the efficiency of society by facilitating coordinated action" (Putnam, 1993, p. 167). Tikly (2004), however, suggests that by concentrating on social capital, non-Western cultures and identities tend to become "essentialized." They come to be seen as fixed in time with no sense of transformation or evolution. We see this reflected in the way that discussions of other places tend not to reflect class and gender differences, and in the lack of focus on ethnic variations in societies.

While in some cases global restructuring and neoliberal ideologies and policies have harmed the interests of women and done little to remove gender inequities, there are key aspects of these agendas that have also set the stage for immense global change with respect to the democratization of both female and male voices. As Bandy (2004, p. 412) suggests:

Liberal capitalism has caused vast power inequities, political corruption, competitive cultures, and violent conflicts of unending variety and scope, [however,] economic liberalism has fostered democratic public spheres by expanding aggregate wealth, creating mass urban publics, championing liberal freedoms, promoting representative states, and sparking citizens' movements.

Development does not just encompass improving access to women's educational, occupational, and health-care choices. Instead, development must also focus on the recognition and promotion of human rights. These rights need to be protected through legal frameworks as they have an instrumental value: they promote both individual and collective agency. "A human right is a claim on society that carries obligations for others to promote, protect, and respect that right" (Fukuda-Parr, 2003, p. 310). Fundamentally, this is not an approach that encompasses a set of policy prescriptions. There is no one route or list of action items that can be advocated in order for societies to improve the lives of their most vulnerable members. Over time and contexts, situations and priorities shift. However, there must be general agreement on a local and global level that the rights and concerns of the poorest and most susceptible individuals must be taken into account. In much of the developing world, that group is primarily composed of women. It is thus imperative that the human development approach that is advocated specifically by UN programs and conventions continue to be incorporated into national and global agendas.

The human development paradigm suggests a capabilities/capacity-improving approach to gender equity that differs from a neoliberal focus on income and economic growth. From this perspective, women's poverty is not just a matter of numbers or based on the income gap between women and men. Under the human development umbrella, women's poverty is concerned with lack of access to education, health care, and the right to decision-making. As a corollary, the human development framework advocates for the fact that improvements in women's health care and educational status benefit to the well-being of others as well—subsequently leading to economic growth.

The changes and initiatives that have been described in this chapter indicate that global conditions and trends are closely tied to local community-based activities. Thus, local NGOs and community-based projects cannot just take into account indigenous issues and characteristics. Instead, these projects need to teach women how to exert their influence on macropolicies. The emergence of a "global justice" movement that is traced by some to the WTO in Seattle in 1999 unites the work of NGOs, trade unions, and other localized social movements with the caveat that many constituencies view NGOs as too dependent on government and private funding (Barton, 2004) (http://www.sdonline.org/35/globalwomensmovements3.htm). They are often also perceived as not representing the poor, as not employing a democratic decision-making structure, and as too elitist. Nonetheless, while feminists are often represented and play an important part in NGOs with respect to organizing, many women from various regions of the world are wary of feminism and see feminist issues as inapplicable to their own lives. As the state declines in importance, many of the movements represented by NGOs focus on broader, global challenges such as environmental degradation, privatization of basic services, and the issues around employment. As transnational organizations such as the International Monetary Fund, the World Bank, and the World Trade Organization continue to expand their reach, national concerns around revolutions and elections are declining in importance to many. In fact, the realization that transnational capital is seen as more powerful than state influence is transforming not just the political and economic landscapes but also the very nature of political organizing and the foci for effecting change. Women need to be part of this discussion and these changes.

Notes

1 See Chapter 3 for a description of the UN conferences and their outcomes.
2 There is a tendency for feminists to shy away from this area of concern as women's biological differences are often downplayed in Western contexts.
3 Kenya has among the highest rates of HIV in the world; about 8.7 percent of women aged 15–49 and 4.5 percent of men ages 15–54 are infected. Young women are disproportionately affected and rates of infection are much higher in urban areas than in rural places (Population Council, 2005).
4 For more specifics, see Bruce et al. (2011).
5 Approximately half the population lives on $1.25 a day and 55 percent are deprived of adequate schooling (UN Human Development Report).
6 For a detailed synopsis of Mahila Samakhya and the basis of its success, see my article "Empowering Girls and Women in the Developing World: Local Solutions to Global Issues" (Trask & Unger, 2011).
7 There are many detailed overviews of the opportunities and challenges associated with microfinance. For instance, see "Microfinance and Gender: New Contributions to an Old Issue" (Darbinger, 2007).
8 Muhammad Yunus was awarded the Nobel Peace Prize in 2006 for his work in providing microcredit to the poor.
9 The Population Council is a research and development organization concerned with population and reproductive health.
10 There is some debate whether CCTs are more effective if there are no conditions attached to the benefit such as in South Africa for example.
11 See Tikly (2004) for a very interesting discussion about the Western bias of development work and development economics in contrast to non-Western tradiations.

9

SUPPORTING WORKING FAMILIES AND GENDER EQUALITY
Policy Responses in the Industrialized World

A recent vignette on a popular U.S. morning show introduced a young working woman in her early thirties excitedly espousing the necessity of having her husband help with the housework while she pursued her career in marketing. She expressed dismay at the idea that at a previous time women were expected to "do it all." "How impossible" was the gist of the interview with her. However, for millions of women, even in the industrialized world, despite progress with respect to gender equality and more supportive work–family policies, an unequal distribution of domestic versus work responsibilities remains the reality of their lives.

As has been extensively discussed throughout this work, women's participation in the paid labor force continues to rapidly grow around the world. Despite this transformation, these significant changes in both economic and social life are unevenly supported by policies that allow women to combine family and work, even in the most progressive countries in the industrialized world. While legal agendas now emphasize equal opportunities and at least some of the more blatant biases with respect to the situation and treatment of female employees have been removed, the balance of employment versus caretaking even in the best contexts remains unresolved. Much of the dilemma remains due to two reasons: 1) most workplace structures and policies are based on the outdated notion that men will be committed to full-time employment; and 2) that women will provide most of the unpaid domestic work and caregiving. While in much of the industrialized world, men are increasingly involved with child care, elder care and the care of the sick and disabled continues to remain within the female sphere of responsibilities. This situation creates an unequal context for the balance of domestic versus work responsibilities for women.

From an ideational and social perspective, in contemporary Western industrialized countries there now exists strong support for the equal treatment of women and men. In virtually every Western country, legal provisions against discrimination based on sex are a foundational aspect of the law: men and women have to be treated equally with respect to the entitlement to social provisions. However, that said, in most cases men and women are not equally situated. At various points in their lifespan, women are much more likely to be engaged in caregiving responsibilities which constrain their participation in paid employment. While there is debate if women "choose" to limit their employment as an adaptive response to their familial situations, there is no arguing that gender still strongly structures their choices. Women's part-time and interrupted employment mean that from a life-span perspective men and women do not finish in the same place with respect to their economic situations. Due to these interruptions, over their lives women become more at risk of landing in poverty and are not always able to claim equivalent employment-based benefits. Specifically, pensions and insurance benefits are affected by periods of low income and/or lack of work. We, thus, have a situation in the Western industrialized world where there is relatively equal access to benefits for those who are in equivalent positions. However, for those individuals who need to either drop out of the workforce or who can only participate partially, their ultimate economic outcomes are usually adversely impacted. Only the Nordic countries differ with respect to these risk factors for women. In the Nordic countries, strong state-supported services allow women who are gainfully employed to balance their work and domestic responsibilities, and the government provides a social safety net for those whose lives may take a downturn. Supportive social services are combined with shorter workdays for parents and generous maternity and family leave provisions, creating a very different situation for working families than in other parts of the industrialized world.

The Dominance of Markets in High-Income Countries—A Negative Trend for Women

In the industrialized world, governments have responded to globalization processes by focusing on reduced social spending, maximizing exports, loosening economic regulations, and reorganizing national economies into transnational trading blocs. Workplaces are being restructured to reflect a more entrepreneurial direction that includes decentralized wage-fixing processes and a devolution toward self-management (Blackmore, 1999). Whereas post-World War II, governments exerted control over markets, increasingly, states have let markets dominate and intervene only in crisis situations. Many industrialized states now see as their primary goal the promotion of a market economy instead of providing services to the citizenry, or as Blackmore (1999) writes, "a shift away from a sense of collective social responsibility." In the United States, the attainment of well-being is increasingly dependent on individual efforts instead of being an agreed upon contract between individuals and the state (deRuyter & Warnecke, 2008).

Blackmore points out that "the promise of seemingly more democratic local self management as espoused in policy texts cross-nationally, masks the overarching framework in which democratic politics and notions of public responsibility are being re-defined in the reduced public sectors of most Western liberal democracies" (p. 35). Thus, what is happening is that the state is moving its responsibility for education, health, and the welfare of individuals away and onto the family.

"There is a re-commodification underway in that all services (public and private) are relegated to the market, and in so doing are removed from politics, as the market is seen to be value free. These services are thus being reconstituted, but with the family, not the state, as the fundamental building block in society" (Blackmore, 1999, pp. 40–41). Those institutions that have historically mediated between markets and individuals, governments, unions, and educational systems are being weakened and reorganized. Their new forms now reflect contemporary market-driven values of corporatization, individual choice, supply and demand, and competitiveness. Moreover, citizens are receiving less state support but are actually more accountable to states because they are expected to increase national productivity through more efficient work schedules and with fewer benefits.

Decentralization and outsourcing and downsizing in the industrialized world have worked against the interests of women. In most instances, women who work part time are not covered by collective bargaining agreements nor are they unionized. This makes them more likely to be "downsized." Moreover, the move to more individualized contractual employer–employee relations has actually increased the gender wage gap as employers set their own parameters about "appropriate" pay scales. While under a welfare regime the state set the primary principles for industrial regulations, in the new world order states do not get involved in such forms of market regulations.

An extremely important aspect of the economic and social transformation that is underway in the industrialized world is the move away from a family wage to individual wages. In a globalized cost-cutting environment, it benefits market and the employer to negotiate pay with employees individually and not to be held responsible for providing "extras" such as health insurance, paid leaves, and other such "perks." Instead, employers increasingly feel entitled to buy purely the actual labor of employees (for example, by paying only minimum wage for hours worked). Blackmore (1999) cautions feminists not to be complacent about the lack of gendered analysis when it comes to these sorts of issues that are associated with globalization. Since globalization is commonly related to the decrease of state powers, an increased role of markets over politics and a focus on competitive individuals instead of community concerns, these processes for the most part do not favor women. Women tend not to fit the ideal of the independent worker who fully exploits his or her own potential in a competitive environment. Yet, this is one of the cornerstones of market theory. Due to their social roles, women are tied to complex social relationships in their roles as caregivers and cannot just realize their own potential in the way that is demanded under a philosophical orientation that favors enterprising, individually oriented workers.

Extensive empirical research indicates that women spend more time caring not just for children but also for the sick, elderly, and disabled. The "caring professions" such as education, health care, and elder care are also characterized by a disproportionately higher number of women (Folbre, 2008). It is important to remember that care is context and person-specific. In other words, some people and certain situations elicit more care than others making it difficult to quantify the amount of time people spend caring for others. Care also has a personal dimension—some individuals enjoy providing care and derive emotional rewards from this activity, while others may find care provision as burdensome. It is this constellation of characteristics that makes care as a commodity difficult to fold into policy discussions and decisions.

In order to better understand some of the critical changes that have been brought about in the lives of women in industrialized societies, it is instructive to examine some of the most important legal and policy transformations that pertain to gender and family issues with respect to the workplace.

Case Study: The European Union and Gender Equality at the Workplace

The transition to having significant numbers of women in the labor force has been accompanied by concerns and legislation about the actual relations between the sexes in work contexts. Specifically, women's rights with respect to protection from harassment and access to equal opportunity have been the focus of important regulations and policies. These policies have even been described as "a watershed in the history of welfare state egalitarianism" (Esping-Andersen, 1999 in Gottfried & Reese, 2003). In practice, however, the application and success of these policies has been variable and very context specific.[1]

The European Union countries present a particularly interesting case study of the development of gender equality policy. Beginning with the 1957 Treaty of Rome, which included an article on equal

---

pay, gender equality policies in the European Union now include a universal focus on hiring, promotion, and working conditions.

Starting in the early 1970s, various European entities employed the European Court of Justice to dispute workplace discrimination. The gender equality objective expanded incrementally to include, by 2002, a definition of sexual harassment as sexual discrimination and this became part of the Directive on Equal Treatment. After nearly 20 years of dispute about whether harassment was "really" discrimination, Article 2, number 3 of the 2002 Directive finally stated that "sexual harassment within the meaning of this Directive shall be deemed to be discrimination on the grounds of sex and therefore be prohibited" (Zippel, 2004, p. 61). Today, specifically, protecting women from sexual harassment has become a cornerstone of all EU gender-focused policies.

In contrast to the United States, where the Supreme Court set the standards around sexual discrimination and harassment, in the EU very few courts initially upheld this directive. Since most member states lacked provisions around legal redress or access to courts for issues dealing with discrimination and harassment, new regulations were sorely needed in this area. In the United States, the legal foundation for sexual harassment laws was built on the laws prohibiting racial harassment. This basis stemmed from the 1964 Civil Rights Act. Interestingly, in the European Union, progress has evolved in a contrasting direction. Sexual harassment and discrimination laws have become the basis for dealing with racial and other types of discrimination.

While passing laws are one aspect of containing sexual discrimination and harassment, their implementation and enforcement are just as crucial. Now that legislation and enforcement banning discrimination are embedded in the contemporary laws of Western industrialized countries, multiple studies indicate that the interaction between a variety of entities including employers, unions, and gender equality "enforcers" such as national- and state-level equality offices and/or courts have led to differential experiences and outcomes for women. For instance, in the United States, women's rights at the workplace have been primarily enacted through court cases that have highlighted those actions that clearly violate women's rights. The cases are commonly associated with class action suits and high fines for the violators. In Germany by contrast, political parties and unions have been the primary agents of social action with respect to enforcing the rights of women in the workplace. Class action suits, an important mechanism in the United States, have had little effect in the German system where employers are not as pressured to respond to incidences of sexual harassment or discrimination (Gottfried & Reese, 2003). In contrast, in Japan, which has a more collectivistic orientation, public trials serve to "shame" employers and companies to adhere to practices of non-discrimination and harassment. In the Japanese case, monetary retribution is not seen as important as the public stigma that is created through allegations of discrimination and harassment.

In part due to what is perceived as undue and excessive legislation in the United States, European policy-makers, employers, and feminists have worked to redefine sexual harassment. In most countries, there has been no legal ban on romantic relationships at the workplace nor is flirtatious behavior perceived as problematic. For instance, the general stance in Germany is that women are autonomous actors who have the right to enter into consensual relationships. In contrast in Spain, sexual harassment from a superior is perceived as problematic but attentions from a peer not necessarily so (Zippel, 2004).

In the United States, the emphasis of an extensive number of rules and policies has been on regulating sexuality in the workplace. However this exclusive focus is heavily criticized by feminists and policy-makers both here and abroad. They point out that prohibiting sexual conduct in the workplace does not resolve issues of discrimination and harassment. Instead, both American and European feminists argue that women need to be better integrated into workplaces. In higher-level professional sectors, many women are segregated from male-dominated spaces and, thus, are not able to achieve top positions. Occupational segregation also occurs between low-paid "female" jobs and higher-paid "male" jobs. Focusing exclusively on sexuality does not redress this issue. With this in mind, the European approach has been to emphasize "fairness" at the workplace instead of the U.S. focus on "sexual conduct." The concept of "fairness" shifts the legal focus to exclusionary practices at work as well as institutionalized structures that discriminate against women and allows for change to occur at a deeper level (Zippel, 2004).

Policy Responses to Support Women's Dual Roles

Orloff (2002) highlights that a major contribution of the feminist movement to policy discussions and changes has been the elimination of women's economic dependence on men, the recognition of their unequal participation in civic society, and women's continuing burden of care labor. In particular, Western feminists have stressed that gaining and maintaining access to paid employment is the most important strategy for guaranteeing gender equality. Recently there has been increased attention to the fact that gender equality is not achieved merely by providing more jobs for women and that integrating women equitably into the labor force is a much more complex process than is usually acknowledged in policy discussions or by employers. In order for workers to truly be integrated into the labor force and to be productive workers, the quality of the jobs with respect to earnings, hours, conditions, and caretaking is critical (Orloff, 2002). As we have seen, globalization creates even more challenges for this goal: as the primary focus on cheaper labor and cost cutting is heightened, the interests of individual workers become even less important than in the past. An exclusive focus on profit and economics also obfuscates the contexts in which workers perform their labor. As workers attempt to balance caretaking and domestic responsibilities with their employment, their actual output may lessen. It thus behooves employers and policy-makers to take into account their workers' familial contexts (O'Connor et al., 1999). In response to this realization, many feminists are working to reshape employment opportunities around the concept that women specifically are also caretakers. They have suggested that extensive public services that provide care outside of the home bolster women's employment while their absence has a significant effect. Many of their efforts have been opposed by conservative parties that stress and encourage market-focused models. Market models constrain women's employment opportunities by placing family considerations second.

To counter conservative trends, feminists in the United States have pointed to the Nordic countries, especially Sweden, where women's employment is prioritized, and care has shifted to institutions other than the family (Orloff, 2002). In the Nordic countries and France, child-care services are public and high-quality. For instance, in the "EduCare" systems in the Scandinavian countries, teachers in child-care centers and preschool programs are required to have university degrees and usually some kind of vocational or polytechnic training. These state-controlled and financed services allow mothers to easily re-enter full-time paid employment after the birth of a child. The United States and Canada operate on a very different model: the norm is for child care to be private and market driven. This has resulted in systems that are often unregulated, low-quality, and location dependent. Women who want to re-enter the workforce are often put into a conflictual situation that forces them to place their children into sub-standard care. In the industrialized world we, thus, have a spectrum with respect to child care from the public models, where high-quality childcare services are encouraged through state regulation, education, and financial backing, to the private model that is often inadequate since workers tend to be underpaid, undertrained, and undervalued leading to high turnover rates. As Gottfried and Reese write, "The quality of care work is likely to be associated with the quality of care" (2003, p. 14). In contrast, to these two extremes lie countries such as Germany and Japan where child care has been separated from public education. Gottfried and Reese (2003) point out that the result has been increased access to private child care but with hours that do not accommodate the whole range of work schedules of two working parents. Strikingly, however, cross-national comparisons indicate that the staff engaged in early childhood provision and education in all of these countries is relatively well compensated. This allows us to see that the valuing of child care plays an integral role in quality provision.

Fertility, Family Values, and Work

Work–family issues have become a major topic of concern, primarily in the European Union countries, due to fertility issues. As a massive decline in birth rates to levels that are far below those necessary for population replacement has become the dominant pattern, policy-makers have sought to stem this trend.[2] While in the past high fertility was associated with countries where there were strong cultural traditions that valued family life and low engagement of women in the paid labor force, this relationship has been transformed. Some of the countries with the strongest familialistic traditions now exhibit the lowest fertility rates in the world, with the average European country coming in at 1.59 children per woman (OECD, 2012). This is a highly problematic trend as it has long-term policy implications. Should a country sustain a long-term period of below replacement level fertility, its population declines rapidly. Castles (2003) notes that over a period of a century, the eventual population could decrease to a quarter of its original size. Austria, Greece, Italy, and Spain are currently on that trajectory, while Germany and Japan are close behind.

Table 9.1 Select Examples of Total Fertility Rate, 2010

Europe	
France	2.0
Germany	1.4
Italy	1.4
Netherlands	1.8
Poland	1.4
Russian Federation	1.5
Spain	1.5
Sweden	1.9
United Kingdom	1.5

(continued)

Table 9.1 (Continued)

Asia	
China	1.2
India	2.6
Philippines	3.1
Japan	1.4
South Korea	1.3

North America	
Canada	1.7
Mexico	2.3
United States	1.9

Middle East	
Egypt	2.7
Israel	2.9
Jordan	3.1
Saudi Arabia	2.8
Turkey	2.4

Central and South America	
Argentina	2.2
Brazil	1.8
Chile	1.9
Colombia	2.4
Peru	2.5

Sub-Saharan Africa	
Ethiopia	4.2
Kenya	4.7
Nigeria	5.5
South Africa	2.5

Source: www.worldfamilymap.org/2012-2013/e-ppendix/table1.

In contrast to the decrease in fertility in countries that have historically supported traditional family arrangements, the English-speaking and Scandinavian countries are exhibiting relatively higher fertility rates. These trends in the Northern countries are accompanied by higher divorce rates, higher cohabitation rates, and higher extra-marital birth rates—thus, indicating a reversal of the commonly held beliefs that fertility should be highest in countries where an emphasis on family is the strongest. How can we explain this surprising phenomenon? Esping-Andersen (1999) and Castles (2003) argue that there is a strong link between cultural trends and economic policies. They point out that the social policies in

Catholic countries that purport to support families make it very complex for women to balance work and family. Women, thus, are choosing employment over having children, leading to the low fertility rates. In contrast, in countries that provide supportive policies for balancing work and children, women today are more encouraged to have children. Their hypothesis is supported by analyses from the OECD. These analyses indicate that changes in fertility rates and women's employment in industrialized countries are very much tied to family-friendly policies that allow women to complete their education and take on paid employment without making their child-care situations their primary worry.[3]

Castles (2003) presents a compelling analysis of this issue. He, correctly, points out that decisions about when and how many children to have, despite being individual and couple-based decisions, are ultimately influenced by context and the values of a particular time. It is not that the trade offs between having a family and being gainfully employed have necessarily become easier. Instead, women and couples decide to mix employment and fertility based on a wide variety of variables. Most importantly, they are constrained by the notions of what constitutes appropriate parenting and the roles of men and women at a particular point in socio-historical space. These values are malleable—what is considered appropriate at one point, may be perceived as detrimental at another. Thus, maternal employment in the post-World War II years was frowned upon in many countries of the West. The labor force participation of mothers with young children was perceived as detrimental to child development, leading to a strong stigma for those women who had to or chose to work outside of the home. He also points out, however, that the fact that so many women *could* stay home and concentrate on child rearing was an aberration in human history resulting from postwar economic surpluses that allowed women to be purely engaged with domestic responsibilities:

> the fact that so many women stayed at home to look after their children from birth to maturity can, with only some minor hyperbole, be likened to a form of conspicuous consumption on the part of industrialized societies made suddenly prosperous by postwar economic growth.
>
> (Castles, 2003, p. 218)

In the contemporary context, with shifting values brought on by the feminist revolution, women are now perceived as having the same needs and rights to work outside of the home as men. Thus, from a policy and social perspective, fertility must somehow be combined with the world of work. Moreover, women's economic contributions are today more prized in the marriage market over their domestic skills. Having a good education and being gainfully employed have become precursors to family formation.

213

Given these shifts in social values, women are much more likely to try to find ways to accommodate having a family with balancing work demands than in the past. This transformation in values explains why countries that accommodate women who work outside of the home with supportive social policies and services are seeing an upswing in fertility rates in contrast to countries that continue to try to enforce a traditional breadwinner–homemaker model. Women are much more likely to be comfortable having children if they know that quality child care is available and that they will be able to re-enter the workforce due to legal protections. It is at this juncture that national policies and academic scholarship converge. Academics allow policy-makers to understand that fertility decisions are ultimately impacted by a range of policy decisions that cover everything from visa restrictions for domestic workers to the education of child-care workers. As the balance between work and family is readjusted, the fertility behaviors of a whole nation are at stake.

Interestingly, it is often countries that profess the importance of family most vehemently that actually do the least in terms of providing policies and services that support women and men as they struggle with the demands of negotiating work and family responsibilities. Instead, today it is in the countries that have more consciously embraced fundamental family and work transformations, that supportive policies have been implemented. As Castles (2003) writes, "the world has been turned upside down because women in the industrialized countries have changed their views as to their proper role in society and because governments, in at least some of these countries have changed their policies to accommodate those views" (p. 220).

Parental Leave and the Regulation of Working Time—Does this Matter?

While awareness of the issues discussed above is high in Western industrialized countries, which policies are appropriate in differing contexts remain highly disputed. Moreover, there are many types of family-friendly policies. For instance, some policies encourage women to stay home after having children by giving them tax credits and child benefits, as in Germany. Or in the French and Swedish examples, the governments provide high-quality subsidized child care, allowing women to easily re-enter the paid labor force after having children. EU policies that allow for longer leave allowances and flexible work arrangements also belong under the umbrella of work–family policies. In order to assess the usefulness of these latter policies let us examine them in greater detail.

Parental Leave

In the industrialized world, by far one of the most important social policies for women and men has been the extension of parental and family leave. In its initial version, maternity leave allowed women to take time off before and after childbirth. As female labor force participation increased, in particular among women with young children (the group that historically stayed home), all industrialized countries adopted some form of maternity leave that was then converted to either parental or family leave. In the United States, the FMLA differs quite significantly from its European counterparts due to two basic provisions: 1) there is a lack of remuneration for the individual who chooses to take a family leave; and 2) child and elder care are combined under the same umbrella. Moreover, there is a great deal of variation between states in terms of the quality and content of family leave regulations.

Parental leave and maternity programs are an important aspect of allowing women to work on more equitable terms by guaranteeing an income even when women are engaged in periods of caregiving. However, by dropping out of the workforce for periods of time, women lose out on the security of retirement benefits as those are predicated on lifelong contributions. Some countries have recently attempted to address this issue by developing caregiving credits. Thus, when an individual drops out of the workforce for a period of time to care for children (or at times other family members), this is counted as insured time and is calculated into the pension benefits.[4] Another significant relatively recent development in the Western context is the recognition that men need to be encouraged to provide care labor. Sweden and Norway lead the way with policies that encourage men through incentives to assist in the care of their infants and young children.[5] Maternal and paternal leave are combined into one program that grants couples about one year to be shared between them. During this period they are paid between 80 to 100 percent of their salaries. By creating a non-transferable entitlement, men are encouraged to use this benefit, resulting in more positive experience at work and at home. Other countries have been slow to follow suit, but as Connell (2005) points out, recent changes in redefining masculinity include male involvement with children as an important component, making these kinds of policy modifications more possible in the future.

In the European Union countries, the policy bodies of the EU have played an important role in standardizing and expanding parental leave programs (Gornick & Myers, 2008). For instance, the EU put into place a Directive on Parental Leave and Leave for Family Reasons in 1995. This ensured that in each member country men and women would receive at least three months of paid or unpaid parental leave that was separate from maternity leave. The directive also set the guidelines for protecting workers from being dismissed due to having to take a parental leave.

These modifications to the basic family policies supported by Western industrialized states are in order with the general global emphasis that has been placed on supporting parents and children. In order to acknowledge the importance of the work performed by parents, the United

Nations Convention on the Rights of the Child (1989), which was ratified by all nations except for the United States and Somalia, instructs that "the nation shall provide appropriate assistance to parents in child-raising." Family allowances, parental leave, publicly supported child care and education, and more flexible work hours are all relatively new adjustments to the demands of balancing work and family life. These benefits, however, still do not adequately cover the total financial and social expenditures that are accrued by working individuals who choose to have children. In today's environment, it is often individuals and couples who choose *not* to have children who are best off financially (Folbre, 2006).

Comparisons of social policies in industrialized countries indicate that in many places family and parental leave policies are much more popular than public child-care support. This highlights the inadequacy of a social infrastructure of care services throughout these countries, with the exception being Sweden. However, the fact that in places where women have relatively easy access to quality child care, fertility rates have risen, indicates that it is not the public versus private nature of child care that matters, but instead it is access and quality that counts. Policy needs to be better informed by empirical research and should, therefore, focus on strengthening both public and private forms of child care, filling in the gaps on either end of the spectrum.

The Regulation of Working Time

While there is much attention given to parental and maternal leaves, tax credits and allowances for children, and the provision of quality child care, much less emphasis has been placed on actually restructuring the workplace. Gornick and Heron (2006) suggest that instead of constantly focusing on social policies and the needs of parents, we should fundamentally rethink the arrangement of work. They suggest a three-pronged restructuring of employment including: 1) reducing the full-time working week to less than the common standard of 40 hours; 2) legally allowing workers to take a certain number of paid days off work; and 3) expanding the benefits associated with part-time work. They suggest by restructuring the number of hours worked per week, employees would feel less vulnerable if they were not able to work overtime and that this would standardize the definition of what is full-time work.[6] Moreover, working parents would be able to be home more, leading to stronger life satisfaction. Re-structuring part-time work would give employees more control over determining work–family schedules without too great a loss in financial compensation. Gornick and Heron (2006) also provide a very interesting analysis of the effects of some of these policy changes by examining data from the United States, Japan, and the countries of the European Union. What they find is that policy reforms aimed at reducing time at work have had a significant effect in Europe. Over the last 20 years, the average amount of time at work from an annual perspective has decreased significantly in most EU countries, with most workers today working an average of 1,530 to 1,600 per year. In the United States in contrast, the amount of hours people spend at work annually has increased over the last 20 years, to approximately 1,800 hours per year. Also, since the national legislation that set the work week was enacted in 1938, there has been no reduction to the number of hours required of employees and this is not a topic that is on the public agenda of lawmakers. In fact, they point out that Americans view time at work as a sign of "industriousness," and as an important aspect of the United State's high per capita GDP. They go on to say:

> Perhaps more significant is that even "work–family" scholars and advocates in the US rarely address the length of the normal full-time working week, the definition of full-year work, or the quality of part-time work. American work–family advocates, instead, typically focus on the need for child care, paid family leave, and (employer-based) programs that permit flexibility in determining which—if not how many—hours workers will spend on the job.
>
> (p. 151)[7]

Gornick and Heron's (2006) cross-country analysis reveals that there are significant differences between the United States, Japan, and the EU countries not just with respect to total number of days and hours worked but also in terms of vacation days, holidays, and remuneration for paid part-time employment. For instance, policies that support and improve part-time work in the European Union are constantly being modified and improved in order to eliminate discrimination against part-time workers. However, labor law in the United States only focuses on the necessity of providing minimum wages to part-time workers. Similarly, Japanese law provides no pay or benefit protection for part-time workers. Gornick and Heron (2006) conclude their analysis by raising the question of cost: if working hours are reduced, and part-time work becomes more common, what is lost in the process? Their work reveals two important consequences of the proposed work modifications: 1) when European workers accept shorter hours, they are often saddled with less standard working schedules; and 2) part-time work ends up with a gender differential. Ultimately, (and we have seen this before in our discussions of work in the developing world), women take on more part-time work than men and may then be disadvantaged in their career and pay trajectories. Conversely, part-time work allows some women to re-enter the labor market instead of staying home as full-time caregivers. Despite all of these limitations, shorter work weeks seem to foster greater gender equality.

As both men and women spend less time at work, they may participate more equally in domestic settings. However, this is a hypothetical determination and requires more empirical study in those places where some of these policies have been implemented.

Conflicting Perspectives on which Policies Really Support Working Parents

While work–family conflict or negotiation has become a dominant paradigm in the study of contemporary social life, the locus of the problem is not agreed upon. Some analysts argue that having working parents (mothers specifically) deprives children from important developmental experiences. Others point to the fact that women are often over extended due to their multiple roles in contemporary societies and that they thus sustain unhealthy levels of stress. Meanwhile, another strand of thought points to the persistent gender disparities in the work realm and the dominant ideal worker model that is predicated on a traditional breadwinner–homemaker arrangement. Still others highlight the high cost of care labor when it is taken out of the home, and either subsidized by the state or given over to the market (Gornick & Heron, 2006).

The range of these arguments helps explain why there is so little agreement about how to better support families and what parents really need in order to assist them in reconciling family life and work demands. Adding in the gendered dimension of work–life negotiation further complicates the situation. Policy-makers and employers alike would prefer simple, uniform answers to the questions about how to support workers and make them more generally productive. In fact, there are some that argue that as we move to a world where gender convergence is increasingly the norm, there is no need to have gender-specific policies.[8] However, as has been argued throughout this volume, women face specific types of vulnerabilities and forms of discrimination with respect to balancing work and family. Ignoring the gender dimension in these discussions is, thus, not a viable option in today's world.

Despite a general yearning on the part of feminists, employers, employees, and all other concerned parties, there is no one-size-fits-all solution to the issue of integrating women's employment, caretaking responsibilities, and policy provisions. In fact, there is no agreement among policy-makers, feminists, or employers and employees about which policies are critical, which ones are women-friendly, and which ones need to be enforced most stringently. Gottfried and Reese (2003) advocate the following:

> Women-friendly policies should promote feminist goals and principles of gender justice by breaking down gender-based hierarchies, they should enhance women's independence and increase

their capacity to support and sustain an independent household, they should empower women, and they should end unequal burdens of labor.

(p. 16)

Integrating Men into Work–Family Discussions

Many tenets of the work–family debate depend on the regional and national context within which the reconciliation of employment and care needs to take place. However, in order to arrive at any sort of viable solution, irrespective of context, men need to be an integral part of the discussion and the solution. In the contemporary global context, men are also adversely affected by the changes to employment opportunities—jobs that used to be available to men, jobs with a family wage and benefits, are increasingly rare and have been replaced by shiftwork and part-time jobs, putting an increasing number of men at economic risk. In order for work–family issues to be better reconciled, men must also increasingly embrace a caretaker identity. As women take on breadwinner responsibilities, a shift to a dual caretaker–breadwinner model is almost inevitable, despite the lag in progress in this arena. A move in that direction would help obscure the current gendered contrast between working for pay and taking on care responsibilities. In order to spur a shift in gender roles and move to greater gender parity, workplaces in the future will need to acknowledge and facilitate through their policies the lives of workers who have caregiving responsibilities—and that includes *both* men and women. Workers need to have the ability to take time off for caregiving without fearing the loss of their jobs, and they need access to programs that assist them with their varied responsibilities. Just as women are encouraged to enter paid employment, men need to be encouraged to take on caregiving responsibilities.

Gornick and Meyers (2008) suggest a new social arrangement for the future. From their perspective, what would be most functional would be a dual-earner/dual-caregiver society. This would entail restructuring society to provide equal opportunities for men and women in the work sphere, equal contributions from both at home, and the availability of high-quality child care provided by both parents and non-parental caregivers. Gornick and Meyers also suggest a policy blueprint that gives paid family leave to both women and men, regulates work time, and subsidizes early childhood education and care. As part of their gender-equalizing policy suggestions they emphasize that both men and women would need access to leave entitlements and that each employed parent would have his or her non-transferable entitlement. This is a model that has already been instituted in Sweden and has succeeded in encouraging men to take on caregiving responsibilities after the birth of a child. Besides some of the other policies that have already been discussed in this chapter, such as better regulated working hours and state subsidized quality childcare, Gornick and Meyer suggest that child care, preschool, and school schedules be better matched to parents' working hours. They rightly point out that for parents who work a standard full-time job, the continuity of child care centers at schools are critically important. They also highlight the fact that for parents who work non-standard hours, alternatives for child care need to be available.

While not as utopian as they assume, given that many of these family-friendly policies are already in place in Sweden, Norway, Finland, Denmark, and France, one fallacy of the Gornick and Meyer (2008) model is that it is predicated on the assumption that all families are composed of dual-earner couples. This ignores the reality—that, increasingly, single-headed families are becoming as common as other family forms. It thus behooves us to institute measures that allow *individuals* to deal with family, work, and caregiving responsibilities and not to always assume that all families are continuously composed of couples. Families need choices with respect to which policies and services will work with their particular situation. Moreover, I suggest reframing the issue to also not always suppose that work, children, and the interests of parents are in constant conflict with each other. There is enough contemporary empirical evidence that maternal satisfaction influences mothers' relationships with their children, and that, at least in the United States, many younger men are intensely involved with their children. Another unexamined assumption is that work–family negotiation is similar across ethnic, racial, and class lines. The reality is that we know little about the role of extended family and fictive kin in mediating work–family demands among different groups in Western industrialized countries.

The social changes within families and work contexts that are discussed in this chapter are reflected in the wide range of policy responses in the Western industrialized world. As we have seen, the range includes caregivers' allowances and shorter workdays or workweeks for caregivers, to the notion that benefits should be provided for all citizens and not be contingent on employment. In some cases, such as in Germany, financial assistance is given to those taking on caretaking responsibilities instead of expanding social services in those areas. Moreover, new conceptualization of the state allows us to understand that policy responses can be introduced and instituted through a variety of mechanisms. As Blackmore (1999) writes:

> Most feminists no longer view the state as being a monolithic set of structures. The state is conceived to be a range of practices, processes, procedures and structures which work, often in contradiction to each other, but which can provide openings for feminist interventions.
>
> (p. 36)

As families, work, states, and policies are re-conceptualized, we will be able to move away from the traditional breadwinner–homemaker model that has provided the basis for so much social policy with respect to work–family issues. Social change tends to be slow, uneven, and at times in conflict. However, the first step is identifying the problems. With respect to work–family reconciliation, this has happened most extensively in Europe and to a lesser extent in the United States and Japan. There are now various models to choose from and there is empirical evidence about which policies are effective, and in which contexts.

Despite the many advances, especially in the European context with respect to reconciling work–family demands, concern remains that some of these policies may also serve to worsen the gender gap, especially by lowering the glass ceiling for women. For instance, evidence from Sweden, Norway, and Finland indicates that despite gender-neutral policies, there is a relatively high level of occupational segregation, especially in high-status jobs. This phenomenon has been attributed to intrinsic gender discrimination: employers are reluctant to hire and promote women into demanding jobs. They worry that women will be more likely to take parental and family leaves than men. Critics of generous work–family policies suggest that while a lack of these provisions creates a strain on employees, women are actually more able to reach top positions when these policies are not in place. Basically, when women do not have the option to take leave, they are more likely to act like men in their work behavior (Gornick & Meyers, 2008). This is an unfortunate side effect of some of the recent policy changes and illustrates that it is not enough just to implement policy changes. Instead, constant evaluation and analysis is an important aspect of the policy process in order to ensure that outcomes are in line with the intentions of the various policies that are put into place.

Synopsis

With the recognition that the world of work is changing rapidly and that role transformations in families are permanent, we will ultimately need to revise and create new services and policies that support individuals and families as they balance their various responsibilities. The raising of children and the care of the sick, elderly, and disabled are more than private responsibilities—they affect the public good. As Folbre (2006) has argued extensively, expanding public supports for care helps achieve economic efficiency and leads to socially optimal outcomes. We also need to be cognizant of the fact that as our proportion of the elderly population grows, it is increasingly skewed toward women. Men tend to be less concerned about issues of caring because as Folbre (2008) highlights "married men may fail to purchase long-term care insurance because they already have it—in for the form of a wife. In part because they are likely to outlive their older husbands, women remain far more vulnerable than men to poverty and infirmity in old age" (p. 377). This is an important observation as the issues around care do not just center on the feminization of caring. Instead, we need to be aware that a high number of those being cared for, or who will need care, are women. Often, they do not have the economic resources that they will require in order to be cared for at the end of their lives in a dignified manner.

Caring promises to be one of the most contentious global problems in the twenty-first century. As women withdraw from caring due to their labor market responsibilities, that space will need to be filled. While women may improve their own economic status by not engaging in caring labor, this now creates a social void that will need to be filled by market forces. In other words, caring labor becomes commodified and the price goes up. However, caring labor is unique—there is a personal dimension in caring labor that is often forgotten. Unlike cleaning a house or other domestic obligations, caring is oftentimes predicated on a bond between the involved individuals. That bond cannot be quantified or necessarily bought. Also, with respect to mainstream ideologies, social pressures remain on women to be the primary carers of both children and others. This also raises the question of how men who take on more gender-neutral caring roles will fare. As men begin to move into the care arena, the question arises of how their employment prospects will be affected by taking on these roles. Folbre (2008), for example, asks if now both men and women will be disadvantaged in a market-based economy that does not value family obligations. In other words, will individuals who take on the responsibility of caring extensively for their children, or others for that matter, be penalized in the workplace for their divided focus? Citing the work of Barbara Bergmann (1981), Folbre (2008) comments:

> Bergmann correctly emphasizes that commitments to care for others reduce competitive success in other tasks. That problem will remain whether or not men and women share responsibilities for child care. Fathers who choose to reduce their paid work commitments will likely face penalties in the labor market. Both mommies and daddies could get stuck on "a parent track" that shunts them away from leadership positions.
>
> (p. 378).

Globalization has provided us with new mechanisms for far-reaching transformations. A globalized world also becomes a new context for us to rethink our social relationships and assumptions about the appropriate distribution of roles. As an overarching goal we could and should aim to raise the quality of life for all citizens—parents, children, caregivers, the elderly, and the disabled. We need to refashion a social contract that does not hand all responsibility for workers' lives to employers and the market, and removes the state out of crucial decision-making. It is imperative that these types of discussions reach mainstream debates and affect policy-makers.

While some who are involved in the work–family discussion suggest that leave rights, work schedules, pay, and subsidized child care should be left to the discretion of employers, experiences from around the world indicate that employers cannot and often will not take on all of those supports for families (Gornick & Meyers, 2008). The costs associated with providing these types of benefits are too great, and in particular for small employers virtually impossible to sustain. Thus, the state continues to play an important role in helping set the policy agenda and providing the financial foundation for alleviating the expenses of work–family reconciliatory benefits. In order to enact policies that truly support working individuals and families, alliances between policy-makers, government officials, employers, and academics are the only truly promising route. There is much evidence from around the world about what works and what does not. Compiling best practices and sharing that information in our networked society is just one path forward to helping reconcile work–family issues. Moreover, this is a discussion that needs both women and men at the table. Work–family policies most definitely have a gendered component to them. But as work is restructured for both women and men, and as gender convergence becomes at least ideationally more normative, the incentives and the benefits that come from rethinking and reworking the intersection of work, caregiving, and domestic responsibilities affect everyone.

Notes

1 See Gottfried and Reese (2003) for a more extensive discussion of the wide variation in sexual harassment laws and enforcement.
2 Total Fertility Rate (TFR) of 2.1 children per woman is considered the basic replacement rate for a population, barring migration flows and a stable mortality rate. In 2010 TFRs were far below replacement in most OECD countries but exceeded 2 children per woman in Iceland, Ireland, Israel, Mexico, New Zealand, and Turkey.
3 The OECD is an economic membership of 34 countries that includes the US and Canada, as well as most of the European countries, and several of the economies of South America and the Asia-Pacific region. Its mission is to promote policies that improve the economic and social lives of the populations in its member states. Most recently, the OECD has also been working closely with the governments of developing nations around the world.
4 See Orloff (2002) for a chart comparing European countries.
5 See, for instance, an interesting study by Haas and Hwang (2007) on how companies in Sweden react to policies that encourage men to participate in child care.

6 This would also help move us away from the notion in certain professions that working double the amount of time of what is considered "normal" is necessary for career success.

7 See their article for a country by country comparison of work weeks and hours at work.

8 Gender convergence refers to the notion that men and women, at least in industrialized societies, increasingly have similar aspirations and opportunities. The concept of gender convergence, while currently in vogue, does not deal with the reality of the differential caregiving burden on women vis-à-vis men.

10

EMPOWERMENT THROUGH GLOBALIZATION

Transformed Gender Roles, Work–Family Supports, and Transnational Collaborations

In June of 2012, Anne-Marie Slaughter published an article in *The Atlantic* entitled, "Why Women Still Can't Have it All." In her piece, Dr. Slaughter chronicles her time in Washington in a high-level foreign policy position, and the grueling schedule that she and her co-workers kept. She writes, "In short, the minute I found myself in a job that is typical for the vast majority of working women (and men) working long hours on someone else's schedule … I realized what should have perhaps been obvious: having it all, at least for me, depended almost entirely on what type of job I had" (2012, p. 87). Slaughter continues her commentary with an analysis of the currently popular observation that the dearth of female leaders both in the United States and abroad can be almost single-handedly accounted for by the fact that either women are "not ambitious enough" or that they retreat from taking on leadership roles once they decide to have children. Critical of this stance, she points to her close assistant who, upon hearing of her research for this essay, sends Slaughter an e-mail that states, "'You know what would help the vast majority of women with work/family balance? MAKE SCHOOL SCHEDULES MATCH WORK SCHEDULES'" (2012, p. 90).

In the academic circles in which I move, this article elicited a great deal of thought-provoking commentary. My colleagues and friends concurred with Dr. Slaughter: despite the many advances and the privileged positions that we occupy, women are still in a different position when it comes to balancing work and family in comparison to men. They referred to the fact that women are judged more harshly at work if they take time off to care for their children, and they are often evaluated by other women with respect to their "mothering" abilities. One of my colleagues even pointed to one of our male co-workers and how she had often heard others expound on the fact that he was a "wonderful" father because he had left work early one time to take his children on a field trip, or at another point taken his son to the doctor. She suggested that if a woman had engaged in this behavior as publically as he had, most of our colleagues would have raised their eyebrows about the fact that she was obviously not carrying her full load at work and that she should have arranged for better child-care options.

Obviously, these are the debates of the privileged few—those of us with flexibility and security built into our jobs. However, they also point to the crux of the issues that have been discussed throughout this work: 1) in both industrialized and developing countries and at all levels of society, there is a critical need for policies that allow individuals to juggle their work and domestic responsibilities; and 2) the dialogue surrounding these issues continues to be different for women than for men. Moreover, as this volume has illustrated, the dilemmas confronting women who work for pay are now global issues. The example of Anne-Marie Slaughter's personal experiences highlights the fact that even for women at the top of the socio-economic and educational ladder, the negotiation of work and domestic responsibilities now dominates their lives. Things become even more complex for those women who do not have adequate financial, social, and educational resources.

Contemporary Circumstances

I have argued throughout this book that the postindustrial economy that is now characteristic of so many societies around the globe and the concurrent changes in families that are allowing and/or forcing an increasing number of women to enter the paid workforce are creating a new arena for negotiating work and family relationships. As more and more women are expected to engage in paid labor outside of the home and simultaneously maintain family life, the negotiation of work and home responsibilities has become more complex and public. This phenomenon has led to a parallel development: the traditional patriarchal gender models that have characterized most societies around the world are beginning very slowly to shift to more egalitarian ones. Concurrently, the transformations of the workplace coupled with the structural changes in families are forcing states and employers to reconsider and, albeit reluctantly, modify their policies and services to assist individuals in reconciling work and family responsibilities. In particular, women's caregiving responsibilities are increasingly recognized as an integral aspect of the work–family intersection (Giele, 2006).

Many of the changes in work and family life can be attributed to the complex influences of globalization. An increasingly feminized global labor force, the spread of ideologies concerned with gender equality and women's empowerment, and a move to dual-earner families and households headed by women are all part of globalizing influences. In contrast to many other analysts however, I do not believe that globalization in and of itself is a negative phenomenon. Instead, I concur with the Nobel economist Joseph Stiglitz who has stated that globalization "is neither good nor bad … It has the power to do enormous good" (2002, p. 20). Today, globalization is understood as a much more extensive force, beyond its former connotation of market integration and the free movement of capital. Instead, globalization is also associated with movement across boundaries, with transnational collaborations, and with the spread of ideas, images, and depictions of new lifestyles. We need to remember that globalization has much to offer both women and men. However, the restructuring that is such an integral aspect of globalization calls for an earnest reassessment of the local, national, and transnational arrangements that characterize economic and social life.

Globalization provides the mechanisms for giving the vulnerable, the weak, the marginalized, and the unheard, a voice. In other words, globalization *can and should* be a used as tool for empowerment. While feminists in particular are wary of the concept of empowerment as they feel that this concept is often co-opted by development agendas that force women to participate in pre-determined economic agendas (Desai, 2010), I use the term here to propose the notion that globalization provides women with mechanisms to have power and to change their lives collectively. The communication technologies that have made globalization in part possible, and the collaborative features that are such an integral part of the process, all have the potential to be used to better the human condition. The challenges that come with globalization are immense—but the potential and the opportunities that accompany this phenomenon are also limitless.

In this work, I have sought to identify some of the most contentious issues that primarily affect women in a globalizing environment, with respect to work–family issues. I have also presented these topics from a worldwide perspective as the situation of women differs based on a myriad of factors. In turn, I have highlighted some examples of initiatives and polices that have made a positive difference in women's lives. By no means is this meant to be a comprehensive list or discussion. Instead, I have sought to demonstrate that while there are complex challenges in the contemporary context, many women have also benefited from well-thought-out initiatives and policies that are a direct consequence of globalization. I offer these examples to illustrate that we can learn from the positive responses to the new situations and issues brought on by a changed world order. By redirecting and reformulating local, national, and transnational policies, intensifying collaborations between individuals and groups within societies and across borders, and creating local, national, and transnational supports, we should be able to harness some of the immense power of globalization to move us to an economic and social agenda that is more just and humane. In this manner, we can assist women and their families to develop their potential, attain personal aspirations, and simultaneously create stronger families, communities, and societies.

Global Responses to Changing Gender Roles

The complex nature of the global social transformations taking place today have led to the debate about the appropriate roles of women and men becoming an increasingly contentious issue in both the industrialized and the developing world. In trying to explain the continuation of ideologies that still privilege traditional gender roles, some analysts continue to promote biological arguments about the "essential" or fundamental nature of women and men. Others suggest that the perseverance of traditional gender roles can be understood by their continued usefulness (Parsons & Bales, 1955 in Hattery, 2001). Feminists, however, have been critical of these types of explanations. Instead, they have persisted in pointing out that the ideological construction of the "breadwinner–homemaker family" with its prescriptive rigid gender roles is socially constructed, and particularly repressive for women (Erickson, 2005; Hochschild, 1989; Thompson & Walker, 1989). This feminist outlook on traditional family and gender role arrangements has been promoted in other parts of the globe. However, in many places, this message has not resonated with all parties. Instead, depending on location, growing social unrest, economic woes, and the incorporation of large numbers of women into the workforce have triggered massive ideological, political, and social counter responses. In particular, attention has often re-focused on the changing role of women in families and societies.

Especially, in non-Western parts of the world, growing national movements are advocating for a restoration of "traditional" values as a response to globalization and Westernization. In these areas, the roles of women and men often become the primary symbol of that which is perceived as important for creating a stable society. Oftentimes, these reactions are linked to fundamentalist religious movements. Adherents point to gender roles, and especially the position of women in the family, as a pivotal aspect of reinstating order in a complex and changing world. For instance, in many countries in the Middle East and Southeast Asia, women's veiling has been identified as a symbolic act on the part of women. By donning a headscarf, many young women broadcast their traditional values while participating in contemporary working life (Macleod, 1993; Secor, 2002).

The movement for "restoring" society and rhetoric that advocates saving the social order from decline are also part of today's American mainstream discourse. Various political movements claim "family values" as one of their primary ideological foundations, and promote the idea that restoring the "traditional" family domain is critical to societal stability. This dialogue persists despite general acknowledgment that today's heterogeneous social environment does not lend itself to returning to a form of family life where men are the primary breadwinners and women mainly engage in homemaker responsibilities.[1]

The debate about the appropriate and essential functions of women and men is, however, even more complex than this discussion indicates. The mass scale export of quintessential American feminist perspectives on "appropriate" gender roles (that is, that women need to be working outside of the home and are empowered through this activity, and that men need to be incorporated into the domestic arena), accompanied with the classification of the sphere of family as the site of women's oppression, have evoked a counter response, specifically from feminists working in developing and non-Western parts of the world. They have pointed out that while national ideologies may perpetuate models of traditional gender constructs and family arrangements, women and men are not passive actors. Instead, women and men are actively engaged in creating new models of gender and families in changing environments (Pyle & Ward, 2003). What happens locally may look quite different from what religious groups or state governments espouse. Moreover, in many non-Western contexts, families have traditionally provided a form of security for women from other types of subjugation such as colonialism or racism. Ideological models that do not take into account the positive, protective features of traditional roles or the importance of families for individuals do not necessarily have resonance in these locales.

Globalization has led to multiple ideological and economic constructs and gender role models being available to individuals around the world. We cannot speak of a universal condition nor can we blame the institutions of the family *or* the marketplace for women's and men's experiences. Instead, contextual approaches reveal that a complex interplay of values, resources, and individual responses shape gender constructions and practices. Globalization has been a factor in stimulating and spreading new concepts, values, and images. However, globalization also provides the mechanisms for transnational dialogues around these issues and for bringing individuals and entities together to work out solutions. An increasing number of policy-makers, feminist groups, transnational NGOs, and private citizens are lobbying for changes to policies and services that will support women and men as they struggle to negotiate the competing demands of gender roles, and work and home responsibilities. Later in this chapter we will examine some of the transnational networks that are effectively instituting supports that promote gender equality and assist women with their work–family negotiations. Prior to that discussion, let us revisit the contentious global debates on families and gender roles, a primary aspect of the work–family intersection.

Global Debates on the State of Families

The changing roles of women have led to a global debate about the state of families. For instance, it is quite popular in the industrialized and developing world to argue that women's presence in the labor force and public life in general has led to the deterioration of families (Popenoe, 1993; Wilson, 2002). Both explicit and implicit arguments focus on the threat to social stability of the decline of the traditional breadwinner–homemaker family model. According to this line of thought, by losing the traditional arrangements of social roles, women decrease their dependence on men, weakening marriage bonds. Ultimately, children suffer as their parents either divorce or they may have a mother who due to her employment status is not totally devoted to them. This leads to dysfunction in future generations and society as a whole is endangered. This perspective ignores cross-cultural and historical examples that illustrate that the traditional breadwinner–homemaker family was a distinctive post-World War II family form and that changes in social life can also provide opportunities for new ways of conceptualizing the processes and responsibilities of family life.

As Gerson (2004) points out, instead of focusing on the absence of employed women in their homes, a different perspective emphasizes the benefits that accrue to children and families when women are engaged in paid employment. For instance, besides providing an income, women are exposed to new ideas, form networks, have a greater say in family decision-making and tend to have greater self-esteem and be more satisfied with their lives. Evaluations of the microcredit programs discussed earlier in this volume indicate that women who begin earning an income most commonly invest that money in their children. The link between education, women, and child well-being is also striking. For example, research indicates that mother's educational attainment is a stronger predictor of children's learning outcomes than father's education. Similarly, children whose mothers have completed upper secondary education have on average higher literacy rates. Strong literacy skills are particularly important for the social and economic success of individuals in low- and middle-income regions and countries, where the restructuring of workplaces are making people with weak skills increasingly economically vulnerable (Fennell & Arnot, 2007).

Children can benefit in other ways from family changes as well. While families today may be slightly less stable, they also offer a wider range of possibilities for their members.[2] Families in which women are more educated with stronger social networks and more financial resources provide new role models to children. These are also often families characterized by greater democratic decision-making processes. This exposes children to models of equality and teaches them about fairness and respect. Studies of transnational motherhood also provide evidence that women's economic empowerment has a positive impact on children (Dreby, 2006). As much as mothers are distressed on an emotional level by the absence from their children for longer periods of time, children learn from the experiences of their working mothers that there are multiple life options available. Children tend also to benefit through the actual income provided by their mothers: they may access greater educational and skills training, they may be able to forge more international connections, and they may receive increased support from extended kin and family friends. Thus, there are tangible and intangible benefits that accrue to families when women become economically and socially empowered.

In examining families from a global perspective, it is also important to take note that families play a somewhat different role in the lives of individuals who live in non-Western areas. A Western bias on individualism tends to obscure the fact that in many parts of the world an individual's chances are still primarily determined by family membership. Even in the West, a recent focus on children living in poverty indicates that familial social and economic capital more often than not determines life-course trajectories (Fennell & Arnot, 2007). Investing in the educational and economic empowerment of women thus has familial and societal implications. By supporting women, states, educational institutions, and employers also ensure the well-being of future generations.

Empirical evidence about the relationship between mothers' work outside of the home and children's well-being indicates that instead of viewing social changes in families from a deficit perspective, we need to be aware that with change also comes new prospects. In all likelihood the social changes that have been described in this book are permanent. This makes it useless to bemoan the loss of past arrangements such as the post-World War II breadwinner–homemaker family characteristic of middle-class families in the United States, and certainly makes it irrelevant to try to revive such a model in the future. Instead, we need to look at the present situation and try to protect future generations by focusing on how to align transformations in workplaces and families with community and state supports. An example of the success of such a policy shift was described in Chapter 9: by recognizing and formally supporting family and workplace changes, the north European countries and France have seen a rise in fertility rates, the greater satisfaction of women and men with their work–family balance, and better services that assist children and families. While many of those countries' solutions obviously are not applicable on a global level, we can learn from their pragmatic approach. Instead of rejecting the familial and social changes that are characteristic of the contemporary experience, they turned their attention and resources to creating culturally appropriate supports for employers, families, and individuals. This approach, so far, has paid off for these societies in economic and social terms.

Work–family negotiations, however, continue to dominate as a significant problem in countless other parts of the globe. In particular, developing countries are facing serious crises in the future with respect to provisions that support families. As Beneria (2007a) points out, the availability to middle- and upper-class families of "cheap" domestic help in many low-income countries is currently obscuring this problem, as well as the fact that legislation is primarily enacted by well-to-do individuals who are not as aware of the situation of lower-income workers. As poorer women increasingly take on higher paying jobs in the market economy, the work–family negotiation that is so complex in higher-income countries portends to become an equally or even more serious problem in these regions.

The Contemporary Workplace and its Mismatch with Family Responsibilities

In many places around the world and at least in the post World War II era, paid employment outside of the home has been under the primary purview of men.[3] However, now that women represent about half the labor force in most industrialized countries, and the same phenomenon is spreading to the developing world, attention has turned specifically to women's experiences. Because the consequences of this transformation extend beyond the marketplace, putting into place appropriate supports is increasingly moving to the forefront of academic, policy, and mainstream discussions. Since women are the ones who traditionally shouldered domestic responsibilities, their work outside of the home has had significant implications for families and communities. Depending on locale and resources, this adjustment has not been easy for many families. These changes in what has been traditionally perceived as the private domain are also increasingly understood to have a public dimension. In other words, in order to assist families and individuals to meet their work and family responsibilities, the social policies and services that support families need to be readjusted. However, as we have seen throughout this book, practical supports for women and families have been slow in coming. Women around the world continue to perform a disproportionate share of household duties and caring labor while now also working outside of the home.

Arlene Hochschild's 1989 description of the second shift currently holds true not just for American women but also for many women in other parts of the industrialized and developing world. Strikingly, even in the most egalitarian industrialized countries of the world, such as the Nordic countries, women often continue to be the primary caregivers and are often found in gender-segregated workplaces. Moreover, actual workplaces in most societies have been slow to change. Employers continue to expect workers to be completely dedicated to their jobs, and caring labor is assumed to be a private matter. This ideal worker model is spreading throughout the world. The contemporary workplace is characterized by the expectation that an individual is committed to his or her career over the long term, without interrupted employment, and with very long working hours. Despite the recognition of the social pressures that dominate the lives of so many working individuals, this model has gained primacy in the market-driven economies that are now found all over the globe.[4]

The contradictions between what is expected at work and in the home leave many women, and to a certain extent today, men, vulnerable. As Gerson (2004) writes, "In a world where personal relationships and job commitments are fluid and unpredictable, women and men alike must balance their commitments to others with the search for self-sufficiency. These dilemmas of commitment and personal independence are transforming the meaning of gender as they leave young women and men to develop work and family strategies" (p. 169).

In the contemporary environment, many women and men must constantly choose where to focus their energy despite the risks entailed in either privileging their jobs or their families. Moreover, the recent recession in the United States has highlighted the fact that the kind of jobs that characterized so much of the post-World War II period, full-time jobs with benefits usually held by men, are rapidly evaporating. Complicating the matter is that in today's volatile economic climate, not being completely dedicated to one's job can have adverse consequences. For lower-income individuals, but also increasingly for middle-class women and men, emphasizing their job over family responsibilities is often their only economically viable choice. This situation creates a double bind for women. They are expected and often for financial reasons need to work, but they are also part of another often more insidious dialogue: one that presumes that their primary identity should come from their relationships with men and as caregivers. For instance, in the contemporary climate in the United States, women are often expected to engage in an intensive mothering model while concurrently supporting themselves and their families through paid work (Hayes, 1996). These phenomena lead to many questions about the impact of economic transformations not just on the labor force but also on identity formation, concepts of femininity and masculinity, shared obligations and responsibilities in families, and more.

What is perhaps most striking is that the changes with respect to gender socialization, family arrangements, and the complexities that are entailed by working outside of the home are becoming characteristic of places that have historically been considered more "traditional." These include rural areas and ethnic enclaves in industrialized societies, as well as locales in the developing world where religion or cultural values emphasize established arrangements and values. As these societies and groups are increasingly incorporated into a global market economy, their ways of life are irrevocably altered; for instance, increasingly rural young women are moving to urban areas for work, or as they are becoming more educated, rejecting customary social arrangements such as early marriage and child bearing. The changes are rapid and pervasive but not necessarily uniform. The local context still matters with respect to the choices that are available to women. It is important to remember that individuals make choices based on their personal set of circumstances and the options available at a specific point in time. Possible alternatives and personal and social resources play a crucial part in decision-making. As Nussbaum (2001) eloquently states: "Certain basic aspirations to human flourishing are recognizable across differences of class and context, however crucial it remains to understand how context shapes both choice and aspiration" (p. 31).

We Need Public Solutions for what are Currently Private Dilemmas

While social conservatives point to cohabitation, the rising age of marriage, divorce rates and the employment of mothers as indicators of global societal decline, an alternative perspective suggests that these phenomena are responses to contemporary conditions that require individuals to be more flexible with respect to private choices. We have come to realize that there is no one family form that works best for everyone, and that there are limitations to all social arrangements. As working couples and single-parent households become more normative worldwide, negotiating work–family issues has become a typical experience for individuals and families. I caution my readers, however, to be suspicious of simplistic analyses that only point to a rearrangement of roles within families as the answer. While it is without question imperative that men also take on domestic responsibilities, this is not a sufficient solution, nor is it always a viable one. As has been elaborated before, many men are caught up in a complex dynamic where their jobs are increasingly susceptible to being eliminated. Connell (2005) in an insightful discussion highlights this observation and states:

> Social and economic pressures on men to compete in the workplace, to increase their hours of paid work, and sometimes to take second jobs are among the most powerful constraints on gender reform. Desire for a better balance between work and life is widespread among employed men. On the other hand, where unemployment is high the lack of a paid job can be a damaging pressure on men who have grown up with the expectation of being breadwinners.

(p. 1813)

Just as women can be empowered through working, men can be disempowered when they lose their jobs. Their families often depend on that income and when men lose their provider role, they suffer from a loss of identity and self-worth. Women are often judged in society by their relationship and mothering abilities, and men continue to be primarily evaluated by their capacity to earn an income and gain status. While this is somewhat of a generalization drawn from the Western middle-class experience, research on marriage among low-income women in the United States indicates that these women often choose to stay single specifically because the men that are available to them would not be able to fulfill the traditional provider role (Edin, 2000). An increasing number of studies from the developing world indicate that similar processes are at work in other societies as well: as women enter the paid labor force and men lose the jobs that traditionally helped them provide for their families, the disruption in family life and loss of identity can be severe, even resulting in increased domestic violence (Connell, 2005).

It is not an adequate solution for scholars, policy-makers, or employers to suggest and encourage primarily private solutions to a problem that has public repercussions and is increasingly global. Negotiating family and work obligations should not just be an issue that is handled on an individual basis. Many families today cobble together solutions that are not satisfactory to them or in the long run efficient for their employers or the societies in which they live. Having supportive policies in place assists individuals and their families, and creates an environment where people can be more productive with more positive morale. Moreover, we need to recognize the broad range of obligations that families are dealing with: while affordable quality child care is without a doubt a central part of the solution to family-caring issues, much less attention has focused on the equally complex problem of the care of the elderly, sick, and disabled. Caring for individuals across the lifespan requires targeted solutions such as flexible work times and the potential to step out of jobs for certain periods of time without detrimental consequences to employees.

Before advancing the idea that work–family issues are primarily solved by a change in the roles of men, we need also to be cognizant of the multiple family forms that characterize so many societies today: there are many situations where there is only one parent present in the family; or as in the case in many places in sub-Saharan Africa that have been ravaged by the HIV/AIDS epidemic, an increased number of families function without any parents. The distribution of roles is one very important piece of the work–family negotiation, but it is not the only part and varies depending on circumstances.

Economic resources also play a critical role in how well families accomplish their basic tasks. For instance, in those circumstances were families have many assets to draw on and can basically pay to "outsource" much of their housekeeping and caregiving, the distribution of roles may look quite different from in those families that are economically challenged. In contrast, there are situations where families have a large network of kin and social connections that assists them with their familial responsibilities, again calling for a different organizational structure. However, most contemporary working women and men do not have any of these means to draw on. They must rely only on themselves, or on the help of a partner to both be economically self-sufficient and help maintain their families. For example, in places like China and India, more and more young people are moving to urban areas due to economic opportunities. Once settled in their new environments, many of these individuals do not have the local supports that would allow them to easily negotiate potential family and work responsibilities (Yan & Neal, 2006). Also problematic for the future is the fact that the elderly that are left behind through rural–urban migrations will need increasing care as societies have larger and larger aging populations.

In addition to the practical family tasks that need to be accomplished, families (even those where economic resources are plentiful), are affected by the ideological values of their time. As I mentioned earlier, debates on mothering and the extent to which mothers need to remain involved with their children persist. In the Philippines, for instance, the prevalence of transnational motherhood has taken political center stage (Parrenas, 2005). Who is a "good" mother and how that is defined is subject to debate and scrutiny. I began this book with an anecdote about an encounter with several thirty-something U.S. working mothers and the work–family conflicts they feel dominate their lives. As that incident indicated, many women—and increasingly men—feel torn about where to direct their energies. Primarily, they must navigate conflicting ideological expectations and economic realities. In non-Western societies the work–family debate may at times be even more complex, as mother–child obligations are also compounded by traditional norms that advocate that filial responsibilities to elderly parents be equally maintained. In Singapore, India, and China, for instance, there are laws in place that require children to care for and regularly visit their aging parents.[5] I highlight these scenarios to illustrate that the contemporary work–family intersection is increasingly complex for individuals around the world, and that this balance is negotiated differently depending on circumstances. It is important to note that today there is no such thing as the "ideal" family arrangement; everyone is struggling to work out their own solutions to what are in reality shared experiences.

How work and family life intersect has changed both historically and cross-culturally. Even today, within the same society, different individuals will have a myriad of experiences depending on a variety of factors that range from educational level to income, to the availability of extended family, and to personality characteristics. We sometimes forget that change is endemic to the human condition. However, what predominantly characterizes our current period is the rapidity, unevenness, and global nature of the changes around us. Everything is more fluid, traditional blueprints are less and less relevant, and every manner of diversity is increasingly characterizing social life. Around the globe we are seeing more and more diverse families, a variety of family arrangements, and a multitude of available roles that individuals are exposed to. Today's children are socialized into this fluid diverse world and often cannot follow in the customary path of their families or communities. Instead, they need new skills. Foremost, they need to be able to access the training and education that will make them employable over a lifetime. Children today need to be socialized to understand that jobs and careers will change and that they need to remain flexible when it comes to taking on various family and community roles. An important part of this process is socializing children to be more gender neutral and egalitarian with respect to expectations and actions. We need to realize that these activities cannot just be under the purview of families. Educational systems and employers are important parts of this equation—and they need to be included in every part of the planning process. In addition, the state continues to play an important role in regulating some of these activities.

Re-Envisioning the Role of the State

Our complex and rapidly changing environment has led to the recognition that transnational, national, and local social policies and programs have not been keeping pace with societal transformations. This situation has led to debates about the role of states and the kind of influence they should exert on employers and the marketplace as well as protecting their citizens. There is also much global debate about how states should interact with transnational entities such as the United Nations, the World Bank, and the International Labor Organization just to name a few. Feminists have also asked specifically gender-based questions: what is the role of states in promoting greater gender equity, and how are women specifically protected from some of the more deleterious effects of globalization (Eisenstein, 2005)?

Transnational influences brought about by globalization have had significant impacts on the role of states with respect to their economies and the services they provide to their citizens. Speaking in general terms, the most common response has been for states to become less involved with the needs of their citizens, and to be less interventionist in relation to markets. The issues discussed in this book, however, indicate that a differing response would be more appropriate: that stronger domestic economic policies and more supports for citizens would raise the quality of life for individuals and would lead to greater productivity. For instance, investing in stronger skills training and education as well as encouraging employers to pay higher wages could lead to greater innovation—thus adding value to human resources, maintaining a global competitive advantage, and subsidizing an equitable standard of living. This requires a greater public investment in training and schools instead of less state support.

As an increasing number of analysts and policy-makers examine the role of states in public life, there has been a tendency to view globalization as a runaway force that cannot be contained. However, as Blackmore (1999) writes, "Policy 'responses' have not been an inevitable consequence of economic globalization, but reflect particular ideological positions which have been made orthodox through the legitimacy imported to them by international monetary bodies and other global discourses" (p. 45). By stepping back and examining the human factor of globalization, we are able to understand that there is an interplay between markets and social life but that this is usually determined at the local and not the global level. Thus, when we are debating policy responses, we need locally specific ones—not just transnational ones that may not have resonance or impact in domestic settings. As Brodie (1996) describes, "globalization is a paradigm shift of governing practices and not some deterministic external inevitable force" (p. 386). The dynamics of globalization and localization are occurring concurrently but often in opposing ways. This dichotomy requires a range of responses operating at various levels—the level of state intervention, locally, and also transnationally. We need to recognize this fact and work toward new ways of organizing and influencing policies, programs, and social directions.

There are of course many paths that states could embark on in order to provide supports for families, specifically with respect to work–family issues. Several of those initiatives and successful policies were examined in previous chapters. However, there are other options as well that have been less publicized or have not yet been fully explored as alternate arrangements. For instance, more governments could publicly prioritize families by creating institutional mechanisms such as Ministries of Family. Such entities would promote policies that enhance the lives of individuals and could have an agenda that supports gender equity and individual empowerment. In the United Kingdom, more attention is being paid to what is referred to as the "third sector" of the economy: nonprofit businesses that are neither standard market driven for profit entities, nor typical voluntary organizations. Instead, these are hybrid small businesses that are affiliated with local governments and offer care resources. By subcontracting to these enterprises, the state is able to offer higher quality services at lower costs. Some analysts see these types of cooperatives and work-owned enterprises as particularly promising for future models of care provision (Folbre, 2008).

Another auspicious state initiated policy scheme is cash transfers to very low-income families to further the education of children and to provide a form of social security for the elderly. So far, cash transfers have primarily gained in popularity as a concrete mechanism for states to support children's education and health. For instance, Mexico Oportunidades is a social protection program targeted to alleviate poverty by giving steady cash payments to families in exchange for agreeing to let their children to attend school, visit health clinics, and receive better nutrition (Ferreira & Robalino, 2010). The grants increase as the children get older, and they are somewhat higher for girls than for boys, because girls tend to have a higher school drop-out rate than boys. A similar program has been instituted in Brazil and is now the largest such initiative in the world (Hall, 2006). Currently, there are four sub-programs including financial stipends to encourage school attendance, money to supplement maternal nutrition, food supplements, and a domestic gas subsidy. This initiative has assisted approximately 30 million of Brazil's poorest individuals. It is important to note that in many countries in Latin America and Southeast Asia, cash support specifically encourages girls to continue their secondary schooling.

Less well known are programs that provide cash transfers and/or food subsidies to families with poor elderly members. For instance, in Mozambique 55 percent of the population lives below the poverty level, and poverty among the elderly is currently at 68 percent (Beales, 2012). In order to help combat this extreme level of poverty, the government has begun to provide food subsidy benefits (the PSA) to the elderly. An impact evaluation of the program revealed that the benefits to families are immense: "Some households manage to save and to access credit in the local market. With the subsidy the beneficiaries were also able to improve their housing and sanitation conditions and comfort in general" (Beales, 2012, p. 9). By subsidizing families with cash transfers, states accomplish two separate goals: they support the education of children in order to prepare them to enter the global labor force, and they promote a social justice agenda that emphasizes the necessity of assisting those individuals that are in need, no matter what age they are.

From a more general perspective, we also need to re-evaluate how we delineate economic growth and state spending. For instance, Folbre (2008) writes:

> As long as economists are allowed to define "output" entirely in terms of market income, proposals to ensure a higher level and quality of care will be deemed "unproductive" and inefficient. For this reason, efforts to incorporate estimates of the value of unpaid care services into alternative measures of gross domestic product and household standards of living are crucial to the development of a stronger care economy.
>
> (p. 384)

In other words, we need to redefine what we consider as "work" and we need to give value to those activities. States can play an active role in this process by explicating the costs of moving care provision into the marketplace.

What these examples illustrate is that states are not becoming obsolete as is argued by some social critics. Instead, states need to redefine their missions and implement new strategies in order to provide supports for their own people and for the global citizenry. A new world order requires a re-conceptualization of the role of the players and of the issues.

Moving into the Future with Transnational Advocacy Networks (TAN)

As states transition to newer or modified roles, we need to look to different paradigms for organizing and building collaborative partnerships. Increasingly, there are innovative functional models that draw on the expertise of states, transnational organizations, and other entities to enact new policies and programs. For instance, some transnational organizations support state activities by providing knowledge expertise. One example is the United Nations Commission for Social Development and, specifically, the department "Focal Point on the Family" that brings together experts and research on family issues from a global perspective. Their findings are then circulated to entities such as the General Assembly Economic and Social Council.[6] These activities allow for best practices to be shared and disseminated, and serve to inform policy-makers of challenges as well as successful initiatives.

Another promising path is embodied in the concept of transnational advocacy networks (TANs). This prototype was introduced in 1998, by Keck and Sikkink, to describe broad partnerships between various entities. Participants share similar values such as around women's issues, human rights, or environmental concerns. TANs include those entities "who are bound together by shared values, a common discourse, and dense exchanges of information and services" (Keck & Sikkink, 1998, p. 2). They are fundamentally different from social movements because they include a wider variety of participants including institutional and non-institutional actors. For instance, they may include "1) international and domestic nongovernmental research and advocacy organizations, 2) local social movements, 3) foundations, 4) the media, 5) churches, trade unions, consumer organization, and intellectuals, 6) parts of regional and international intergovernmental organization, and 7) parts of the executive and/or parliamentary branches of governments" (Keck & Sikkink, 1998, p. 9).

Keck and Sikkink point out that the primary difference between TANs and social movements is that they employ different strategies in order to achieve their goals. In order for social movements to be effective, they need to bring together large groups of individuals for collective action. TANS are fundamentally dissimilar. They fashion networks between different entities and across borders. This allows TANs to influence policy arenas through a variety of mechanisms and to draw on multiple bodies of knowledge, varied discourses, and transnational experts (Ferree & Mueller, 2004).

Case Study: The European TAN on Gender Equality

Zippel (2004) provides a fascinating case study of how an effective TAN can effectively create social change. She points to the European TAN on gender equality and analyzes both who the players are as well as their relationships to one another. For instance, this particular TAN includes small, national women's organizations that are commonly focused on one issue and EU policy-makers that are concerned with women's issues and are interested in transnational connections. In the EU context, transnational connections are extremely pertinent due to the cultural differences and laws that exist between countries. In contrast to a democratic system like the United States that is driven by political parties, EU politics and policies are dominated by bureaucratic administrative structures. As Zippel (2004) points out, in this sort of a system, public opinion matters less than transnational expertise. Policy-makers need to primarily rely on information about the potential effects of policies on member states. Policies are formulated at a supranational level and their actual impacts are often ambiguous at the outset of the process (Sperling, Ferree, & Risman, 2001). In fact, once the global and the local intersect, the results may turn out to be quite different from what was originally predicted.

In order to legitimize themselves, supranational bodies like the EU necessitate the creation of "new" fields of policy. Gender equality has been one of these newly adopted spheres. Thus, the European gender equality TAN has been supported through a variety of venues including conferences, research, expert groups, and consultants. A TAN can provide the individuals and the expertise that can then stimulate information sharing and the actual policy-making process: "By providing alternative discourses, TANs can help transform what are regarded as radical demands into concrete policy initiatives, contributing their expertise to debates and to policy making in general" (Zippel, 2004, p. 64).

Zippel, however, also points out that not all TANs are successful. Many are plagued by power dynamics and disagreements among the various entities and players about a cohesive, collective strategy. In particular, local grass-root entities and elite professionals are often in conflict with one another due to their unequal relationships. For instance, Sperling, Ferree, and Risman (2001) describe how a TAN between U.S. women feminists and female activists in Russia ultimately became an object of struggle with both parties advocating for very different outcomes. Still, TANs provide one of the most promising venues in particular for local grass-root organizations to make an impact on a national and transnational level. Through the nature of their composition, they provide innovative, effective pathways to influence policy-makers. Zippel (2004) also highlights the fact that TANs strengthen the position of the various participants as they are empowered by gaining information and access to new bodies of knowledge, alternative discourses, and potentially unfamiliar policies. However, the process tends to be complex. For instance Sperling, Ferree and Risman (2001) quote a Russian participant as stating, "'We understand that we need to learn from the world's experience, and the world also needs to learn something from us. But to find a way to do this is very hard'" (p. 1182).

Their varied composition allows TANs to move through multiple cycles of influence. They can exert pressure on national states and on transnational bodies, and thereby influence policy-making at those levels. As incremental changes are implemented, TANs can recalculate or modify their original goals, or aim toward new ones and begin their cycle anew. For instance in the U.S.–Russian TAN described by Sperling, Ferree, and Risman (2001), the negotiation between the two groups ultimately results in a new focus. The redirected TAN prioritized organizing "the women in the Northern Caucasus against the war in Chechnya," an activity that was far removed from the original aims of the collaboration (p. 1169). This is one example that illustrates that TANs are not static entities, but constantly evolving enterprises whose aims and actual impacts vary with execution.

As new supranational levels of political and administrative structures become more important, TANs will in all likelihood also gain in importance in achieving social action goals. TANs highlight some of the mechanisms of globalization, and allow us to see that social action and policy formation will increasingly play themselves out on a global stage. They also illustrate that the relationship between transnational activities and local practices are negotiated and do not proceed in a unidirectional manner.

Where Do We Currently Stand with Respect to the Global Status of Women?

Ultimately, this book has focused on a complex and controversial question: have the changes brought about by globalization, specifically their greater incorporation into the global labor force, been positive for women? Yet, as has been discussed in great detail, there is no clear or uniform answer. In part, this ambiguity stems from the complexity of the issues. With respect to the work–women–globalization intersection, there are contradictory factors and differing occurrences at work. We cannot speak of a uniform experience for women within one society, let alone between places or regions. Social location, resources, and personal characteristics play critical roles in determining an individual's experiences.

From a general perspective, I would argue that we are witnessing wide-ranging improvements in women's lives. The ability to become financially self-sufficient, the prospect of increased educational and skills-based training, the chance to network and collaborate transnationally, and the sharing of information have definitely affected millions of women in a positive manner. But that said, millions of other women have been cast into greater poverty due to the precarious nature of their jobs. Importantly, this phenomenon is not limited to the non-Western parts of the world nor is there a steady forward-moving trajectory. For instance, women may have acquired skills and a job, and their lives may have improved for a period of time. However, as a consequence of the cost-cutting measures that so often accompany globalizing processes, they may then have lost their jobs as work moves to newer, less expensive or less regulated environments. These types of situations have forced some women to become part of a growing transnational sex industry, or they may have had to enter into other dangerous and exploitative forms of employment. Under those conditions, women usually have little recourse to protection nor are they empowered in any form. Moreover, most working women have not received any form of relief from their domestic responsibilities. Thus, when we speak of women in the labor force and their increased participation in the global economy, we are not speaking of universal positive experiences, nor are we necessarily speaking of Western concepts of self-actualization and emancipation.

It is important to note that even in those areas where there is a greater focus on gender equality and gender mainstreaming, issues with respect to discrimination and prejudice persist. For instance, Beneria (2005) correctly points out that "the existence of discriminatory practices and the effects of segregation on women's wages needs to be emphasized as these issues take on an international dimension" (p. 275). As the labor market shifts to employing a larger number of women, we need to take a cautionary stance. Incorporating more and more female workers is not necessarily a sign of gender equality but instead in many places is an indicator of the availability of cheap female labor. As Third World countries, in particular, move to export-focused economic strategies, employing large numbers of women becomes a popular approach for states and transnational corporations to deal with the pressures of international competition. While these jobs may provide women with new opportunities, they are oftentimes also predicated on the subordinate position of females in their societies (Beneria, 2005). Women are increasingly employable in certain sectors of the global economy because they are thought to be more disciplined and malleable, to have "nimble" fingers that allow them to work with fine and small objects, and they provide flexible labor as they take on part-time and unstable work. Women's "flexibility" meshes well with a contemporary labor market that oscillates in terms of places and types of production. That same labor market, for the most part, does not account for women's private responsibilities that ultimately impact social reproduction and the continuance of social life. Especially for low-skilled women, their wages remain below those of men and they are often forced to accept substandard working conditions. Even the issue of equal pay for equal work is complex in our new environment: we are often dealing with contexts where men and women are doing different types of work (Beneria, 2005). And when there is gender segregation, women are often compensated at a lesser rate, that is, their work is seen as less valuable and is paid at a different rate. Where we have whole industries that have been feminized, women are on the whole earning much less than their male counterparts.

While the transformations of the global labor market are dramatic with respect to the feminization of the labor force, the situation in the domestic realm has not changed in a similarly rapid manner. Among middle-class families in industrialized countries, men are increasingly taking on domestic responsibilities, however, these trends have been slow to catch on, and are much less common among lower-class non-Western families. Instead, in many places women's double and triple shifts continue to persist or have become more common. As Amartya Sen (1990) suggested, "Conflicts of interest between men and women are unlike other conflicts, such as class conflicts. A worker and a capitalist do not typically live together under the same roof—sharing concerns and experiences and acting jointly. This aspect of 'togetherness' gives gender conflict some very special characteristics" (p. 147). Many men, of all walks of life, feel displaced by the dramatic social changes occurring around them, and they are either resentful or ambivalent about domestic rearrangements that do not necessarily benefit them.

This set of circumstances does not bode well for societies with growing elderly populations that have traditionally relied on women as caregivers. With an increased number of women in the paid labor force, the care of the elderly, the disabled, and the ill will place new pressures on states and on families. This is an enormous social burden for women, especially in non-Western societies where there are few if any provisions currently in place.[7]

What Does the Future Hold When it Comes to Gender Equality?

Globalization and the interconnectedness that is at its very core allows us to now come together across borders, social classes, and racial, ethnic groups. In a global dialogue on the situation of women, it is thus critical to be inclusive and to take into account constituents from all parts of the world. In both scholarship and mainstream discussions we need a dialogue that highlights women's shared experiences and commonalities, as well as the specific challenges that are faced by particular groups. Instead of dichotomizing the discussion by just concentrating on the West or the developing world, engaging the various groups around common concerns is a more productive process. The future lies in forming alliances and collaborations through shared commitments to common interests and concerns. Importantly, these alliances and collaborations must also include men. As Connell (2005) states,

> Inviting men to end men's privileges, and to remake masculinities to sustain gender equality, strikes many people as a strange or utopian project. Yet this project is already under way. Many men around the world are engaged in gender reforms ... The diversity of masculinities complicates the process but is also an important asset. As this diversity becomes better known, men and boys can more easily see a range of possibilities for their own lives, and both men and women are less likely to think of gender inequality as unchangeable.
>
> (p. 1817)

All of this said, I again would like to emphasize that this discussion does not by any means presume that women in the industrialized and developing worlds all share a common experience (nor that all men necessarily support a gender equality agenda). As we have seen, there may be overlap in how different groups manage their public and private lives, but there is also significant variation. Despite this dissimilarity, differences do not mean that various groups of individuals cannot share their experiences with one another. In fact this is a crucial step in overcoming the gender disparities that are still so prevalent in many regions. It is precisely through dialogue and collaboration that we may now be able to make the substantive progress on behalf of improving women's situations. As Blackmore (1999) states, "It is the *articulation* and shifting relations between class, race and gender, local and global, state and individual, which need to be focused upon theoretically and in empirical research, and not just the shared common universal experience of womanhood" (p. 47).

I have made the case in this volume that women are affected in unique ways through globalization, and their experiences span a wide spectrum. Even within the same group, women's work opportunities and domestic challenges may vary widely. It would be presumptuous to suppose that we all share the same concerns or the same prospects—or that we all even have similar expectations for our domestic or work lives. However, this analysis has highlighted the fact that we are currently at a very specific juncture in time. While globalizing forces are spreading values that focus on personal choice and responsibility, the reality of most women's situations are much more complex. As Blackmore (1999) states, "theories of rational choice which assume that individuals have the equal capacity, resources and knowledge to make 'rational' choices [and] disregard differential power relations and social relationships of responsibility, and indeed the *social* interdependencies which make *market* relations possible" (p. 48). Women, *and* men, are embedded in varied contexts often with limited access to power. They do not always have the resources or the ability to make the choices that a free market, rational choice model predicates. We need to recognize that the philosophical underpinnings that currently form the foundation of the free market economic system that we have exported to all corners of the globe may in fact not be the model that is most fitting for building a more socially just future or even ultimately creating more efficient market economies. Moreover, we need to factor race, ethnicity, and social class into our analysis of women's lives. Power differentials in the larger environment *as well as* in families play a critical role in determining the lived experiences of women. However, it is also essential that we do not place women in a "needs" or victim position but instead highlight the interdependence of men and women. For instance, research illustrates that in Western contexts, structural as well as interactional (relationship and communication skills) move women and men to a more equal division of labor (Deutsch, 2007).

Currently, structural changes, such as women earning greater pay, may create the opportunity for transformations to occur at the interactional level. But it is important to note that these adjustments do not necessarily mean that change will occur or that it will happen in a uniform manner. Moreover, globalization is creating an environment where the public and private arenas are being redefined. The more porous boundaries between work and home life are focusing attention on how these arenas intersect and raising questions about the ultimate sustainability of a system that subordinates social concerns to economic ones. The increasingly global nature of this problem indicates that in the long run this will not be a private matter to be handled only on an individual basis. Instead, the immense importance of working out sustainable solutions for individuals to handle both their economic and domestic responsibilities needs to rapidly become a policy and social justice prerogative, not just for Western nations that are suffering fertility declines but also for all the players in the global market economy.

As we have seen, women play critical and complex roles in contemporary social transformations. The gendered nature of the changes need to become a primary aspect of mainstream dialogue in order to effect the policies and programs that ultimately create a more productive workforce and that stem some of the more deleterious effects of globalization. It is important to note, too, that women have achieved access to some current opportunities precisely due to their unequal relationships to men. Yet, as we have seen, their advancement comes at times with the danger of exploitative work conditions, and relatively if any alleviation of their domestic responsibilities.

As has been explored in this volume, demand for female workers has been a major driver in propelling women into the paid labor force. However, other factors have influenced this phenomenon too. For instance, a rising divorce rate in the West highlighted the dangers of women who were homemakers being completely economically dependent on men. Moreover, the spread of the women's movement introduced new ideas about the autonomy of women and the importance of financial independence. As educational opportunities for women have opened up, their career choices have also been impacted. Whether it be in the highly industrialized countries of the West or in developing nations such as in South Asia or sub-Saharan Africa, increased education and skills building is making girls and women more marriageable, and introducing concepts of self-empowerment. As women become gainfully employed, they tend to marry later and have fewer children, leading to a certain lessening of their domestic responsibilities. It is important to note, however, that access to education just by itself is not enough. What is needed in order to attain true gender equality is an examination and recognition of power relationships and the education of both women and men with respect to these issues. Women's empowerment is dependent on education and on a shift in gender relations (Fennell & Arnot, 2007). This new way of understanding gendered realities points to the fact that for many poor women and men schooling may not always provide the way "out" that we assume in the West. Instead, we need to look at social networks, social capital, and the cycle of social reproduction in efforts to create change.

A global comparison of the situation of women indicates that relatively well-educated women with sufficient incomes today tend to outsource many of their domestic responsibilities. In order to find time for their jobs, they purchase either child care or domestic services or both. Much of this outsourcing is to other women, often from other countries, leading to complex global interactions. Women who do not have these financial resources often have to find other ways of coping. Most commonly they rely on extended family or fictive kin to help them shoulder their domestic burden. In contrast to Western middle-class women, poorer women in the developing world rarely receive much assistance with respect to care and housework from the men in their lives. The feminist revolution that has changed the lives of women in the West and that has brought notions of economic and self-empowerment to other parts of the world has thus far failed to bring about many changes with respect to the behavior and roles of men in many non-Western societies. This promises to be a complex problem in the future.

In Western societies, social values and, to a certain extent, family-friendly policies are promoting the role of men in participating in the various aspects of family life and responsibilities. But in much of the developing world, the roles of men and women continue to be defined by cultural values that stress the importance of the male breadwinner. This flies in complete opposition to the reality of our contemporary world where more and more women are working outside of the home. As has been illustrated, for a host of complex reasons, women have become the preferred labor force, at least for certain sectors of work. The implications for men have been under studied and are not properly understood. However, the fact that some women suffer greater domestic abuse due to this trend is well documented in the literature (Connell, 2005). This rise in domestic abuse indicates that a certain percentage of men are uncomfortable with the shift in gender roles that is rapidly pervading their societies.

Another global consequence of women's increased participation in the paid labor force is that their fertility levels are declining. Concurrently, however, the demands of the elderly around the world are growing. And in places such as certain communities in sub-Saharan Africa where the HIV/AIDS epidemic is at crisis levels, care labor is a major social problem. It is this crisis in care that will dominate our next century. In the West, much attention is being paid to child care and the implications of family-friendly policies that assist women and men balance work–family obligations. But the issues surrounding care of the elderly, sick, and disabled are just as complex, and at times even less easily resolved.

Synopsis

The discussions in this volume have illustrated that negotiating work and home responsibilities is an immense dilemma for women the world over. As Anne-Marie Slaughter (2012) describes in the initial example in this chapter, women at all levels of society continue to debate how to make the mixture of employment, children, and other family responsibilities work, despite a rhetoric that encourages them to "have it all but maybe not at the same time." The real problem, however, is that most women do not have the luxury of choice or the resources to ease the responsibilities that come with participating in the paid labor force and taking care of domestic obligations. Moreover, most women negotiate their increased sphere of responsibilities in contexts where the policies and supports that they need are frequently missing. This same problem also, of course, affects men. But, as we have seen, despite a rhetoric of parity, women's and men's situations tend to be somewhat different. In addition, even with extensive analysis we still do not fully understand the long-term social ramifications of women's employment outside of the home. For instance, while the main focus of much work–family research is on family dynamics or the relationship between families and the workplace, other implications of this phenomenon have been virtually ignored. As women enter the paid labor force, they often drop out of the community and volunteer work that they have engaged in historically. Thus, other spheres besides the intimate sphere of the household are affected as women's roles change. It is these long-term social consequences that we also need to be cognizant of.

One positive phenomenon that we can deduce from this discussion is that the increased number of women in the paid labor force indicates that gender stereotypes are *beginning* to break down and that we are moving to a world of greater gender equality despite the persistence of certain types of prejudice and discrimination. While not by any means a uniform phenomenon, women's ability to earn an income is very slowly breaking down the patriarchal arrangement of familial roles. In the West, more egalitarian household arrangements are spreading and shared decision-making in families is becoming the norm. While this is not necessarily the case in other regions around the globe, images about other possible lifestyles are now spreading and may have future impacts. Moreover, despite the criticism of feminist economists that poor women in the developing world are primarily being exploited by working under dismal conditions for minimal wages, ethnographic evidence indicates that having employment where none was available before can ultimately lead to improvements in women's lives (Ganguly-Scrase, 2003; Fraser, 2007). It is inaccurate and misleading to apply a purely economic lens to understanding social life, and specifically gender relations. Conversely, we cannot just examine gender through a lens of subordination based on the cultural valuing of one group over another. Instead, we need to understand gender relations from a multi-pronged approach that considers the economic *and* socio-cultural underpinnings of these interactions.

In order to move toward a more just, egalitarian model of gender relations and greater gender parity, we need to aim for cultural change that focuses on establishing "women as full partners in social life, able to interact with male peers" (Fraser, 2007, p. 31). This can only be accomplished by re-evaluating the role of certain economic activities, as well as revaluing those activities that have been associated primarily with women, such as caregiving. In other words, we need to change cultural codes that equate low-paying service jobs as "women's work" and consign activities such as caregiving to the "female" realm. Women need both access to resources and status recognition for activities that have been customarily consigned to a subordinate cultural sphere.

I would like to end by emphasizing the concept of individual agency. Individual agency remains a crucial aspect of any analysis of women's lives and aspirations. We are all not just cogs in the great machinery of globalization. Instead, as Koggel (2003) suggests "This dynamic approach endorses an account of women as agents, who, in the process of interacting with and reacting to changing local and global factors, themselves reshape meanings and therefore change the conditions of their own lives" (p. 174). Ultimately, women's empowerment is about women being able to govern their own choices and decisions. While we may be constrained by contexts, beliefs, and resources, ultimately we are still the architects of our own lives. Globalization is providing each of us with new tools with which to fashion our biographies—and these biographies may end up looking quite different from that which we currently may imagine.

Notes

1 As Stephanie Coontz (2000) describes in *The Way We Never Were: American Families and the Nostalgia Trap*, however, this was never the situation even for most families in the United States.
2 It is not clear that families are really less "stable" today as historically so many families were marked by high degrees of mortality.
3 A notable exception is West Africa where women have traditionally worked as traders and been prominent in market relationships.
4 This is not to say that people stay at the same jobs for 30 or 40 years as in the past. Instead, benefits accrue by staying in the labor market and not interrupting employment for family responsibilities.
5 In China the Filial Responsibility Act requires children to take care of their parents financially and to visit them on a regular basis.
6 See for instance the reports for 2012 at http://social.un.org/index/Family/InternationalObservances/TwentiethAnniversaryofIYF2014/Resources.aspx.
7 For instance, in Nigeria 1 percent of the labor force receives social security and in the global labor force three out ten workers receive any kind of a pension. Moreover, ageism is a serious problem in both high- and low-income countries (Beales, 2012).

REFERENCES

Acker, J. (2004). Gender, capitalism, and globalization. *Critical Sociology, 30*, 17–41.

Afshar, H., & Barrientos, S. (1999). *Women, globalization and fragmentation in the developing world.* London: Macmillan.

Allan, H., & Larsen, J. (2003). *We need respect: Experiences of internationally recruited nurses in the UK.* Royal College of Nursing: London. www.rcn.org. uk/downloads/international/irn-report-we-need-respect.pdf.

Amsden, A.H. (1989). *Asia's next giant: South Korea and late industrialization.* New York: Oxford University Press.

Apple, M. (2005). Are new markets in education democratic? Neoliberal globalism, vouchers, and the politics of choice. In M. Apple, J. Kenway, & M. Singh (Eds.), *Globalization education: Policies, pedagogies, and politics* (pp. 209–230). New York: Peter Lang.

Aumann, K., Galinsky, E., & Matos, K. (2011). *The new male mystique. Families and Work Institute.* http://familiesandwork.org/site/research/reports/main.html#new.

Baliamoune-Lutz, M. (2006). Globalisation and gender inequality: Is Africa different? *Journal of African Economies, 16*, 301–348.

Bandy, J. (2004). Paradoxes of transnational civil societies under neoliberalism: The coalition for justice in the maquiladoras. *Social Problems, 51*, 410–431.

Barber, B., & Olsen, J. (1997). Socialization in context: Connection, regulation and autonomy in the family, school, and neighborhood and with peers. *Journal of Adolescent Reseach, 12*, 287–315.

Bartolomei, M.R. (2010). Migrant male domestic workers in comparative perspective: Four case studies from Italy, India, Ivory Coast, and Congo. *Men and Masculinities, 13*, 87–110.

Barton, Carol. (2004). Global women's movements at a crossroads: Seeking definition, new alliances, and greater impact. *Socialism and Democracy, 18*(1), 151–184.

Baumrind, D. (1980). New directions in socialization research. *American Psychologist, 35*, 639–652.

Baxter, J., & Kane, E. (1995). Dependence and independence: A cross-national analysis of gender inequality and attitudes. *Gender and Society, 9*, 193–215.

Beales, S. (2012). Empowerment and older people: enhancing capabilities in an aging world. *Expert Group Meeting on "Promoting people's empowerment in achieving poverty eradication, social integration and productive and decent work for all."* New York: United Nations.

Beck, U. (1992). From industrial society to the risk society: Questions of survival, social structure and ecological enlightenment. *Theory, Culture & Society, 9,* 97–123.

Beck, U., Giddens, A., & Lash, S. (1994). *Reflexive modernization: Politics, tradition and aesthetics in the modern age.* Stanford: Stanford University Press.

Beck-Gernsheim, E. (1998). On the way to a post-familial family: From a community of need to elective affinities, *Theory, Culture & Society, 15,* 53–70.

Beek, K.A. (2001). Maquiladoras: Exploitation or emancipation? An overview of the situation of Maquiladora workers in Honduras. *World Development, 29,* 1553–1567.

Beneria, L. (2003). *Gender, development, and globalization: Economics as if all people mattered.* New York: Routledge.

Beneria, L. (2005). Gender and the global economy. *Treballs de la Societat Catalana de Geografia, 23,* 21–37.

Beneria, L. (2007a). Paid/unpaid work and the globalization of reproduction. *The International Working Group on Gender, Macroeconomics, and International Economics.* IWG-GEM Working Paper.

Beneria, L. (2007b). *The crisis of care, international migration and the capabilities approach: Implications for policy.* Working Paper Series no. 4-07. Mario Einaudi Center for International Studies. Ithaca, NY: Cornell University Press, pp. 1–17.

Bergeron, S. (2001). Political economy discourses of globalization and feminist politics. *Signs, 26,* 983–1006.

Bergmann, B. (1981). The economic risks of being a housewife, *American Economic Review, 71,* 81–86.

Bhagwati, J. (2004). *In defense of globalization.* New York: Oxford University Press.

Bianchi, S., Robinson, J., & Milkie, M. (2007). *Changing rhythms of American family life.* New York: Russell Sage Foundation.

Blackmore, J. (1999). Localization/globalization and the midwife state: Strategic dilemmas for state feminism education? *Journal of Education Policy, 14,* 33–54.

Bosch, A. (2001). Uncovering pathways for girls' education: Gender equity and early childhood development. *Development, 44,* 41–46.

Bose, C. (2011). Eastern sociological society presidential address: Globalizing gender issues: Many voices, different choices. *Sociological Forum, 26,* 739–753.

Boserup, E. (1970). *The role of women in economic development.* New York: St. Martin's Press.

Bouis, H., Palabrica-Costello, M., Solon, O., Westbrook, D., & Limbo, A. (1998). *Gender equality and investments in adolescents in the rural Philippines.* Research Report 108. International Food Policy Research Institute.

Bourdieu, P. (1991). *Language and symbolic power* (J. B. Thompson, ed., M. Adamson, trans.). Cambridge: Polity Press.

Bowman, P.J., & Howard, C. (1985). Race-related socialization, motivation, and academic achievement: A study of Black youths in three generation families. *Journal of the American Academy of Child Psychiatry, 24,* 134–141.

Brady, M., Saloucou, L., & Chong, E. (2007). *Girls' adolescence in Burkina Faso: A pivotal point for social change.* Population Council Report. New York: Population Council.

Brenner, J. (2000). *Women and the politics of class*. New York: Monthly Review Press.

Brodie, J. (1994). Shifting the boundaries: Gender and the politics of restructuring. In I. Bakker (Ed.), *The strategic silence: Gender and economic policy* (pp. 46–60). London: Zed.

Brodie, J. (1996). New state forms, new political spaces. In R. Boyer, & D. Drache (Eds.), *State against markets: The limits of globalization* (pp. 383–398). New York: Routledge.

Bruce, J., Haberland, N., Joyce, A., Roca, E., & Sapiano, T.N. (2011). First generation for gender and HIV programs: Seeking clarity and synergy. *Poverty, gender and youth*. Working Paper, No. 23. New York: Population Council.

Bureau of Labor Statistics. (2012). www.bls.gov/emp/ep_table_201.htm.

Bureau of Labor Statistics. (2013). February 10. http://economix.blogs.nytimes.com/2012/09/07/share-of-men-in-labor-force-at-all-time-low/.

Carrington, V. (2001). Globalization, family and nation-state: Reframing 'family' in new times. *Discourse: Studies in the cultural politics of education, 22*, 185–196.

Castles, F.G. (2003). The world turned upside down: Below replacement fertility, changing preferences and family-friendly public policy in 21 OECD countries. *Journal of European Social Policy, 13*, 209–227.

Castells, M. (2000). *The end of millennium*. Malden, MA: Blackwell.

Caughy, M.O., O'Campo, P.J., Randolph, S.M., & Nickerson, K. (2002). The influence of racial socialization practices on the cognitive and behavioral competence of African American preschoolers. *Child Development, 73*, 1611–1625.

Cerny, P.G., & Evans, M. (2004). Globalisation and public policy under New Labour. *Policy Studies, 25*, 51–65.

Chang, G. (2000). *Disposable domestics: Immigrant women workers in the global economy*. Cambridge, MA: South End Press.

Chant, S. (2010). Towards a (Re)conceptualisation of the "Feminisation of Poverty": Reflections on gender-differentiated poverty from the Gambia, Philippines and Costa Rica. In S. Chant (Ed.), *The international handbook of gender and poverty: Concepts, research, policy* (pp. 111–116). Northampton: Edward Elgar Publishing Limited.

Chen, E., & Rao, N. (2011). Gender socialization in Chinese kindergartens: Teachers' contributions. *Sex Roles, 64*, 103–116.

Chin, C.B.N. (1997). Walls of silence and late twentieth century representations of the foreign female domestic worker: The case of Filipino and Indonesian female servants in Malaysia, *International Migration Review, 31*, 353–385.

Chisamya, G., DeJaeghere, J., Kendall, N., & Khan, M. (2011). Gender and education for all: Progress and problems in achieving gender equity. *International Journal of Educational Development, 32*, 743–755.

Chodorow, N. (1978). *The reproduction of mothering: Psychoanalysis and the sociology of gender*. Berkeley: University of California Press.

Chopra, R. (2006). Invisible men: Masculinity, sexuality, and male domestic labour. *Men and Masculinities, 9*, 152–167.

Chossudovsky, M. (2003). *The globalization of poverty and the new world order*. 3rd ed. Shanty Bay, Ontario: Global Outlook.

Chow, E. (2003). Gender, globalization and social change in the 21st century. *International Sociology, 18*, 443–460.

253

Claassen, R. (2011). The commodification of care. *Hypatia, 26*, 43–64.

Colclough, C. (2007). Global gender goals and the construction of equality Conceptual dilemmas and policy practice. In S. Fennell, & M. Arnot (Eds.), *Gender education and equality in a global context: Conceptual frameworks and policy perspectives*. London: Routledge.

Committee on the Elimination of All Forms of Discrimination against Women (CEDAW). (2003). *Consideration of state parties: Canada: 5th periodic report* (draft report, unpublished) (31 January).

Connell, R.W. (1998). Masculinities and globalization. *Men and Masculinities, 1*, 3–23.

Connell, R.W. (2005). Change among the gatekeepers: Men, masculinities, and gender equality in the global arena. *Signs, 30*, 1801–1825.

Coontz, S. (2000). *The way we never were: American families and the nostalgia trap*. New York: Basic Books.

Crompton, R. (2006). Employment and the family: The reconfiguration of work and family life in contemporary societies. Cambridge: Cambridge University Press.

Cunningham, M. (2008). Influences of gender ideology and housework alloca-tion on women's employment over the life course. *Social Science Research, 37*, 254–267.

Curtol, F., Decarli, S., DiNicola, A., & Savona, E.U. (2004). Victims of human trafficking in Italy: A judicial perspective. *International Review of Victimology, 11*, 111–141.

Daly, M. and Lewis, J. (2000). The concept of social care and the analysis of contemporary welfare states. *British Journal of Sociology 51*(2), 281–298.

Dannecker, P. (2005). Transnational migration and the transformation of gender relations: The case of Bangladeshi labour migrants. *Current Sociology, 53*, 655–674.

Darbinger, M. (2007). Gender-sensitive microfinance? Critical commentary on the targeting of women in microfinance. *Dialogue. Microfinance and Gender: New Contributions to an Old Issue, 37*, 117–144.

Davids, T., & van Driel, F. (2005). *The gender question in globalization: Changing perspectives and practices*. Burlington, VT: Ashgate.

Delius, P., & Walker, L. (2002). Aids in context. *African Studies, 61*, 5–12.

Dembele, D.M. (2003). PRSPs: Poverty reduction or poverty reinforcement? *Pambazuka News: An Information Service for Social Justice in Africa*. December 11. www.pamazuka.org.

Denis, A. (2003). Globalization, women and (in)equity in the South: Constraint and resistance in Barbados. *International Sociology, 18*, 491–512.

Derne, S. (2005). The (limited) effect of cultural globalization in India: Implications for culture theory. *Poetics, 33*, 33–47.

Derne, S. (2008). Globalizing gender culture: Transnational cultural flows and the intensification of male dominance in India. In K. Ferguson and M. Mironesco (Eds.), *Gender and globalization in Asia and the Pacific: Method, practice, theory* (pp. 121–137). Honolulu: University of Hawaii Press.

DeRuyter, A., & Warnecke, T. (2008). Gender, non-standard work and the development Regime: A comparison of the USA and Indonesia. *Journal of Industrial Relations, 50*, 718–735.

Desai, M. (2010). *Hope in hard times: Women's empowerment and human development*. Human Development Research Paper, 14. New York: United Nations.

Deutsch, F. (2007). Undoing gender. *Gender & Society, 21*, 106–127.

De Walque, D. (2007). How does the impact of an HIV/AIDS information campaign vary with educational attainment? Evidence from rural Uganda. *Journal of Development Economics, 84*, 686–714.

Dollar, D., & Gatti, R. (1999). *Gender inequality, income and growth: Are good times good for women*. World Bank Policy Research Working Paper 2881. Washington, DC: World Bank.

Doyal, L. (2002). Putting gender into health and globalization debates: New perspectives and old challenges. *Third World Quarterly, 23*, 233–250.

Dreby, J. (2006). Honor and virtue: Mexican parenting in the transnational context. *Gender & Society, 20*, 32–59.

Duncan, S. (2003). Mothers, care and employment: Values and theories, *CAVA Working Paper No. 1*. Leeds, UK: University of Leeds Press.

Dunkle, K., Jewkes, R., Brown, H., Gray, G., McIntryre, J., & Harlow, S. (2004). Transactional sex among women in Soweto, South Africa: Prevalence, risk factors, and association with HIV infection. *Social Science and Medicine, 59*, 1582–1592.

Edgar, D. (2004). Globalization and Western bias in family sociology. In J. Scott, J. Treas, & M. Richards (Eds.), *The Blackwell companion to the sociology of families* (pp. 3–16). Malden, MA: Oxford University Press.

Edin, K. (2000). What do low-income single mothers say about marriage? *Social Problems, 47*, 112–133.

Ehrenreich, B., & Hochschild, A. (Eds.). (2003). *Global woman: Nannies, maids and sex workers in the new economy*. New York: Metropolitan Books.

Eisenstein, H. (2005). A dangerous liaison? Feminism and corporate globalization. *Science & Society, 69*, 487–518.

Ekberg, G. (2004). The Swedish law that prohibits the purchase of sexual services. *Violence Against Women, 10*, 1187–1218.

Eliot, L. (2009). *Pink brain, blue brain*. Boston, MA: Houghton Mifflin Harcourt.

Elyachar, J. (2002). Empowerment money: The World Bank, non-governmental organizations, and the value of culture in Egypt. *Public Culture, 14*, 493–513.

England, P., & Folbre, N. (1999). The cost of caring. *Annals of the American Academy of Political and Social Science, 5*, 39–51.

Erez, E. Ibarra, P.R., & McDonald, W.F. (2004). Transnational sexual trafficking: Issues and prospects. *International Review of Victimology, 11*, 1–9.

Erickson, R. (2005). Why emotion work matters: Sex, gender and the division of household labor. *Journal of Marriage and Family, 67*, 337–351.

Erulkar, A., Bruce, J., Dondo, A., Sebstrad, J., Matheka, A., Khan, B., & Gathuku, A. (2006). *Providing social support, savings and microcredit opportunities for young women in areas with high HIV prevalence*. Working Paper. New York: Population Council.

Esping-Andersen, G. (1996). *Welfare states in transition: National adaptations in global economies*. London: Sage/UNRISD.

Esping-Andersen, G. (1999). *Social foundations of post-industrial societies*. Oxford: Oxford University Press.

Esping-Andersen, G. (2000). The sustainability of welfare states into the twenty-first century. *International Journal of Health services*, 30, 1–12.

Fennell, S., & Arnot, M. (2008). *Gender education and equality in a global context: Conceptual frameworks and policy perspectives*. New York: Taylor & Francis.

Ferguson, K., Merry, S.E., & Mironesco, M. (2008). Introduction. In K. Ferguson, & M. Mironesco (Eds.), *Gender and globalization in Asia and the Pacific: Method, practice, theory* (pp. 1–14). Honolulu: University of Hawaii Press.

Fernandez-Kelly, M.P. (1997). *Maquiladora: The view from inside*. In N. Vasvanathan, L. Duggan, L. Nisonoff, & N. Wiegersma (Eds.), *The women, gender and development Reader* (pp. 203–215). London: Zed Books.

Ferree, M. (1979). Employment without liberation: Cuban women in the United States. *Social Science Quarterly*, 60, 35–50.

Ferree, M., & Mueller, C. (2004). Feminism and the women's movement: A global perspective. In D. Snow, S. Soule, & H. Kriesi (Eds.), *The Blackwell companion to social movements* (pp. 576–607). London: Blackwell.

Ferreira, F., & Robalino, D. (2010). Social protection in Latin America: Achievements and limitations. *World Bank Research Working Paper, No. 5305*. Washington, DC: World Bank.

Ferris, E. (2007). Abuse of power: Sexual exploitation of refugee women and girls. *Signs*, 32, 584–591.

Finch, J., & Mason, J. (1993). *Negotiating family responsibilities*. London: Routledge.

Folbre, N. (2006). Measuring care: Gender, empowerment, and the care economy. *Journal of Human Development*, 7, 183–199.

Folbre, N. (2008). Reforming care. *Politics & Society*, 36, 373–387.

Fraser, N. (1994). After the family wage: Gender equity and the welfare state. *Political Theory*, 22, 591–618.

Fraser, N. (2000). Rethinking recognition: Overcoming displacement and reification in cultural politics. *New Left Review*, 3, 107–120.

Fraser, N. (2007). Feminist politics in the age of recognition: A two-dimensional approach to gender justice. *Studies in Social Justice*, 1, 23–35.

Freeman, C. (2000). *High tech and high heels in the global economy. Women, work, and pink-collar identities in the Caribbean*. Durham, NC: Duke University Press.

Freeman, C. (2001). Is local:global as feminine:masculine? Rethinking the gender of globalization. *Signs*, 26, 1007–1037.

Freeman, J. (1975). *The politics of women's liberation: A case study of an emerging social movement and its relation to the policy process*. New York: David McKay.

Fukuda-Parr, S. (2003). The human development paradigm: Operationalizing Sen's ideas on capabilities. *Feminist Economics*, 9, 301–317.

Fukuyama, F. (1992). *The end of history and the last man*. New York: The Free Press.

Gamburd, M.R. (2000). *The kitchen spoon's handle: Transnationalism and Sri Lanka's migrant housemaids*. Ithaca, NY: Cornell University Press.

Ganguly-Scrase, R. (2003). Paradoxes of globalization, liberalization, and gender equality: The worldviews of the lower middle class in West Bengal, India. *Gender and Society*, 17, 544–566.

Garcia-Linera, Á. (1999). *Reploretarización: Nueva clase obrera y desarrollo del capital industrial en Bolivia (1952–1998)*, La Paz: Muela del Diablo Editores.

Gerson, K. (2004). Understanding work and family through a gender lens. *Community, Work & Family*, 7, 163–178.

Giddens, A. (1991). *Modernity and self-identity: Self and society in the late modern age*. Cambridge: Polity Press.

Giddens, A. (2001). *Sociology*. Cambridge: Polity Press.

Giddens, A. (2003). *Runaway world: How globalization is reshaping our lives*. New York: Routledge.

Giele, J.Z. (2006). The changing gender contract as the engine of work-and-family policies. *Journal of Comparative Policy Analysis*, 8, 115–128.

Glenn, E.N. (1994). Social constructions of mothering: A thematic overview. In E.N. Glenn, & G. Chang (Eds.), *Mothering: Ideology, experience, and agency* (pp. 1–32). New York: Routledge.

Glick Schiller, N. (1999). Terrains of blood and nation: Haitian transnational social fields. *Ethnic and Racial Studies*, 22, 340–366.

Gore, C. (2000). The rise and fall of the Washington Consensus as a paradigm for developing countries. *World Development*, 28, 789–804.

Gornick, J.C., & Heron, A. (2006). The regulation of working time as work-family reconciliation policy: Comparing Europe, Japan, and the United States. *Journal of Comparative Policy Analysis*, 8, 149–166.

Gornick, J., & Meyers, M. (2008). Creating gender egalitarian societies: An agenda for reform. *Politics & Society*, 36, 313–349.

Gottfried, H., & Reese, L. (2003). Gender, policy, politics, and work: Feminist comparative and transnational research. *Review of Policy Research*, 20, 3–20.

Gough, I. (2000). Welfare regimes in East Asia and Europe: Comparisons and lessons. Paper at "Towards the New Social Policy Agenda in East Asia," Parallel Session to the Annual World Bank Conference on Development Economics Europe.

Grameen Bank. (n.d.). www.grameen-info.org/.

Guerin, I., & Palier, J. (2007). Microfinance and the empowerment of women: Will the silent revolution take place? *Dialogue*, 37, 27–34.

Gupta, A., & Sharma, A. (2006). Globalization and postcolonial states. *Current Anthropology*, 47, 277–307.

Haas, L., & Hwang, C.P. (2007). Gender and organizational culture: Correlates of companies' responsiveness to fathers in Sweden. *Gender and Society*, 21, 52–79.

Haberland, N. (2007). Supporting married girls: Calling attention to a neglected group. *Promoting Healthy, Safe and Productive Transitions to Adulthood*. Brief no. 3. New York: Population Council.

Hakim, C. (2000). *Work-lifestyle choices in the 21st century*. Oxford: Oxford University Press.

Hall, A. (2006). From Fome Zero to Bolsa Familia: Social policies and poverty alleviation under Lula. *Journal of Latin American Studies*, 38, 689–709.

Hallman, K. (2005). Gendered socioeconomic conditions and HIV risk behavior among young people in South Africa. *African Journal of AIDS Research*, 4, 37–50.

Hallman, K., & Roca, E. (2007). Reducing the social exclusion of girls. *Promoting Healthy, Safe and Productive Transitions to Adulthood*. Brief No. 27. New York: Population Council.

Hannum, E., & Adams, J. (2007). Girls in Gansu, China: Expectations and aspirations for secondary schooling. In M. Lewis, & M. Lockheed (Eds.), *Exclusion, gender and schooling: Case studies from the developing world* (pp. 71–98). Washington, DC: Center for Global Development.

Harcourt, W. (2010). Editorial. Global crisis, the commons, and community well-being. *Development, 53*, 1–5.

Hartmann, H. (1987). Changes in women's economic and family roles in post-World War II United States. In L. Beneria, & C.R. Stimpson (Eds.), *Women, households, and the economy* (pp. 33–64). New Brunswick, NJ: Rutgers University Press.

Hattery, A. (2001). *Women, work and family: Balancing and weaving*. London: Sage.

Hawkesworth, M.E. (2006). *Globalization and feminist activism*. Lanham, MD: Rowman & Littlefield.

Hayes, S. (1996). *The cultural contradictions of motherhood*. New Haven: Yale University Press.

Hellum, A. (1999). *Women's human rights and legal pluralism in Africa*. Aschehoug, Tano: Mond Books.

Hernández, D.J., Denton, N.A., & Macartney, S.E. (2007). Family circumstances of children in immigrant families: Looking to the future of America. In J.E. Lansford, K. Deater-Deckard, & M.H. Bornstein (Eds.), *Immigrant families in contemporary society*. Duke series in child development and public policy (pp. 9–29). New York: Guilford.

Herz, B., & Khandker, S. (1991). *Women's work, education and family welfare in Peru*, World Bank, Discussion Papers #161.

Hill Collins, P. (1994). Theorizing about motherhood. In E.N. Glenn, G. Chang, & L.R. Forcey (Eds.), *Mothering: Ideology, experience, and agency* (pp. 45–65). New York: Routledge.

Hill Collins, P. (1998). It's all in the family: Intersections of gender, race, and nation. *Hypatia, 13*, 62–82.

Hirdman, Y. (1998). State policy and gender contracts: Sweden. In E. Drew, R. Emerek, & E. Mahon (Eds.), *Women, work and the family in Europe* (pp. 36–46). London: Routledge.

Hochschild, A.R. (1989). *The second shift: Working parents and the revolution at home*. New York: Viking.

Hochschild, A.R. (2001). Global care chains and emotional surplus value. In A. Giddens, & W. Hutton, (Eds.), *On the edge: Living with global capitalism* (pp. 130–146). London: Vintage.

Hodge, D., & Lietz, D. (2007). The international sexual trafficking of women and children: A review of the literature. *Affilia, 22*, 163–174.

Hofmann, E., & Marius-Gnanou, K.M. (2007). Credit for women: A future for men. *Dialogue, 37*, 7–12.

Hondagneu-Sotelo, P. (1994). *Gendered transitions: Mexican experiences of immigration*. Berkeley: University of California Press.

Hondagneu-Sotelo, P., & Avila, E. (1997). "I'm here, but I'm there." The meanings of Latina transnational motherhood. *Gender and Society*, *11*, 548–571.

Hughes, D. (2000). The "Natasha" trade: The transnational shadow market of trafficking in women. *Journal of International Affairs*, *53*, 625–651.

Hughes, D., Rodrigues, J., Smith, E., Johnson, D., Stevenson, H., & Spicer, P. (2006). Parents' ethnic-racial socialization practices: A review of research and directions for future study. *Developmental Psychology*, *42*, 747–770.

Human Rights Watch (2002). *World Report*. New York: Human Rights Watch.

Hynes, H.P. (2004). On the battlefield of women's bodies: An overview of the harm of war to women. *Women's Studies International Forum*, *27*, 431–445.

International Labor Organization (ILO). (2013). Statistics and databases. www.ilo.org/global/statistics-and-databases/lang--en/index.htm.

International Organization for Migration. (2000). *Perspectives on trafficking of migrants*. Geneva: IOM.

International Organization for Migration. (2012). *Facts and figures: Global estimates and trends*. www.iom.int/cms/en/sites/iom/home/about-migration/facts--figures-1.html.

Jaggar, A. (2002). A feminist critique of the alleged southern debt. *Hypatia*, *17*, 119–142.

Jain, K. (2001). Muscularity and its ramifications: Mimetic male bodies in Indian mass culture. *South Asia*, *34*, 197–224.

Joffres, C., Mills, E., Joffres, M., Khanna, T., Walia, H., & Grund, D. (2008). Sexual slavery without borders: trafficking for commercial sexual exploitation in India. *International Journal for Equity in Health*, *7*, 1–11.

Jolly, R. (2003). Human development and neoliberalism: Paradigms compared. In S. Fukuda-Parr, & A.K. Shiva Kumar (Eds.), *Readings in human development: Concepts, measures and policies for a development paradigm* (pp. 106–116). New Delhi: Oxford University Press.

Jones, K. (2007). Theorizing gender, sexuality and politics in an era of global change. In S. Adrian, M. Gustavson, & N. Lykke (Eds), *GEXcel Work in Progress Report, Volume 1* (pp. 87–106). Linkoeping: Linkoeping University.

Kabeer, N., & Mahmud, S. (2004). Globalization, gender and poverty: Bangladeshi women workers in export and local markets. *Journal of International Development*, *16*, 93–109.

Kamerman, S. (2010). Child, family and state: The relationship between family policy and social protection policy. In S. Kamerman, S. Phipps, & A. Ben-Arieh (Eds.), *From child welfare to child well-being: An international perspective on knowledge in the service of policy making* (pp. 429–437). New York: Springer.

Kaplan, T. (2001). Uncomon women and the common good: Women and environmental protest. In S. Rowbotham, & S. Linkogle (Eds.), *Women resist globalisation: mobilising for livelihood and rights* (pp. 28–45). London: Zed Books.

Karoly, L.A., Kilburn, M.R., & Cannon, J.S. (2005). *Early childhood interventions: Proven results, future promise*. Santa Monica, CA: RAND Corporation.

Karraker, K.H., Vogel, D.A, and Lake, M.A. (1995). Parents' gender-stereotyped perceptions of newborns: The eye of the beholder revisited. *Sex Roles*, *33*, 687–701.

Kassim, A. (2013). Companion of India rape victim: I begged attackers to stop. CNN. www.cnn.com/2013/01/04/world/asia/india-rape-case.

Kaufman, M., & Crawford, M. (2011). Research and activism review: Sex trafficking in Nepal: A review of intervention and prevention programs. *Violence Against Women, 17*, 651–665.

Keck, M., & Sikkink, K. (1998). *Activists beyond borders: Advocacy networks in international politics.* Ithaca, NY: Cornell University Press.

Keddie, A. (2010). Neo-liberalism and new configurations of global space: Possibilities, tensions and problematics for gender justice. *Journal of Gender Studies, 19*, 139–152.

Kelkar, G., & Nathan, D. (2002). Gender relations and technological change in Asia. *Current Sociology, 50*, 427–441.

Kelly, L., & Regan, L. (2000). *Stopping traffic: Exploring the extent of and responses to trafficking in women for sexual exploitation in the UK.* Home Office, Policy Research Series, no. 125. Policy and Reducing Crime Unit. London: Research, Development and Statistics.

Keough, L. (2006). Globalizing "postsocialism" mobile mothers and neoliberalism on the margins of Europe. *Anthropological Quarterly, 79*, 431–461.

Khondkar, M. (2002). Women's empowerment in Bangladesh: Credit is not a panacea. London: One World Action. www.oneworldaction.org/genderand-microfinance.html#asia.

Kilkey, M. (2010). Men and domestic labor: A missing link in the global care chain. *Men and Masculinities, 13*, 126–149.

Koggel, C. (2003). Globalization and women's paid work: Expanding freedom? *Feminist Economics, 9*, 163–183.

Kolarova, M. (2006). Gender and globalization: Labour changes in the global economy. *Czech Sociological Review, 42*, 1241–1257.

Kristof, N., & WuDunn, S. (2009). *Half the sky: Turning oppression into opportunity for women worldwide.* New York: Vintage.

Kuiper, E., & Barker, D. (2006). *Feminist economics and the WB: History, theory and policy.* New York: Routledge.

Lalor, K. (2008). Child sexual abuse and HIV transmission in Sub-Saharan Africa. *Child Abuse Review, 17*, 94–107.

Lewis, M., & Lockheed, M. (2007). *Exclusion, gender and schooling: Case studies from the developing world,* Washington, DC: Center for Global Development.

Li, D., & Tsang, M.C. (2005). Household decisions and gender inequality in education in rural China. *China: An International Journal 1*, 224–248.

Lim. L.Y. (1990). Women's work in export factories: The politics of a cause. In I. Tinker (Ed.), *Persistent inequalities: Women and world development* (pp. 101–119). New York: Oxford University Press.

Lloyd, C.B., Mete, C., & Grant, M. (2007). Rural girls in Pakistan: Constraints of policy and culture. In M. Lewis, & M. Lockheed (Eds.), *Exclusion, gender and schooling: Case studies from the developing world* (pp. 99–118). Washington, DC: Center for Global Development.

Long, L.D. (2002). Trafficking in women and children as a security challenge in Southeast Europe. *Journal of Southeast European and Black Sea Studies, 2*, 53–68.

Long, L.D. (2004). Anthropological perspectives on the trafficking of women for sexual exploitation. *International Migration*, *42*, 5–31.

Lorber, J. (1994). *Paradoxes of gender*. New Haven, CT: Yale University Press.

Loveband, A. (2004). Positioning the product: Indonesian migrant women workers in Taiwan. *Journal of Contemporary Asia*, *34*, 336–348.

Mabala, R. (2006). From HIV prevention to HIV protection: Addressing the vulnerability of girls and young women in urban areas. *Environment and Urbanization*, *18*, 407–432.

Macleod, A. (1993). *Accommodating protest: Working women, the new veiling and change in Cairo*. New York: Columbia University Press.

Mahler, S., & Pessar, P. (2006). Gender matters: Ethnographers bring gender from the periphery toward the core of migration studies. *International Migration Review*, *40*, 27–63.

Mahmud, S., & Amin, S. (2006). Girls' schooling and marriage in Bangladesh. In E. Hannum, & B. Fuller (Eds.), *Children's lives and schooling across societies* (Research in the Sociology of Education 15) (pp. 71–99). London: Emerald.

Marchand, M., & Runyan, A.S. (2000). Introduction. Feminist sightings of global restructuring: Conceptualizations and reconceptualizations. In M. Marchand, & A.S. Runyan (Eds.), *Gender and global restructuring: Sightings, sites and resistances* (pp. 1–22). London: Routledge.

Mattingly, D. (2001). The home and the world: Domestic service and international networks of caring labor. *Annals of the Association of American Geographers*, *91*, 370–386.

Mauss, M. (1923/1990). *The gift*. New York: W.D. Halls.

McHale, S. Crouter, C., & Tucker, C. (2003). Family context and gender role socialization in middle childhood: Comparing girls to boys and sisters to brothers. *Child Development*, *70(4)*, 990–1004.

McLaren, P., & Faramandpur, R. (2005). *Teaching against global capitalism and the new imperialism: A critical pedagogy*. Lanham, MD: Rowman & Littlefield.

Mead, M. (1935). *Sex and temperament*. New York: Dell.

Mead, M. (1939). *From the south seas: Studies of adolescence and sex in primitive societies*. Oxford: Morrow Publishers.

Mensch, B., Ibrahim, B., Lee, S., & El-Gibaly, O. (2000). *Socialization to gender roles and marriage among Egyptian adolescents*. Policy Research Division Working Paper No. 140. New York: Population Council.

Mensch, B., Ibrahim, B., Lee, S., & El-Gibaly, O. (2003). Gender-role attitudes among Egyptian adolescents. *Studies in Family Planning 34*, 8–18.

Mitropoulos, A. (2001). Habeas corpus. *Arena Magazine*, *55*, 52–54.

Moghadam, V. (2005). *The feminization of poverty and women's human rights*. SHS Papers in Women's Studies/Gender UNESCO Research, no. 2. New York: UNESCO.

Mohanty, C. (2003). *Feminism without borders*. Durham, NC: Duke University Press.

Momsen, J., & Kinnaird, V. (eds.) (1993). *Different places, different voices: Gender and development in Africa, Asia, and Latin America*. London: Routledge.

Monzini, P. (2004). Trafficking in women and girls and the involvement of organized crime in western and central Europe. *International Review of Victimology*, *11*, 73–88.

Morel, N. (2007). From subsidiarity to 'free choice': Child- and elder-care policy reforms in France, Belgium, Germany and the Netherlands. *Social Policy & Administration*, *41*, 618–637.

Mummert, G. (2005). Transnational parenting in Mexican migrant communities: Redefining fatherhood, motherhood and caregiving. *The Mexican International Family Strengths Conference*. Proceedings. Cuernavaca, Mexico.

Munshi, S. (2001). *Images of the modern woman in Asia: Global media, local meanings*. Surrey: Curzon Press.

Nationmaster. (2013). www.nationmaster.com/graph/lab_wor_mot-labor-working-mothers.

Nicholson, M. (2006). Without their children: Rethinking motherhood among transnational migrant women. *Social Text*, *88*, 13–33.

Nussbaum, M. (2001). *Women and human development: The capabilities approach*. Notre Dame, IN: Notre Dame University Press.

Ochieng, B., & Erulkar, A. (2008). *Highlighting marital HIV risk and promoting premarital VCT in Nyanz Province, Kenya*. Frontiers Final Report. Washington, DC: Population Council.

O'Connell, P. (2007). On reconciling irreconcilables: Neo-liberal globalization and human rights. *Human Rights Law Review*, *7*, 483–509.

O'Connor, J., Orloff, A.S., & Shave, S. (1999). *States, markets, families: Gender, liberalism, and social policy in Australia, Canada, Great Britain and the United States*. Cambridge: Cambridge University Press.

OECD. (2012). www.oecd.org/els/familiesandchildren/oecdfamilydatabase.htm.

Okin, S.M. (1989). *Justice, gender and the family*. New York: Basic Books.

Orloff, A.S. (2002). *Women's employment and welfare regimes: Globalization, export orientation and social policy in Europe and North America*. Social Policy and Development Programme Paper Number 12. United Nations Research Institute for Social Development. New York: United Nations.

Orozco, M. (2002). *Attracting remittances: Practices to reduce costs and enable a money transfer environment*. Washington DC: Multilateral Investment Fund of the Inter-American Development Bank.

Oza, R. (2001). Showcasing India: Gender, geography, and globalization. *Signs*, *26*, 1067–1095.

Palkovitz, R.J. (2002). *Involved fathering and men's adult development: Provisional balances*. Hillsdale, NJ: Lawrence Erlbaum Press.

Parrenas, R.S. (2001). Mothering from a distance: Emotions, gender and intergenerational relations in Filipino transnational families. *Feminist Studies*, *27*, 361–390.

Parrenas, R.S. (2005). *Children of global migration: Transnational families and gendered woes*. Stanford: Stanford University Press.

Parrenas, R.S. (2010). Transnational mothering: A source of gender conflicts in the family. *North Carolina Law Review*, *88*, 1825–1855.

Parrenas, R.S. (2012). The reproductive labour of migrant workers. *Global Networks*, *12*, 269–275.

Parsons, T. (1949). The social structure of the family. In R. Anshen (Ed.), *The family: Its function and destiny* (pp. 173–201). New York: Harper.

Parsons, T., & Bales, R. (1955). *Family, socialization and interaction process.* Glencoe, IL: Free Press.

Pearson, R. (2004). Women, work and empowerment in a global era. *IDS Bulletin, 35,* 117–120.

Pels, T. (2003). The question of respect: Socialization and misconduct of Moroccan boys in the Netherlands. *The Netherlands Journal of Social Sciences, 39,* 126–141.

Penttinen, E. (2008). *Globalization, prostitution, and sex-trafficking: Corporeal politics.* London: Routledge Publishers.

Pessar, P. (1986). The role of gender in Dominican settlement in the United States. In J. Nash, & H. Safa (Eds.), *Women and change in Latin America* (pp. 273–294). South Hadley, MA: Bergin and Garvey.

Peterson, V.S. (1997). Whose crisis? Early and postmodern masculinism. In S. Gill, & J.H. Mittelman (Eds.), *Innovation and transformation in international relations theory* (pp. 185–206). Cambridge: Cambridge University Press.

Peterson, V.S., & Runyan, A.S. (1993). *Global gender issues,* 1st ed. Boulder, CO: Westview Press.

Pew Research. (2010). Pew Research Global Attitudes Project. Philadelphia: Pew Global. www.pewglobal.org/2010/01/12/widespread-anti-immigrant-sentiment-in-italy/.

Pieterse, J.N. (2000). *Global futures: Shaping globalization.* London: Zed Books.

Plan UK. (2009). *Because I am a girl: The state of the world's girls 2009. Girls in the global economy: Adding it all up.* London: Plan UK.

Polanyi, K. (1944). *The great transformation: The political and economic origins of our times.* New York: Beacon Press.

Pollin, R. (2003). *Contours of descent: U.S. economic fractures and the landscape of global austerity.* London: Verso.

Popenoe, D. (1993). American Family Decline, 1960–1990: A Review and Appraisal. *Journal of Marriage and the Family, 55,* 527–555.

Population Council. (2005). *Accelerating girls' education: A priority for governments.* Gender, Family, and Development, Working Papers. New York: Population Council.

Portes, A., Castells, M., & Benton, L.A. (1989). *The informal economy: Studies in advanced and less developed countries.* Baltimore: Johns Hopkins Press.

Poster, W., & Salime, Z. (2002). The limits of microcredit: Transnational feminism and USAID activities in the United Sates and Morocco. In N. Naples, & M. Desai (Eds.), *Women's activism and globalization: Linking local struggles and transnational politics* (pp. 189–219). New York: Routledge.

Putnam, R. (1993). *Making democracy work: Civic traditions in modern Italy.* Princeton, NJ: Princeton University Press.

Pyle, J. (2006). Globalization and the increase in transnational care work: The flip side. *Globalizations, 3,* 297–315.

Pyle, J., & Ward, K. (2003). Recasting our understanding of gender and work during global restructuring. *International Sociology, 18,* 461–489.

Qayum, S., & Ray, R. (2010). Male servants and the failure of patriarchy in Kolkata (Calcutta). *Men and Masculinities, 13,* 111–125.

Raffaelli, M., & Ontai, L. (2004). Gender socialization in Latino/a families: Results from two retrospective studies. *Sex Roles, 50,* 287–299.

Raghuram, P. (2008). Migrant women in male-dominated sectors of the labour market: A research agenda. *Population, Space and Place, 14,* 43–57.

Raijman, R., Schammah-Gesser, S., & Kemp, A. (2003). International migration, domestic work, and care work: Undocumented Latina migrants in Israel. *Gender & Society, 17,* 727–749.

Rampell, C. (2010). Single parents around the world. *New York Times,* March 10. http://economix.blogs.nytimes.com/2010/03/10/single-parents-around-the-world/.

Razavi, S. (2011). Rethinking care in a development context: An introduction. *Development and Change, 42,* 873–903.

Razavi, S., & Miller, C. (1995). From WID to GAD: Conceptual shifts in the women and development discourse. *United Nations Development Programme.* New York: United Nations.

Razavi, S., & Pearson, R. (2004). Globalization, export-oriented employment and social policy: Gendered connections. In S. Razavi, R. Pearson, & C. Danloy, (Eds.), *Globalization, export orientated employment and social policy* (pp. 1–29). New York: Palgrave.

Ridgeway, C.L. (2009). Framed before we know it: How gender shapes social relations. *Gender & Society, 23,* 145–160.

Risman, B. (1998). *Gender vertigo.* New Haven, CT: Yale University Press.

Risman, B.J. (2004). Gender as social structure: theory wrestling with activism. *Gender and Society, 18,* 429–450.

Rodriguez, N. (2006). The battle for the border: Notes on autonomous migration, transnational communities, and the state. *Social Justice, 23,* 21–37.

Rodrik, D. (1997). *Has globalization gone too far?* Washington, DC: Institute for International Economics.

Rollins, J. (1985). *Between women: Domestics and their employers.* Philadelphia: Temple University Press.

Rose, D.R. (2001). Gender and judaism. In D. Vannoy (Ed.), *Gender mosaics: Social perspectives* (pp. 415–424). Los Angeles, CA: Roxbury Publishing.

Rosen, E.I. (2002). *Making sweatshops: The globalization of the U.S. apparel industry.* Berkeley, CA: University of California Press.

Ryan, L. (2007). Migrant women, social networks and motherhood: The experiences of Irish nurses in Britain. *Sociology, 4,* 295–312.

Sassen, S. (2002). Global cities and survival circuits. In B. Ehrenreich, & A.R. Hochschild (Eds.), *Global woman: Nannies, maids, and sex workers in the new economy* (pp. 254–274). New York: Henry Holt.

Sathar, Z.A., & Lloyd, C. (1993). Who gets primary schooling in Pakistan: Inequalities among and within families, Population Council Working Papers No. 52. New York: Population Council.

Schuler, S.R. (2007). Rural Bangladesh: Sound policies, evolving gender norms, and family strategies. In M. Lewis, & M. Lockheed (Eds), *Exclusion, gender and schooling: Case studies from the developing world* (pp. 179–203). Washington, DC: Center for Global Development.

Scott, L.D. (2003). The relation of racial identity and racial socialization to coping with discrimination among African Americans. *Journal of Black Studies, 33,* 520–538.

Secor, A.J. (2002). The veil and urban space in Istanbul: Women's dress, mobility, and Islamic knowledge. *Gender, Place and Culture: A Journal of Feminist Geography*, 9, 5–22.

Seguino, S. (2005). *Gender inequality in a globalizing world.* Working Paper No. 426. The Levy Economics Institute.

Segura, D.A. (1994). Working at motherhood: Chicana and Mexican immigrant mothers and employment. In E.N. Glenn, E. Nakano, G. Chang, & L.R. Forcey (Eds.), *Mothering: Ideology, experience, and agency* (pp. 211–227). New York: Routledge.

Sen, A. (1990). Gender and cooperative conflicts. In I. Tinker (Ed.), *Persistent inequalities* (pp. 123–149). Oxford: Oxford University Press.

Sen, A. (1997). *Choice, welfare, and measurement.* Boston: Harvard University Press.

Sen, A. (1999). *Development as freedom.* New York: Anchor Books.

Shahra, R. (2011). Rethinking care in a development context: An introduction. *Development and Change, 42,* 873–903.

Shukla, S. (2003). *India abroad: Diasporic cultures of postwar America and England.* Princeton: Princeton University Press.

Shurmer-Smith, P. (2000). *Doing cultural geography.* London: Sage.

Simmons, P. (1997). "Women in development": A threat to liberation. In M. Rahema, & V. Bawtree (Eds.), *The post-development reader* (pp. 244–255). London: Zed.

Singh, S., Wulf, D., Samara, R., & Cuca, Y. (2000). Gender differences in the timing of first intercourse: Data from 14 countries. *International Family Planning Perspectives 26,* 21–28.

Slaughter, A.M. (2012). Why women still can't have it all. *The Atlantic,* (July/August 2012). www.theatlantic.com/magazine/archive/2012/07/why-women-still-cant-have-it-all/309020/.

Smith, D.E. (1993). The standard North American family: SNAF as an ideological code. *Journal of Family Issues, 14,* 50–65.

Spade, J.Z., & Valentine, C.G. (2004). *The kaleidoscope of gender.* Belmont, CA: Wadsworth/Thompson Learning.

Sperling, V., Ferree, M.M., & Risman, B. (2001). Constructing global feminism: Transnational advocacy networks and Russian activism. *Signs, 26,* 1155–1186.

Stack, C. (1974). *All our kin.* New York: Harper & Row.

Standing, G. (1999). Global feminization through flexible labor: A theme revisited. *World Development, 27,* 583–602.

Statisticbrain (2013). www.statisticbrain.com/working-mother-statistics/.

Sternberg, R.M. (2010). The plight of transnational Latina mothers: Mothering from a distance. *Migration and Health,* Field Actions Science Reports. Special Issue 2, 1–4.

Stiglitz, J. (2002). *Globalization and its discontents.* London: W.W. Norton.

Sullivan, O. (2006). *Changing gender relations, changing families: Tracing the pace of change over time.* New York: Rowman & Littlefield.

Supp, B. (2009). Quiet revolution: Can globalization help women out of traditional roles? *Spiegel Online International.* www.spiegel.de/international/world/quiet-revolution-can-globalization-help-women-out-of-traditional-roles-a-605813.html.

Suurmond, E. (2010). Good motherhood and the need for a transnational perspective. *Journal of Social Intervention: Theory and Practice, 19*, 100–111.

Tang, K., & Peters, H. (2006). Internationalizing the struggle against neoliberal social policy: The experience of Canadian women. *International Social Work, 49*, 571–582.

Thomas, A.J., & Speight, S.L. (1999). Racial identity and racial socialization attitudes of African American parents. *Journal of Black Psychology, 25*, 152–170.

Thompson, L., & Walker, A. (1989). Gender in families: Women and men in marriage, work, and parenthood. *Journal of Marriage and the Family, 51*, 845–871.

Thompson, P. (2003). Disconnected capitalism. *Work, Employment and Society, 17*, 359–378.

Tikly, L. (2004). Education and the new imperialism. *Comparative Education, 40*, 173–198.

Torregrosa, L. (2013). The internationalization of women's issues. *New York Times.* www.nytimes.com/2013/01/09/us/09iht-letter09.html?_r=0.

Trask, B.S. (2010). *Globalization and families: Accelerated systemic social change.* New York: Springer.

Trask, B.S., & Unger, D. (2011). Empowering girls and women in the developing world: Local solutions to global issues. In J. Hagen, & A. Kisubi (Eds.), *Best practices in human services: A global perspective* (pp. 301–318). Oshkosh, WI: Council for Standards in Human Service Education.

Udry, J.R. (2000). Biological limits of gender construction. *American Sociological Review 65*, 443–57.

UNESCO. (2003/4). *Gender and education for all: The leap to equality.* Global Monitoring Reports. New York: UNESCO.

UNESCO. (2005). *Progress of the world's women 2005: Women, work and poverty.* www.un-ngls.org/women-2005.pdf.

UNESCO. (2006). *Global education digest 2006: Comparing education statistics across the world.* Montreal: UNESCO Institute for Statistics.

United Nations. (1967). *Declaration on the elimination of discrimination against women.* www.unhcr.org/refworld/docid/3b00f05938.html.

United Nations. (2000). *Protocol to prevent, suppress and punish trafficking in persons, especially women and children.* www.uncjin.org/Documents/Conventions/dcatoc/final_documents_2/convention_%20traff_eng.pdf.

United Nations. (2009). *The millennium development goals report.* New York: United Nations.

United Nations. (2010). *The world's women 2010: Trends and statistics.* Publication of the Department of Economic and Social Affairs. New York: United Nations.

United Nations. (2013). *Gender mainstreaming.* United Nations Entity for Gender Equality and the empowerment of women. New York: United Nations. www.un.org/womenwatch/osagi/gendermainstreaming.htm.

United Nations Development Program. (1995). *Human Development Report 1995.* New York: Oxford University Press.

United Nations Development Program. (UNDP). (1999). *Human development report 1999: Globalization with a human face.* New York: Oxford University Press.

United Nations Development Program. (2001). *Human development report 2001*. New York: Oxford University Press.

United Nations Office on Drugs and Crime. (2005). *Fact sheet on human trafficking*. www.unodc.org/unodc/en/trafficking_victim_consents.html.

UNAIDS. (2004a). *Facing the future together. Report of the Secretary General's Task Force on Women, Girls and HIV/AIDS in Southern Africa*. New York: UNAIDS.

UNAIDS. (2004b). *Epidemic update*. Geneva: UNAIDS.

UNICEF. (2010). *Bangladesh: Statistics*. www.Unicef.org/info-bycountry/bangladesh_bangladesh_statistics.html.

Unterhalter, E. (2008). Global values and gender equality in education: Needs, rights and capabilities. In S. Fennell, & M. Arnot (Eds.), *Gender education and equality in a global context: Conceptual frameworks and policy perspectives* (pp. 19–34). London: Routledge.

Updegraff, K. Delgado, M., & Wheeler, L. (2009). Exploring mothers' and fathers' relationships with sons versus daughters: Links to adolescent adjustment in Mexican immigrant families. *Sex Roles, 60,* 559–574.

USAID (2003). *Women's property and inheritance Rights: Improving lives in changing times:* Final synthesis and conference proceedings paper. Washington DC: USAID.

U.S. Department of State. (2004). *Trafficking in persons report*. www.state.gov/g/tip/rls/tiprpt/2004/34021.htm.

Villaruel, A.M. (1998). Cultural influences on the sexual attitudes, beliefs, and norms of young Latina adolescents. *Journal of the Society of Pediatric Nurses, 3,* 69–79.

Visvanathan, N. (2011). Introduction. In N. Visvanathan, L. Duggan, N. Wiegersma, & L. Nisonoff (Eds.), *The women, gender & development reader*, 2nd ed. (pp. 3–13). London: Zed Books.

Wamoyi, J., Fenwick, A., Urassa, M., Zaba, B., & Stones, W. (2011). "Womens' bodies are shops": Beliefs about transactional sex and implications for understanding gender power and HIV prevention in Tanzania. *Arch Sex Behavior, 40,* 5–15.

West, C., & Zimmerman, D. (1987). Doing gender. *Gender and Society, 1,* 125–151.

Wichterich, C. (2000). *The globalized woman: Reports from a future of inequality*. New York: Zed Books

Wilson, J.Q. (2002). *The marriage problem*. New York: Harper Collins.

Wood, W., & Eagly, A.H. (2002). A cross-cultural analysis of the behavior of women and men: Implications for the origins of sex differences. *Psychological Bulletin. 128,* 699–727.

Yan, R., & Neal, A. (2006). The impact of globalization on family relations in China. *International Journal of Sociology of the family, 32,* 113–125.

Yeoh, B., Huang, S., & Willis, K. (2000). Global cities, transnational flows and gender dimensions, the view from Singapore. *Tijdschrift voor Economische en Sociale Geografie, 91,* 147–158.

Yunus, M. (2002). A national strategy for economic growth and poverty reduction. *The Daily Star*. www.dailystarnews.com/200206/200227/n2062709.htm#BODY2062701.

Zhan, H., & Montgomery, R. (2003). Gender and elder care in China: The influence of filial piety and structural constraints. *Gender and Society, 17,* 209–229.

Zimmerman, C., Yun, K., Shvab, I., Watts, C., Trappolin, L., Treppete, M., et al. (2003). *The health risks and consequences of trafficking in women and adolescents. Findings from a European study.* London: Gender Violence and Health Centre, London School of Hygiene and Tropical Medicine.

Zippel, K. (2004). Transnational advocacy networks and policy cycles in the European Union: The case of sexual harassment. *Social Politics, 11,* 57–85.

AUTHOR INDEX

References to notes consist of the page number followed by the letter 'n' followed by the number of the note, e.g. 203n7 refers to note no. 7 on page 203.

SUBJECT INDEX

References to tables are shown in **bold**. References to notes consist of the page number followed by the letter 'n' followed by the number of the note, e.g. 78n3 refers to note no. 3 on page 78.

see also female empowerment; feminism; feminist principles, global spread of; feminist scholarship; women's rights

women's networks: and migration 138–140; *see also* transnational movements; transnational women's conferences

women's rights: and capitalism 75–76; and microfinance 198; and neoliberalism 63; NGOs, United Nations and women's rights (Canada case study) 62–63; United Nations legislation 61–62; *see also* female empowerment; feminism; feminist principles, global spread of; feminist scholarship; women's movement

work *see* female labor force; labor; women, work-family life and global transformations; work-family issues; working time

work-family issues: choice and economic context 13; and employers 223; and gender inequality 225–226; and global debates on the state of families 230–232; and globalization-related changes 3–8, 222–223, 226–228; and men 3, 219–221, 223, 225–226, 234–235; mismatch between workplace and family responsibilities 232–234; need for public solutions 234–237, 248–249; role of the state 238; *see also* empowerment through globalization; policy responses

(industrialized world); women, work-family life and global transformations

working time: part-time work and gender inequality 205, 244; part-time work and work-family balance 13, 29–30, 163; regulation of 216–218

World Bank (previously International Bank for Reconstruction and Development): and declining national concerns 202; development agenda and feminist economics 73; development and gender equity 68, 69; educational initiatives in Bangladesh 188, 189; female education and economic growth 171; initiatives aimed at controlling women's fertility 74; migrant remittances 127; need for gender dimension 41; neoliberalism 37–38, 40, 173–174, 200–201; and role of the state 237; Social Funds 195

World Health Organization (WHO): gender mainstreaming 78n6; HIV rates (sub-Saharan Africa) 178

World Trade Organization (WTO), 1999 Seattle Ministerial Conference and "global justice" movement 202

Yousafzai, Malala, and education of girls 55

Yunus (Grameen) Bank 194

Zambia: HIV/AIDS 115; male domestic workers 162; rape of girls 182; school environments/commutes and sexual exploitation 115–116